REGNUM GLOBAL VOICES

Salaam: Development as Mission

Series Preface

The **Global Voices** series takes the missiological work of writers who have written in their own language and makes this accessible to the English-speaking world through translation and republishing. The key principle here is that the translated work reflects the context, experience and thinking of the local context. In so doing, Regnum Books seeks to amplify voices less easily heard outside their own contexts. Work of this nature will make a significant contribution to the development of 'polycentric missiology'; namely, mission thinking and practice that truly reflects the contexts, concerns and contributions of the global church in all its rich diversity.

REGNUM GLOBAL VOICES

Salaam: Development as Mission

Christian Giordano & Charo Pérez

Translated and edited by David Greenlee

First published 2022 by Regnum Books International

Regnum is an imprint of the Oxford Centre for Mission Studies
St. Philip and St. James Church, Woodstock Road
Oxford OX2 6HR, UK
www.regnumbooks.net
09 08 07 06 05 04 03 7 6 5 4 3 2 1

British Library Cataloguing in Publication Data

A catalogue record for this book is available from the British Library

ISBN: 978-1-5064-9732-7
eBook ISBN: 978-1-5064-9733-4

Typeset by Words by Design

The authors welcome comments and your reflections.
Please send them to desarrollo-salaam@losgiordano.org. Thank you.

Distributed by Fortress Press in the US, Canada, India, and Brazil

Acknowledgments

Above all, God deserves our thanks. For many years, faith in Him has inspired our lives, and now has given birth to this book. Also, this work would never have been published without the practical help and constant support we have given each other as a team.

We also owe a debt of gratitude to those pastors and leaders whose many contributions have helped to see this book in print. We acknowledge and offer our sincere thanks to all of them.

Index of Figures

Contents

Definitions

Central Asia: The territory made up of Turkmenistan, Uzbekistan, Tajikistan, Kyrgyzstan, Kazakhstan, and Afghanistan.

Church: For the context of our study, a community of ten or more baptized believers in Jesus Christ who demonstrate membership in a group that has a nucleus of one or more Christian families, has (or is in process to have) national leaders, meet in national households, and have assumed responsibility for the ministerial and financial aspects of their church community.

Development projects: A broad term that includes all types of medium and long-term activities, managed in a project style (with phases, budgets, evaluations, etc.), aimed at the common good. For our purposes, the term refers to purely developmental and humanitarian projects including immediate response to emergencies as well as other efforts of a social, cultural, or business nature. When we refer to *Iberoamerican development projects,* we point to development projects carried out by Iberoamerican evangelical missionaries through an Iberoamerican (or Latin American) missionary agency.

Folk or Popular Islam: The grassroots practice of Islam in many Muslim communities and countries. Having many animistic elements, it affects most rites and facets of daily life and is accepted as a part of the religion, with (in the eyes of practitioners) no perceived contradictions to official or orthodox Islam. Its predominant theme is power and how to manipulate the spirits.

Gender, issues of gender: In our use, this is limited to issues such as how men and women relate to each other within the church, family, and society; for example, if they are together or separated during meetings, and roles that might be reserved for men.

Iberoamerican, Latin American: Native of one of the countries of America that once formed part of the kingdoms of Spain and Portugal. Belonging to or relating to these peoples and to Spain and Portugal. Geographically, Iberoamerica does not include the United States, but when used as a qualifier it does include the Hispanics of the U.S. In this text, Iberoamerica and Latin America have been used as synonyms.

Integral mission: Integral mission is the non-compartmentalized expression of the gospel, capable of integrating evangelization and discipleship, as well as economic, ecological, and political transformation in a comprehensive, dynamic, and coherent witness, following the ideal of the kingdom of God. It is more intuitive and lived from the heart and less a category that is readily shaped by an intellectual or academic definition.

Integrality: Characteristic of being whole or complete. In this work, it describes the daily internalization of integral mission; thus, the degree of integrality is the degree of practical application of a theoretical understanding of integral mission in a person or project.

Islamia: A generic term to refer to countries in which Muslims are a majority of the population and the Christian church experiences severe limitations. A synonym could be "the Muslim world."

North Africa: For the purposes of this book, the area of Africa comprising the present-day countries of Mauritania, Morocco, Algeria, Tunisia, and Libya, as well as the disputed area of Western Sahara.

Sahel: For our purposes, we refer to the area of Africa directly South of the Sahara: Senegal, Mauritania, Mali, Niger, and Chad.

Sufism: Mystical current of Islam that seeks a close relationship with the Divine, often through music and poetry. It is organized in brotherhoods governed by a master.

Worker: Equivalent to "evangelical missionary." It should be understood that in the Muslim context there is a disparity between the word missionary, which carries a very negative and offensive stereotype, and the person and work—often much appreciated—of the Iberoamerican missionaries. Hence, our frequent use of the term "worker" to describe them.

1. Our Roadmap

We remember that week in the spring of 2001 as if it were yesterday, not twenty years ago. Juan, a visitor from Argentina, arrived at our home in Granada, a historic city in Southern Spain, site of the famous Alhambra. We sensed the visit was significant, but only in hindsight did we realize that this was the first international step of a life-changing journey for Juan and his family.

For several years, they had been conscientiously preparing to serve as missionaries in a Muslim country. Their church and its pastor, Brother Marcelo, were unreservedly supportive. In fact, the pastor and church had engaged in a process in which all of them had been taking ever deeper and more intentional steps toward this goal, along with Juan and his wife. They drew in other churches in their beautiful land of Argentina; their missionary sending project gaining strength as it took shape.

Juan, Brother Marcelo, and the various pastors spent many hours reading and gathering information, absorbing the new ideas of missionary practice that were coming to Argentina at that time. They wanted to do their best to contribute to the establishment of a Christian church in a specific place in the Muslim world. Taking the process very seriously, they contacted several missionary agencies to help them think through both the logistics and the practical and ministerial care of their workers once they reached the field. PM International (PMI) seemed to them to be the most suitable agency, the agency Christian served as project director. But they had an important question: since PMI was carrying out several development and humanitarian projects, was establishing new churches the mission's priority? The church leaders and PMI's staff agreed that they should take two trips: to the mission field and to the agency's headquarters. This included an initial exploratory trip by Juan, and another journey by several of the Argentinean pastors a few months later.

In that long-ago conversation, Juan bombarded me (Christian) with questions and ideas, raising his points of concern as well. Where would his wife and he live? They would be part of a team; what was team life like? What did they need to do to get a residence visa? When he had learned the language, would he be able to preach? To disciple? To sing with the new believers? They were three very intense days, full and delightful days, in which we ate together, drank lots of coffee, and spent many hours simply talking.

Some of Juan's questions were more about stories and cultural things. He had already visited North Africa before visiting PMI's office in Granada, in the South of Spain. The smells, the music, the way of traveling and bargaining were all deeply recorded in Juan's mind and in his senses. But there were other, deeper questions – questions about missionary methods, about doctrine, and about approaches in forming a church.

Some months later, I had the pleasure of accompanying the group of pastors who supported Juan. There was Brother Marcelo, delighted to be accompanied by his denomination's leaders, their presence a demonstration of their commitment to Juan and his plan to serve as a missionary. This time, the pastors first discussed "official" business with PMI's leaders in Granada, and then I took them in my van to North Africa. We toured a number of cities, met with several missionaries, and visited some of the development projects. As my time with Juan had been, the days with the pastors were filled with talking.

When they met with missionaries, the pastors asked many questions, mainly concerning evangelism and the church. But as I listened, I sensed a change. Things of which they had been sure, built up over years of successful ministry, were now being shaken by a radically different way of understanding the church and evangelism. It was not just a matter of outward forms. These veteran pastors understood that it was much more than that. Most of them had traveled and preached extensively in Latin America and Europe, and were used to seeing cultural differences, but now they were encountering a deeper change. On the one hand, they grasped the presence and witness of the Holy Spirit in the missionaries and projects they had visited. But on the other hand, their doctrinal assumptions were brought into question.

I well remember a time when the group's conversation turned to reflection, a sort of conclusion to what they had seen and experienced as they met the PMI missionaries and saw their work. One of the pastors said: "Well, it is clear that what you are doing is pre-evangelism." I wanted to strangle him! I restrained myself, of course. To make things worse, he was a highly respected servant of God, known across Latin America, and recognized by many as an apostle. What frustration! Hadn't they understood anything?

The next day, a little calmer, I reminded myself that a few years earlier I had also experienced similar confusion. My process was different than that of those important leaders; I was neither a denominational leader, nor was I famous or Latin American. But I did remember well the years in which my theology and missionary practice changed, little by little. I remembered how, sometimes, I had stopped to list the many ways in which my understanding of the Bible, of mission, of evangelism, of the church, and even of society had become different from what my parents and my church had taught me. I had faced the changes little by little, in a process spread over several years of practice and biblical reflection. For these Argentinean leaders, the encounter had been like hitting a train head-on. They realized that not only their missionary, Juan, would deal with this new missionary reality and expression of the church but, as they supported him, they would deal with it as well.

As a result of my encounters with Juan, his church leaders, and quite a number of others, I decided to write a little book explaining the process of change my companions in PMI and I had lived through and the missionary model that we were following. *Peregrinaje en la Misión* (Pilgrimage in Mission) appeared in 2009, divided into two parts.[1] The first section is historical and theological. In the second, I return to those themes but do so through the narrative of Juan's story and the process of establishing a church in a Muslim country.

Now, many years later, my wife Charo and I are together writing the history of this singular group of people, the development projects they carried out, and the churches that are being formed. We have chosen to not just recount the stories but to add our reflection to these narratives. Why this approach? Principally because we ourselves have been learning and have learned a lot during these forty-plus years of direct involvement in missionary work. Even though we daily recognize that we have much still to learn and understand, we want to put into writing our thoughts and reflections, the lessons we have learned. We do not want to avoid sharing them, because sharing is a fundamental part of both the Christian life and simply of being human.

The second reason we are writing this account is because we have discovered that reading both about their successes as well as their failures is attractive to the great majority of Christians interested in the mission of God. Yes, the great majority. Earlier we had thought that this would only be of interest to those who are involved in mission in countries where Muslims form the majority. But over the years we have discovered that many of these successes as well as failures are not unique to these settings but are shared across the continents. They are familiar to the great majority of Christians and their churches committed to the mission of God, whatever the location.

First Questions

In the face of growing global tension between the West and Islam, what paths are there for a transparent and healthy collaboration for development, for the common good?

Can Latin American expatriates in Muslim countries work in harmony with their Muslim colleagues while maintaining their identity as practicing Christians, or should they minimize that identity for the sake of greater harmony as they live and work together? In fact, a growing number of Latin American expatriates are evangelical or Protestant missionaries, some of them collaborating in development projects or engaged in pastoral and evangelism work.

---

[1] This book, in Spanish, is available at http://musulmania.com/resources/14_Peregrinaje_en_mision.pdf.

In practice, we observe that much of the evangelism in Muslim lands is either so subtle that it goes unnoticed or, if it is clear and open, it quickly leads to religious confrontation. Likewise, many of the Latin Americans involved in mission use projects (development, cultural, relief, business) as a sort of enticement or lure for evangelism and as a pretext to obtain visas that they would otherwise not be granted.

Is there a possibility of Christian evangelism in Muslim lands that is both frank and respectful while resulting in a reasonably low level of religious confrontation? Moreover, a question on which there are very polarized positions, is it permissible to combine the implementation of development projects with the establishment of churches? If so, how does the concept of integral mission contribute to the theory and practice of such a combination of churches and projects?

In this book, we explore how several Latin Americans have carried out development projects and established Christian churches in North Africa, the Sahel, and Central Asia, and have done so with a very low level of religious confrontation. One aspect of the novelty and appeal of this book lies precisely in the absence of serious religious intolerance in the settings we have studied.

The major themes we will explore are: (1) a biblical theology of development, (2) the particularities of the Latin American concept of integral mission in Muslim contexts, (3) the establishment, contextualization, and relevance of the churches that have emerged, linked directly or indirectly to these projects, (4) all within the pervasive and multifaceted cultural framework of Islam, and (5) some lessons we have learned coupled with a missionary proposal.

Social Context

We have focused specifically on what some would call least-reached settings: communities where the project is itself a pioneering effort and where there is no Christian church. The settings are in societies where over ninety-five percent of the community are Muslims, each with strong components of popular or folk Islam and Sufism. Since Islam is far from uniform, the narratives take into account the cultural, social, and religious diversity of each environment.

The projects we describe are located in North Africa, Senegal, and Uzbekistan. Details about the North Africa settings are omitted since both the churches and the projects could suffer serious consequences if the information were mishandled. In the case of Uzbekistan, although religious persecution is currently severe, the events analyzed are from the past and their description does not pose any present risks to Uzbeks or foreigners. We have added data on projects and churches in Mauritania, Algeria, Turkey, India, and the Middle East, not in extensive descriptions but as useful elements at a comparative level.

The projects analyzed are distinctly Latin American in their style: they are carried out with many financial limitations, the missionaries implementing the projects do not always have the level of professional training they might desire, the personal relationships and empathy with the beneficiaries are high, and, as will be shown, the final result is much better than what could initially be expected. The Spanish maxim *hacemos mucho con poco* (making a little go a long way) can be justly applied.

Background

There are approximately one thousand Iberoamerican evangelical missionaries in Muslim-majority countries, of whom between seventy and ninety percent, depending on the country, are directly involved in development projects.[2] The projects include a variety of approaches: rural programs including water, sanitation, and agricultural development along with schools, medical or health assistance, care for the disabled and groups at risk of exclusion, vocational training, language teaching, cultural cooperation, business or entrepreneurial projects, and, to a lesser extent, emergency disaster relief.

As we will explore in detail in later chapters, the concept of development and its related terminology emerged after World War II, with the attempt by the countries of Europe and North America to bring their former colonies into the process of modernization and industrialization. They hoped to bring about standards of "social welfare" as measured by the various indicators established by the United Nations Development Program (UNDP).

The Christian church and its many agencies or organizations joined the ideology of this "development" without critiquing it. The developmentalist economic model did not begin to be questioned until the mid-1960s when Paul VI promulgated the 1967 encyclical *Populorum Progressio*. It took another decade for practical or alternative options to emerge: on the one hand, liberation theologies in their various forms, and, on the other hand, the long process of the Lausanne Movement in search of "integrality." From Latin America, the concept of integral mission has been advocated. In recent years, various theologies centered on the kingdom of God have opened the doors to ecological and relational issues, while the Jubilee 2000 Campaign for the abolition of foreign debt opened a new aspect, a new participation of evangelicals in politico-economic issues. Today, while some unreservedly approve of the UN Sustainable Development Goals, others doubt that the very concept of development can be interpreted theologically.

In Muslim countries, expressions of mission from Latin America are polarized. A majority of Latin American missionaries look for veiled ways to obtain residence visas and dedicate themselves to a supposed evangelism, for which they may use projects of various kinds as a hook and a cover. Nevertheless, a minority has opted for integral mission; they carry out projects with the understanding that the projects themselves are a needed and valid part

[2] These figures are based on the best information we have available from confidential sources. Published data is not available.

of their missionary task. However, it is not always clear how to combine projects with non-proselytizing evangelism and church planting. Sometimes the project and evangelism are like the rails of a railroad: they do not touch. At other times, project and church reinforce each other, although the how and why of this relationship is not clear.

Is there such a thing as a biblical theology of development suitable for this century and for the Muslim contexts in which Latin American workers serve? Is it appropriate to even attempt to establish churches in relationship to development projects? What are the differences between proselytism and evangelism? Can one be non-proselytizing and at the same time establish Christian churches? These are some of the questions that we attempt to answer in this book.

Point of Departure

The questions we raise are important for us personally. Christian has spent thirteen years leading development projects carried out by a hundred Iberoamerican missionaries in Muslim countries in Asia, North Africa, and the Sahel while Charo has worked for ten years in the logistics and administration of PMI, an agency specialized in integral mission among the followers of Muhammad. Before that, we had already spent nineteen years together establishing new churches in Spain.

Although we write from a Christian perspective, we do not share the animosity perceived in broad Christian sectors towards Islam. On the contrary, we profess a sincere appreciation for Muslim culture and Islam in general.

We are also aware that the formation of churches is a fundamental missionary goal for a significant proportion of the missionaries and organizations that support the projects we studied. Although we do not share this point of view, as participant observers we have tried to faithfully reflect and interact with the positions of the people who are part of this study. According to our understanding, the glory of God is the ultimate goal of mission, and the establishment of the church should be understood as the penultimate goal.

Our Roadmap

Our intent has been to write for a broad audience of Christians interested in mission, development, and Islam. That is, we hope that our content will be accessible to pastors, missionaries, theological students, and development workers. With that in mind we have avoided academic jargon and, while giving appropriate references, limited the use of footnotes. We have also translated all foreign language quotations. For those readers interested in a detailed bibliography and references to methodological issues, please consult Christian's *En Busca de una Misiología Integral* (In Search of an Integral Missiology).[3]

The stories of the people, projects and churches we describe are part of a universe of meanings, a specific environment. That is why we have divided this book into three parts. The first part will introduce us to the various understandings of development and integrality with a theoretical emphasis. This approach will help readers understand both the proposal we eventually offer as well as the history behind two expressions that too often are worn out or merely used as catchphrases: integral mission and development.

The second part of the book is comprised mainly of narrative. Four chapters are devoted to describing the projects and churches as well as their social and religious contexts. Another chapter provides a preliminary overview, comparisons, and reflections. This will help us draw lessons from the experiences of the people, projects, and churches.

Finally, the third part of the book is devoted to presenting a proposal we term Development-Salaam. We open this part with a chapter of biblical analysis, seen from the eyes of a development worker, followed by a biblical and qur'anic exposition and comparison of the concepts of *shalom* and *salaam*. It will be followed by a chapter offering an outline of a theology of Development-Salaam. In that chapter, we draw together ideas that should guide the life and mission of the church and of the people involved in working for the common good and for peace. We conclude the third part with two chapters which offer specific ways forward at the practical, methodological, and identity level of our missionary proposal.

At the end of each chapter, we have added questions for reflection. They can be used in the classroom or by individual readers as they formulate their own answers and analysis. They are intended as a bridge between the Muslim settings described and the Western or English-speaking world, to help apply the lessons or insights to the readers' context. We also offer with each chapter a brief list of resources for further reading, these are publications that expand on the topics covered in that chapter.

---

[3] Available at *https://hdl.handle.net/1871.1/5c4e0640-8da2-48da-9ff5-d965c1fa5458*. For the print or electronic version of this volume, contact the authors at *desarrollo-salaam@losgiordano.org*.

PART ONE

Theoretical Foundations

In this first section, we enter into a vital discussion of the theoretical foundations underpinning our interpretation of the concepts of mission and development. This first largely theoretical part of the book allows us to:

- Explore the nature of *integrality* and the missiological stream of integral mission.
- Understand development from secular and humanist perspectives and how development is carried out by government and other official entities and NGOs.
- Understand the various theologies of development that flow from both Catholic and Protestant thinking.

2. Integral Mission and Integrality

Integrality: the Concept and the Practice

What does it mean to be *integral*? It has to do with wholeness and connection, with drawing together all of something's many elements, facets, and possibilities. *Integrality*, in turn, is the quality of being complete and whole. It is a term we frequently use in describing the people and projects we are considering, each of which fits broadly into the category of integral mission. In these settings our reference to integrality will point to the quality of being whole, to lived-out expressions of integral mission as expressed in the Micah Declaration and related documents. It refers to the "undivided witness" in which no artificial barriers are erected between the demonstration and the explanation of the gospel.[1]

The concept of integral mission is so wide that it escapes definition; its range of meanings are captured by various expressions. In fact, as described by various writers, integral mission is generally described in detail rather than concisely defined. We can compare this attempted definition to a question such as: What is life? What does it mean to be alive? Answering those questions requires more than a simple definition, broad as it might be. Therefore, together with those other theologians and missionaries, we prefer to describe rather than define the term; we will try to uncover its meaning by entering into dialogue with the term.

Integrality is also an abstract term. It is difficult to measure – but no more so than other abstract terms. The principal difficulty in defining and measuring it lies, we think, in the fact that it is a relative concept. First, it is a reactive personal perception. It can be *perceived* only in contrast with its absence. It is *personal*; that is, different people perceive its absence to different degrees. It is a *reaction* to a sense of inconvenience or discomfort in the face of partiality, reductionism, or the absence of specifics. Secondly, the perception of integrality is an ideal; we try to achieve it even while we are limited by a large number of circumstances

[1] Micah Network, "The Micah Network declaration on integral mission," September 21, 2001, https://live-micah-global.pantheonsite.io/wp-content/uploads/2020/10/integral_mission_declaration_en.pdf; Paul Bendor-Samuel, "Epilogue: Called to Undivided Witness," in *Undivided Witness: Jesus Followers, Community Development, and Least-Reached Communities*, ed. David Greenlee, Mark Galpin, and Paul Bendor-Samuel, Regnum Practitioner Series (Oxford: Regnum, 2020), 163-68.

and the specifics of the context. And while academics, theologians, writers, and others are able to describe it in theory, in practice the perception of being integral – and, therefore, the capacity to implement it – will be distinct in each time and place and never more than partially achieved.

We qualify mission as being integral then because earlier we had perceived it as being "disintegral" or incomplete.

Integral Mission in General

We will focus our thinking on describing the differences between the Latin American vision of integral mission and its expression in the settings we refer to as *Islamia*.[2] However, by way of introduction, we will first briefly discuss several concepts rooted in theology that will help us understand the basic elements of what we mean when we refer to integral mission.

Transformation and integral mission imply that:

- Sin is not simply individual or personal (committed by people) but is also structural, collective, and organized.
- Equally, salvation has personal, collective, and structural dimensions. Because of this, "we can never say that the gospel is an individual message and that the communal dimensions of it are a natural consequence of that individual approach."[3]
- Salvation and transformation go hand in hand. It is the *re-creation* of everything: persons, institutions, societies, culture, relationships, and more through Christ in the power of the Spirit.
- The kingdom of God is not just in the hearts of believers nor can it be limited to a future hope, even though these are both aspects of the kingdom. The kingdom of God is the lordship – the governance – of Jesus Christ in all areas of life: of persons, of societies, and of the entire cosmos. This is the daily passion of every believer who prays: "Your kingdom come" (Matt. 6:9, Luke 11:2), asking that the future should become reality today, a kind of "celestification of the earth."[4] The kingdom "has come and is coming." The kingdom, then, is an ideal, a "not yet," a "present," and a "now" toward which mission works and expresses itself.
- The missionary task includes, therefore, preaching the gospel as well as its practical demonstration, the exercise of loving works, fighting for justice

---

[2] As a reference to countries with a majority Muslim population we have adapted this term from Federico A. Bertuzzi, ed., *Ríos en la Soledad: Latinos Respondiendo al Llamado Macedónico de los Pueblos Islámicos*, CLAME 90 (Santa Fe, Argentina: Proyecto Magreb, 1991), 18.

[3] Valdir Steuernagel, "Wholistic Mission," Mission Commission of the World Evangelical Alliance, Global Missions Summit, June 18-24, 2006, 11.

[4] Archbishop (Yannoulatos) Anastasios, *Mission in Christ's Way: An Orthodox Understanding of Mission* (Brookline, Mass. and Geneva: Holy Cross Orthodox Press and World Council of Churches Publications, 2010), 6.

and the dignity of every human, as well as caring for God's creation. The work of mission is the essential task of the church in its corporate form. The church is not the final object of mission but its beginning. At the same time, from an integral perspective, we should be clear that "a better human future must include a vibrant, growing, living Christian community."[5]

- The church cannot ignore human needs, not any of them. She is the visible sign, and anticipation of the kingdom that is coming.

To these understandings, we add three phrases from noted authors, the first from Latin America, the second from Asia, and the third of Mexican-North American roots:

> Wholistic mission is not primarily about content but about attitude and about journey.[6]

> Integral mission flows out of an integral gospel and an integrated people. There is a great danger that we transform the mission of the church into a set of special "projects" and "programs", whether we call them "evangelism" or "socio-political action," and then look for ways to integrate these methodologically. Rather, the mission of the church is located in the adequacy and faithfulness of its witness to Christ.[7]

> A missiology of transformation entails the new formation, the re-creation of whole persons – of all and every aspect of their lives, each in their particular context in terms of knowing, being, doing, serving, and relating to one other: it has simultaneously personal, social, structural, and national implications. It involves reconciliation with God, self, creation, others, and the sociocultural economic and political structures.[8]

Latin American Integral Mission: A Brief History

A significant contribution to the recovery of the evangelical social conscience came about through work begun in the early 1960s by Latin American evangelical leaders and theologians, most of whom were linked with the International Fellowship of Evangelical Students (IFES). One result of the concerns, reflection, and gatherings of these leaders was the birth of the Latin American Theological Fraternity (FTL) during a December 1970 gathering of twenty-five leaders in Cochabamba, Bolivia. The previous year, listeners had

---

[5] Bryant L. Myers, *Walking with the Poor: Principles and Practices of Transformational Development*, rev. ed. (Maryknoll: Orbis, 2011), 177.
[6] Steuernagel, "Wholistic," 21.
[7] Vinoth Ramachandra, "What Is Integral Mission?" (Micah Network Integral Mission Initiative, 2012), 10, https://www.yumpu.com/en/document/view/33518643/what-is-integral-mission-by-vinoth-ramachandra-micah-network/3.
[8] Charles E. Van Engen, *Transforming Mission Theology* (Pasadena: William Carey Library, 2017), chap. 6.

given a seven-minute standing ovation to Samuel Escobar's presentation at CLADE I, the first congress of the Latin American Council of Evangelicals, a talk very similar to his landmark speech at the Lausanne Congress five years later. Something was happening in Latin America; a widespread yearning among evangelical leaders for an understanding of the gospel that represented a true spiritual and social response to the situation of corruption, widespread poverty, and disenchantment. During this time, the expression "integral mission" was coined, used widely by René Padilla along with others associated with the FTL.

While the expression "integral mission" is now widely accepted not only in Latin America but in all evangelical circles related to development, the depth of its understanding and application in Latin America is still in question. Some have wanted to believe that its impact has almost transformed the evangelical church in the continent. Others, probably more realistic upon analyzing its thirty-five years of history, have recognized that "It is widespread, it is true, although it cannot be claimed that in all cases it has been assimilated, nor that it has had the most appropriate application, [one that would] enable us to dream of the human and social transformation that the gospel demands of us."[9] The reality is that the two major Latin American evangelical sectors involved in mission, those linked to the FTL and those related to COMIBAM (the Iberoamerican Cooperation in Missions network), have brought their positions much closer in recent years, although not necessarily their vocabulary. As I wrote in 2008:

> COMIBAM and the FTL represent two complementary points of view on the issue of mission both of them from a clear evangelical theological position.
>
> On the one hand, the movement represented by the FTL has been accused of speaking a great deal about mission while focusing almost exclusively on local Latin American issues, setting global and cross-cultural aspects of mission almost completely aside.[10] In actual practice, when the FTL environment speaks about mission, they nearly always refer to the mission of the church within its own cultural world.
>
> On the other hand, COMIBAM seems to have reduced the missionary task to "saving souls" and "planting churches," limiting it to merely sending of missionaries to non-Christian nations.[11] They have often done so without spending time reflecting theologically or methodologically about their work, and they have

---

[9] Harold Segura Carmona, "La Misión Integral Treinta y Cinco Años Después," *Espacio de Diálogo*, March 2005, 2, http://www.cenpromex.org.mx/revista_ftl/ftl/textos/harold_segura.htm. Trans. D Greenlee.

[10] See for example Pablo Davies in: P. Carrillo Luna, *Seminario Raimundo Lulio* (Granada: LAM and PMI, 2005), 54–55.

[11] From the publisher's description of the book *Ser, Hacer y Decir: Bases Bíblicas de la Misión Integral*, Kairos Ediciones, http://www.kairos.org.ar/novedad.php?ID=2026, accessed April 3, 2006

given ideological priority – their language reflects this choice – to the proclamation of the Word of God and the evangelization of the last frontiers of the earth.

In the author's opinion, as both movements are gaining experience and their mutual interaction is increasing, their differences are softening. Today, some of these differences are merely semantic issues.

An interesting and informal meeting that took place in Miami in April 1995 is an example of the growing understanding. Eight leaders each from FTL and COMIBAM spent three days together, discussing "the perspective of each regarding the themes of missiology, Latin American reality, integral mission, and the local church and mission."[12] They did so in a spirit of brotherhood. Federico Bertuzzi, one of the participants, recalled in a conversation with us in May 2006:

"That meeting in Miami was conducted with mutual respect, and it was a good fit! Each organization presented three perspectives on selected topics. We realized that when there was divergence on any point, we were not really that far from each other. COMIBAM was lacking a more articulated social conscience and FTL had missed the cross-cultural emphasis. [...] Our relationship improved. [...] And our discourses have changed over the years, especially since the end of the Cold War."[13]

For many, however, integral mission means merely adding good works to the verbal proclamation of the gospel. At first glance, words and actions may appear to be the same, but their meaning and motives differ greatly, as our descriptions of several development in later chapters will show.

Differences between the versions of integral mission in Latin America and in Islamia

Below, we will attempt to draw out the differences between the understanding of integral mission in Latin America and as it is understood and put into practice in *Islamia*. We group the ideas into large "baskets" or sections, several of them closely interrelated. Our question here is: How do these differences manifest themselves in the Muslim-Latino hybridization experienced by Latino workers in the *Dar al-Islam* (Arabic for the house of Islam, the house of peace), those territories where Islamic law rules, or where the majority of the population is Muslim?

Discomfort and reaction: A new formulation of integral theology and missiology emerged in Latin America in the 1970s, formulated in reaction to discomfort over accepting the approaches of either liberation theology or the conservative-fundamentalist positions of evangelical sectors. Harold Segura

---

[12] Bertuzzi historical archive. "Consulta Misiológica FTL-COMIBAM, 1995: Comunicado de Prensa" (Miami: FTL and COMIBAM, 1995), 6/23, http://recursosmisioneros.com/docs/eventos/Miami_1995.pdf.

[13] Christian Giordano, "Identity, Context and Message: Iberoamerican Mission in Muslim Lands" (M.Th., London, Brunel University, London School of Theology, 2008), 13-15, https://doi.org/10.13140/RG.2.1.2644.4241.

calls it a "third way in missiology."[14] Its proponents reacted to concrete approaches and situations; they not only wanted "*to say*, but also [...] to *disavow* or contradict."[15] Latin American integral mission reacts to liberation theology and the model of mission it has received: a specialized and individualistic expression of mission exercised from a position of power and resources.

On the other hand, some Latin American missionaries in Muslim countries reacted, almost two decades later, both against the classical missiological model and to the pressures of cultures more integrated than their own.

The starting point: The FTL's discourse was rooted in a modernity-based worldview, expressed in the language of the elites and university students. It sought evangelical answers to the social challenges of Latin America, but, in the end, it did not connect with the ecclesial bases, the great Latin American evangelical masses. Its starting point was theological and ideological. On the other hand, the Latin American missionaries in *Islamia* were not generally sent by churches related to the FTL but linked to COMIBAM, which was more conservative and more inclined to proclamation. While the FTL concentrated on its own Latin American context, COMIBAM focused on cross-cultural mission. Latin American missionaries who have practised integral mission in Islamic contexts are mostly *practitioners* rather than thinkers or theologians, and their starting point has been Muslim culture: the unity of all based on the unity of God. Thus, the missiological reflection of missionaries in *Islamia*, whose thinking and practice are guided by concepts of integral mission, is basic and practical; it is almost utilitarian rather than theological. Above all it asks the Bible different questions, questions arising from the clash between their Latin American Christian convictions and the daily reality they observe in Muslim societies. Its starting point is anthropological and cultural as well as empirical.

The journey: On the other hand, integral mission is a journey or a process; it is personal, contextual, incarnational, and hermeneutical; it is always flawed and incomplete. As the Spanish saying on individual experience goes: *Cada uno habla de la feria como le va en ella* (Each one talks about the fair according to how one fares).[16] It is far from being a static vision. It is a process. Progress or change take place at both the personal and group levels. The main exponents of the FTL have pointed out some of its most notable changes or evolutions. For example, Samuel Escobar, a well-known Latin American missiologist, mentioned the change of emphasis in a 2011 conversation we held with him:

> In the initial period, integral mission had a Christological structure that was key to understanding the needs of human beings as well as the content of the gospel and

---

[14] Harold Segura Carmona, *Ser Iglesia en la "Era del Vacío"* (El Paso: Mundo Hispano, 2011), 24.

[15] Segura Carmona, *Ser Iglesia,* 41, emphasis in original.

[16] Which means, "Everyone see things in his own way" Ramón García-Pelayo y Gross, ed., *Diccionario Moderno Español-Inglés Larousse* (Paris: Larousse, 1986).

> the style of missionary work. Our ongoing work is based on a trinitarian approach that also takes into account the reality of a global church.

For Harold Segura, the change of focus was from soteriology to ecclesiology.[17] If in the early days the concern was to combat a gospel only for the soul (what kind of gospel to proclaim?), it soon became concerned with the kind of church that lives that gospel: "The integral church is one that understands that all areas of life are 'mission fields' and seeks ways to affirm the sovereignty of Jesus Christ in all of them."[18]

But every journey is also *personal*, lived differently by each person, hence the section "My Pilgrimage in Mission" in the *International Bulletin of Mission Research*, one of the most important mission journals.

Additionally, the journey is *contextual*: human beings only exist in a concrete context. That has always been one of the characteristics of integral mission. Of course, the Latin American and Muslim contexts differ diametrically, hence the need to rethink integral mission when it is exercised in Islamic, European, and other contexts.

The journey is also *incarnational*. This is a theme that the early proponents of integral mission emphasized from the beginning, especially from biblical-theological perspectives. Incarnation was encouraged, the example of Christ was studied, and applications and principles were drawn from it, even though, due to the circumstances themselves, its practice was limited. In comparison, however, incarnation and contextualization have been strong points of the practice of Latin American missionaries in *Islamia*.[19]

Incarnation and *hermeneutics* go hand in hand. Lived experiences make one re-read both context and Scripture, both history and its meaning, and the community and its interpretation of the events in question. There is no such thing as pure interpretation, disconnected from the person of the interpreter.[20] Hermeneutics is always personal and contextual, and therefore changeable.

Finally, the journey remains *unsuccessful and incomplete*; it is an attempt that aspires to an ideal. It is marked by mistakes, inconsistencies, and contradictions; room always remains for critical evaluation and regret. As missiologist Timothy

---

[17] Segura Carmona, *Ser Iglesia*, 29–30.

[18] C. René Padilla, *The Local Church, Agent of Transformation: An Ecclesiology for Integral Mission* (Buenos Aires: Ediciones Kairos, 2004), 22.

[19] Federico A. Bertuzzi, ed., *Latinos en el Mundo Islámico* (Miami: UNILIT, 1991); Bertuzzi, *Ríos de Soledad*; Christian Giordano, *Peregrinaje en la Misión*, Colección Musulmania 14 (Granada: PM Internacional, 2009), http://musulmania.com/resources/14_Peregrinaje_en_mision.pdf; Carrillo Luna, *Seminario Raimundo Lulio*.

[20] In the field of the theology of mission, Charles Van Engen has added personal experience to the three traditional fields of interpretation: Scripture, the historic and communal interpretation of the church, and context. See Van Engen, *Transforming*, chap. 2.

Halls commented in a 2011 interview, "Integral mission does not defend its integrality but seeks it."

There is no doubt that the journey has been much more extensive and spread over a longer period of time in Latin America than in *Islamia.* In this sense, both the Latin missionaries and the churches that have emerged from their work in Muslim lands are beginning the journey thirty or forty years later than their siblings in Latin America. It will likely lead them to similar overarching results but with important differences, especially in ecclesiological, anthropological, and soteriological aspects.

Incarnation and Contextualization: As we have said, incarnation and contextualization have been strong points of the missionaries in *Islamia.* Latin American theologians of integral mission spoke a lot about incarnation; they started from the example of the incarnation of the Son of God, developing new theological approaches, and building on their own upper-middle class social position: university students with good education. The reflections of Orlando Costas encouraging us to follow Jesus "outside the gate" continue to be a source of inspiration.[21]

On the other hand, integral mission in Muslim lands is expressed with an unequivocal commitment to incarnation, especially at the cultural level, that is linked to a critical contextualization in the host culture. It starts by accepting the particular culture as being just as worthy and valuable as the worker's culture of origin or the biblical cultures. It is achieved, first, both with a determined attitude to learn and adapt wholeheartedly and to the maximum extent possible and, second, with the help of the tools of cultural anthropology. These technical tools, as well as the help of the Holy Spirit and the missionary community, contribute to a critical contextualization, that is to say, one that distinguishes those elements of the culture that need to be redeemed by the gospel from those things that may arise because they are bothersome to missionaries and their families. Contextualization and incarnation affect, of course, learning of both the language and social customs, but they go much further, modeling the very way of doing mission, the way of making decisions, Bible reading – we will return to this topic – as well as aspects of the life of the missionary community itself (e.g. dress, social status, and standard of living) and of the family (e.g., one's children being born in the country rather than abroad and the possibility of their marrying within the country).

Again, the emphasis in Latin America was theological and in *Islamia* it was pragmatic. However, regarding the contextualization of the gospel (not so much of the missionary) differences also seem to be intuited. The position of René Padilla and Samuel Escobar has been that of the "translatability" of the gospel, a position also supported by Kwame Bediako, Lamin Sanneh, John Mbiti, and

---

[21] Orlando E. Costas, *The Integrity of Mission: The Inner Life and Outreach of the Church* (San Francisco: Harper & Row, 1979); Orlando E. Costas, *Christ outside the Gate: Mission beyond Christendom* (Maryknoll: Orbis, 1982).

Andrew Walls. It is still too early to state it definitively, but the tendency of the Latin American missionaries who pursue integral mission in Muslim lands seems to lean more towards the "local theologizing" advocated by Shoki Coe, Robert Schreiter, Dean Gilliland, Stephen Bevans, Ashish Chrispal, Tite Tienou, and Andrew Kirk.[22] In any case, evaluating how Iberoamerican missionaries understand contextualization is a topic that requires further study. It should be kept in mind that most of these missionaries have not had formal studies in anthropology, much less an explanation of the different schools or positions regarding contextualization. The COMIBAM III study, carried out on behalf of that missions network, found that only forty-five percent of those working in the Muslim megasphere had a bachelor's degree, and that only thirty-three percent had taken a course in cultural anthropology. On a general level, the study report indicated that "churches do not normally invest much in training their workers prior to their departure to the field or in retraining them after they arrive at their cross-cultural site."[23]

Epistemology: The sources of knowledge of the academy are often modernist and in some cases postmodernist and may fit poorly with indigenous worldviews (including Islamic worldviews). The same can be said of the methodologies employed, mostly conceived from (and for) a Eurocentric mentality.[24] We would venture to say that the model of "modern missions" – an Anglo-Saxon expression to describe the Eurocentric Protestant missionary movement of the last two hundred years – has had a detrimental character of separation or disconnection, in the sense that it has exported the compartmentalized way of understanding the Christian faith proper to Western culture. But Muslim worldviews (and indigenous ones in general) do not tolerate well such disconnection since it is

---

[22] Translatability originates in the external agents that "bring the gospel." It takes on autochthonous forms according to the local cultural facts. It is mainly a movement in one direction: from the Bible and the gospel to the culture understood in a static way, as a cultural fact. That is to say that it contemplates only one movement: the adaptation of the gospel to a given context. In contrast, "local theologizing" aims to go two steps further: (1) understanding culture in a broad way, i.e., all the events of life and society (politics, economics, injustice, relationships, etc.) and (2) fostering a constant two-way dialogue between Bible and society. The concept thus includes the idea that theology is always being made, changing with social changes. In 1972, Shoki Coe, then director of the Theological Education Fund, called it "contextualization" to distinguish it from indigenization.

[23] Levi deCarvalho et al., "Fortalezas y Debilidades del Movimiento Misionero Iberoamericano" (Equipo Investigación Misiopedia, 2006), 40, http://recursosmisioneros.com/resources/Fortalezas_debilidades.pdf A summary of this report in English is available at https://www.globalconnections.org.uk/sites/newgc.localhost/files/papers/Comibam%20missions%20-%20strengths%20and%20weaknesses%20%20-%20Jan%2007.pdf.

[24] Keyan G. Tomaselli, Lauren Dyll, and Michael Francis, "'Self' and 'Other': Auto-Reflexive and Indigenous Ethnography," in *Handbook of Critical and Indigenous Methodologies* (Los Angeles and London: Sage, 2008), 347-72.

neither integral nor cohesive. Certain academic methodologies – too often, it seems – insist on dissecting things in order to analyze and explain them, but inevitably kill them in the process.

Integral mission is, in this sense, an attempt at reconnection; the desire to bring together pieces and aspects that should never have been separated. It has been received, in general, as an innovative and restorative alternative, although with diverse acceptance. Latin American integral mission is expressed within a culture that is less dichotomistic and individualistic than that of North America but still compartmentalized in comparison to Muslim cultures. In a continuous linear representation from compartmentalization to being integral (holism), Latinos would be in the middle. Anglo-Saxon and Germanic cultures would be at one extreme (compartmentalized or dichotomistic) and Arabs would be at the other extreme (being integral or holistic). For the compartmentalized mentality, it is a matter of joining Word and works (the capital letter is intentional) but it does not reach beyond that. At the other extreme, for Muslim and strongly holistic cultures in general, the integration of all things is a reality that is taken for granted, an *a priori*. The Latin American concept of integral mission would be in the middle. Let us remember that the origin of integral mission was modern, not postmodern, but that situation is changing, especially since the 2012 CLADE V congress of Latin American evangelicals called by the FTL. There, North American Hispanics raised new questions and approaches that implied epistemological changes. Likewise, internal voices are emerging that raise postmodern points of view and "wisdoms," especially from the voices of new, younger leaders.[25]

On the other hand, Latin missionaries in *Islamia* face the challenge of explaining the gospel to pre-modern cultures that are being marked both by postmodernity (in its younger and internationalized strata) and globalization.

Extended vs. Minority: We are surprised by the contrast between two statements: one from a book, the other from an interview. Harold Segura picks up a comment of Padilla that "There are good grounds to affirm that the idea of integral mission is established within the Latin American evangelical community."[26] In effect, even though many of the important implications of integral mission have remained hidden, a large proportion of Latin American evangelical churches have broadly adopted the idea and practice of uniting preaching with good works. However, although the vocabulary is that of integral mission, the practice is often superficial or even the opposite of what integral

---

[25] Oscar García-Johnson, *Mestizo/a Community of the Spirit: A Postmodern Latino/a Ecclesiology*, Princeton Theological Monograph Series 105 (Eugene: Pickwick Publications, 2009); FTL-Brasil, "Seguir a Jesus em seu Caminho de Vida. Reflexiones para CLADE V." (FTL-Brasil, June 25, 2012), http://ftl-al.org/images/stories/Contribuicao_da_FTL-B_-_Documento_Final-finalmente.pdf.

[26] Harold Segura Carmona, "La Misión Integral: 41 Años Después," *El Blog de Bernabé* (blog), October 11, 2011, 32, https://www.elblogdebernabe.com/2011/10/la-mision-integral-41-anos-despues-por.html. Trans. D. Greenlee.

mission means, as when social work is instrumentalized for proselytizing purposes, without social transformation.

This contrasts with the lack of depth of penetration of the concept among Latin American mission agencies and their personnel, especially as far as mission among Muslims is concerned. From North Africa, one of our colleagues surprised us in saying: "[In the whole country] we are almost the only ones who practise integral mission. [...] I think ninety percent of the workers are involved in proclamation, without considering the integral nature of the gospel." This has also been the experience of the Latin American-rooted mission agency PM International, which finds itself "rowing against the current" among related mission agencies focused on Muslims. Even among the agency workers themselves, the concept is not clear. For many, integral mission is only equivalent to uniting words and works, without being aware that this is only the visible part of the iceberg, to put it comparatively.

Paradoxically, those Latin American workers who serve among Muslims and who have opted for integral mission often feel they are misunderstood by the very churches that have sent them and faithfully support them. The question arises: Wasn't the church committed to integral mission? Moreover, they chose to send their valuable workers with a missionary agency that openly positions itself in that missiological line. The reality is that, as we pointed out above, most of the evangelical churches in Latin America have signed up to a questionable understanding of what it means to be integral. This partial understanding has not gone beyond uniting "Word and works" and has remained limited to service, to social diakonia. For this reason, they expect their missionaries to *use* good works, the projects in which they are involved, to produce converts and new churches, but they assign a reduced value to the projects themselves, considering them to be merely pre-evangelization. As a result, the missionaries find themselves between a rock and a hard place: having to struggle both with the mission field and with teaching their church what integral mission truly implies.

Transformation: To speak of integral mission implies being aware of the broad dimensions of salvation and of the global transformation that God is working toward at individual, community, socio-political, ecological, and other levels. Salvation, understood integrally, includes the transformation of individuals, and in turn the formation of communities of faith that model the kingdom of God – that is, integral churches. These in turn actively contribute to transforming their society according to the model of the kingdom. This perspective does not contradict or deny individual salvation (although it does contradict individualistic views of salvation), but rather broadens the concept to include the communitarian and social dimensions of salvation.

Even so, there are many who reduce this concept to mean merely carrying out some assistance project. For them, integral mission means little more than good works. But this is a distortion of words. Much of what we see both in the churches in Iberoamerica and in the mission field is not integral mission, even though that is what people try to call it. Perhaps the same confusion exists with the English terms holistic and wholistic mission, which is why the Micah Network, after some debate, decided to use, also in English, the expression integral mission.

However, since the nature of being integral always is contextual, in specific moments and concrete contexts we may emphasize its social or communitarian aspects. For example, the current situation in Latin America, where Evangelicals carry demographic and social weight, demands that they do not neglect the transformation that the church should promote in society as a whole and its structures. However, where the church is very much a minority or persecuted, it will be necessary to emphasize the communitarian aspect, the integral nature of small ecclesial communities. This is the case of the minority churches of North Africa to mention just one example. Although the present emphases may differ, the final ideal is the same: the kingdom of God. But if transformation is not present, then the gospel has been curtailed, reduced, and thoughtful people will miss the integral nature of the gospel.

The integral nature of humans: Another difference between the FTL's descriptions and the version of integral mission lived out by missionaries is seen in how the integral nature of the gospel is applied to people. As Samuel Escobar reminded us in a personal conversation in 2011, from its beginning, the FTL insisted on "an integral vision of the human being that is biblical and that seeks to understand them in their fullness and to serve them also in their fullness, avoiding traditional dichotomies that separate the spiritual from the rest of the person created in the image of God." It has been a repeated and well-developed theme, mainly from the point of view of biblical anthropology.

On the other hand, those missionaries serving among Muslims, and Latin American organizations, that have opted for integral mission have emphasized the *applied* integral nature of the missionary; that is, (1) how much they are able to adapt or incarnate themselves in the host culture and (2) how deeply the implications of integral mission have penetrated them. This does not mean that they have left aside the integral vision of the human being as such nor that of society, but rather that they have *added* a personal emphasis, an emphasis on the missionaries themselves. We have already mentioned above the practical and theological importance of incarnation in the eyes of such missionaries. They attach importance not only to learning the language and culture; they also want the host culture to penetrate into the depths of their being, as far as possible.

This is seen in the very identity of the missionaries and their families, who have learned not to attempt to camouflage their identity as missionaries sent from some churches in Latin America. It implies reformulating personal and – when the missionary has a family – family identity, since the identity as a "full-time Christian missionary" that they bring from Latin America is misunderstood and counterproductive in their new host culture. Rather than camouflaging an identity, they forge a new one; quite a psychological and mental challenge! This applied integral nature includes re-reading the Bible through the cultural lens of the new culture, and re-formulating both the gospel message and its presentation. We will return to this topic later.

This reformulated identity reflects the desire to avoid living out a kind of "ministerial schizophrenia" stemming from having two identities, the hidden identity of being a missionary and the public identity of being a teacher, a doctor, or possibly a development worker. They have left aside the bivocational model to choose to be integral, reformulating their identity as teachers or doctors or workers, followers of *Isa al-Masih* (Jesus the Messiah). This reformulated identity is monovocational, transparent, real, and balanced; added to it are one or more social roles known and integrally part of the host culture.

The poor: In our recent reading of evangelical missiology, frequently we find an emphasis oriented toward the poor. It is an imbalance that ignores the rich, as if they do not need salvation – or are beyond its reach! Perhaps the imbalance is unconscious or unintentional, but it is nonetheless evidence of a misconception of both the person of God and the nature of poverty and its solution. This imbalance is seen in the Micah Statement of Integral Mission:

> Mutual learning, encouragement and strengthening as we serve the cause of God's Kingdom among the poor. [...] Jesus modeled identification with the poor and inclusion of the other. [...] We serve [...] as we journey with the poor. [...] We commit ourselves to prayer, advocating on behalf of the poor. [...] We want to see the poor through the eyes of Jesus [...] like sheep without a shepherd.

The document, which contains some twenty-five mentions of the poor and four of the rich continues:

> We are called to work for reconciliation between rich and poor, between the oppressors and the oppressed. [...] Wealthy Christians – both in the West and in the Two-Thirds World – must use their wealth in the service of others. We are committed to the liberation of the rich from slavery to money and power.[27]

Looking at things from another perspective, Bryant Myers reminds us that rich and poor are relational concepts that depend on each other, that both have the same problem, albeit with a different polarity: a mistaken identity, and that the solution to poverty can never be achieved by working only with or on behalf of the poor.[28]

The way many of our Iberoamerican colleagues serving in Muslim countries express themselves falls along the lines expressed by Myers: they develop their work, relationships, and ministry, all linked together, both among the wealthy as well as the poor and needy. This witness of breaking down social barriers has a very powerful impact in highly stratified societies.

Manifestations of the Spirit: Being surrounded by Islamic societies and brotherhoods (often of Sufi inspiration) that do good and develop an intense welfare activity, Latin American missionaries have seen the crucial importance

---

[27] Micah Network, "Micah Declaration."

[28] Myers, *Walking with the Poor*, 2011, 145-48.

of including the manifestation of the Holy Spirit as part of their understanding of the integral gospel. Integral mission is not only talking about God, doing good and becoming incarnate, but also the demonstration of the power that comes only from God. This supernatural manifestation can take many forms including dreams, visions, healings, convictions, and miracles. Among those holding Muslim worldviews, these manifestations and visible presence of the Holy Spirit are very important; they typically take for granted that such manifestations are a normal part of divine confirmation in the events of daily life. It is a *sign*. It is a power that brings transformation in depth, it is the "perfect gift [...] from above, coming down from the Father of the heavenly lights" (James 1:17). It is the power that the devil has always tried to imitate, as in the case long ago of the magicians of Egypt contesting the first three plagues (Ex. 7; 8) and the work of Muslim sorcerers today, although their power can never be compared to God's power. As we were told in an interview which we conducted in Senegal:

> On the morning of April 11, we went to visit the village again. As usual, we consulted the patients and then the village chief, Malik, invited us for coffee. We drank coffee with milk and lots of sugar and ate some moldy bread. I confess that it was a bit difficult, but I decided not to look at the bread and to eat quickly. [...] A few minutes later we went to visit Marieta, the patient for whom many were praying during the month of March. We entered her house, and to our surprise we found her with a big smile on her face, a clear sign of her physical and emotional improvement. On examining her, we noticed a notable decrease in her tumor. She happily explained to us that her pain had greatly diminished. It was very gratifying to hear her husband's testimony: "For months, my wife went to doctors and hospitals and took various medications without any improvement. Tired of spending money, she went in search of healers and traditional African treatment, which also did not produce any results. However, after you examined her, through the medicines and your prayers, she has improved a lot; an improvement she had never experienced before. I ask you to continue to pray for her, and my house is open to receive you always." Joyful to see the miracle worked by Jesus in this woman, we preached the Word, and laying our hands on her, we prayed again for her complete recovery.[29]

Re-reading the Bible: Integral mission in Muslim lands also includes a re-reading of the Bible through the eyes of the host cultures. This starts with understanding everyday events, which may be very similar to those of biblical times: "coming in and going out of the gate" (John 10:9b), judges and the council of notables sitting by the gate (Ruth 4:1-2), public negotiations, the kind of hospitality that takes a whole day to cook a dinner from its living ingredients (Gen. 18:2-8), using oil as medicine and for anointing (Luke 10:34, Ps. 23:5), and bargaining (Gen. 18:22-32), to cite a few examples. The stories of Jeremiah,

---

[29] José Rocha Júnior, "Dois Cafés da Manhã" (Privately circulated manuscript, Dakar, Senegal, April 21, 2005).

Abraham, Joshua, and David take on new life; we understand them with new nuances, tinged with the concepts of honor, fealty, family loyalty, hospitality, and so on.

A colleague in North Africa told us: "I have discovered that God himself taught Samuel how to lie – or how to tell a half-truth. He feared that Saul would kill him when he went to anoint David. God instructed him: 'Say that you are going to offer a sacrifice'" (1 Sam. 16:1-2). My friend, raised in a strict Dutch Mennonite family, had just discovered a biblical reading through a lens of North African culture. This re-reading had come about thanks to the "noise of her own world, of her own experience […] that wants to bring to bear on the actual experience of the reader or listener."[30]

Thus, speaking of the hermeneutics of genitive and "bad" or uncomfortable texts, Professor Hans de Wit draws attention to the fact:

> Given the presence of bad [uncomfortable] texts, the question arises as to the *cultural* factor present in our interpretation of the Bible. Who decides what is good or morally correct? Judgments about what is morally correct are not constructed in isolation from the moment in which one lives as a reader. […] We must be aware of how and to what extent our way of reading bad biblical texts obeys *culturally* determined patterns and values.[31]

Deep hermeneutical change can come from contact with national believers and their interpretations of Scripture, the associations of ideas they make and how they apply them. From there, new conceptions of discipleship, church and leadership emerge. But there is still more. Re-reading the Bible with "Muslim" eyes leads to discovering new facets not only *in the way* the gospel message is presented, but also *in the content* of the gospel. Of course, the gospel is one for all time (Gal. 1:9) – and we thought we knew it all and very well! But how many truths have we never dreamed existed until we re-read the Word with other "cultural glasses," helped by our national brothers and sisters?

This is not the time to go into details, but there is increasing awareness of what some call the gospel of honor and shame. The same could be said about themes of cleanliness and impurity that permeate the entire Bible (and especially Leviticus) – but are rarely discussed in comparison to the theme of shame and honor. This cleanliness-impurity pair is a very powerful issue in Muslim culture and spirituality. What more could we learn in exploring themes such as the concept of sin and salvation, the person of God, the new Jerusalem, and so on?

---

[30] Hans de Wit, *En la Dispersión el Texto es Patria: Introducción a la Hermenéutica Clásica, Moderna y Posmoderna*, (San José, Costa Rica: Universidad Bíblica Latinoamericana, 2002), 12.

[31] de Wit, *En la Dispersión,* 528. Emphasis in original, trans. D. Greenlee.

Conclusion

While we have pointed out differences between the Latin American and the hybrid Latin-Muslim versions of integral mission, are these two expressions really different? We believe they are not; we are dealing with the same concept, even though it has different nuances and emphases. When integral mission is lived out among Muslims, many of the lived-out theological principles are also found, even in seed form, in the writings of some of the Latin American exponents of integral mission.

What these comparisons between versions of integral mission corroborate is how much the context affects the practice of mission.

In that regard, we have pointed out eleven important differences between integral mission as expressed in Latin America and lived out in *Islamia* by Latin American missionaries:

- the response to different situations,
- a different starting point,
- a journey that is just beginning,
- the emphasis on contextualization and incarnation placed at different points,
- a different epistemology,
- a minority (theological and practical) point of view,
- the concept of social transformation exercised from almost underground,
- the focus of human wholeness placed primarily on the missionary (along with a re-defined missionary identity),
- a variety of relationships with both poor and rich,
- convincing manifestations of the Holy Spirit among or observed by our Muslim friends close to and observing the lives and work of missionaries, and, finally,
- a re-reading of the Bible through Muslim eyes.

Furthermore, there is a prevailing confusion over the use of certain words that prevails in the Latin American missionary world, as seen when some consider that simply carrying out some activity of service is qualified as integral mission.

Questions for Reflection and Discussion

1. What has your own journey been like – simply as a human? Specifically, as a Christian? Looking back, in what ways has your doctrine, practice, or emphasis changed?
2. How does the Bible become real and alive for you?
3. Which of these statements do you agree with more?
   - The Bible relates to the realities of daily life.
   - The Bible relates to spiritual themes.
4. What experience have you had of manifestations of the Holy Spirit? Do you think they are important, or accessories? Why?

For Further Reading

Adeney, Miriam. *Wealth, Women, and God: How to Flourish Spiritually and Economically in Tough Places*. Pasadena: William Carey Library, 2015.

Escobar, Samuel. *In Search of Christ in Latin America: From Colonial Image to Liberating Savior*. Downers Grove: InterVarsity, 2019.

Muller, Roland. *The Messenger, the Message, the Community: Three Critical Issues for the Cross-Cultural Church-Planter*. Osler, Sask., Canada: CanBooks, 2006. www.canbooks.com.

Padilla, C. René. *Mission between the Times: Essays on the Kingdom*. 2nd ed. Carlisle: Langham Monographs, 2010.

Peristiany, Jean George. *Honour and Shame: The Values of Mediterranean Society*. Chicago: University of Chicago, 1974.

Van Engen, Charles E. *Mission on the Way: Issues in Mission Theology*. Grand Rapids: Baker, 2000.

Van Engen, Charles E. *God's Missionary People: Rethinking the Purpose of the Local Church*. Grand Rapids: Baker, 2003.

Wright, Christopher J. H. *The Mission of God: Unlocking the Bible's Grand Narrative*. Downers Grove: IVP Academic, 2006.

3. The Ideology of Development

In this and the next two chapters, we will explore various theoretical schools of thought related to development along with recent approaches of state-sponsored and official international agencies, such as the International Monetary Fund and the World Bank.

The concept of *development* is very broad. It refers to a process that is common in nature and, indeed, in any growing or evolving process. Further, development assistance or humanitarian aid can be understood by focusing on their various aspects. Over time and depending on those writing, development has been described in many different ways. For the sake of clarity, we have chosen to group the various approaches or positions into three broad categories:

1. A secular, or official focus;
2. An alternative focus; and
3. A religious focus, which we will consider in the next two chapters.

1. Secular or State-Sponsored Development Focus

At a very general level, the concept of development and its associated terminology emerged after World War II, with the attempt by European and North American countries to bring their former colonies into the process of modernization, industrialization, and standards of social welfare measured according to the various indicators established by the United Nations Development Program (UNDP).[1]

Official Development

Some have pointed to U.S. President Harry Truman's inaugural address on January 20, 1949, as the beginning of the state-sponsored development vision, espoused by the state, and specifically by rich Western countries to solve the problems of "poor countries."[2] The triggering effect was twofold. On the one

---

[1] Wolfgang Gern, "Development," in *Dictionary of Mission: Theology, History, Perspectives*, ed. Karl Müller, American Society of Missiology Series, no. 24 (Maryknoll: Orbis, 1997), 102-8; Vinay Samuel, "The Development Movement: An Overview and Appraisal," *Transformation* 13, no. 4 (December 1996): 12-16.

[2] Richard Peet and Elaine Hartwick, *Theories of Development: Contentions, Arguments, Alternatives*, 2nd ed. (New York and London: Guilford Press, 2009), 222.

hand, World War II had left much of Europe and parts of Asia devastated. On the other, the dynamics of the Cold War resulted in the countries that fought on the losing side in World War II coming under pressure from those on the winning side to align their policies and worldview with that of the United States and "democracy." The aim was to establish a new world order, a new relationship of powers and values.

Modernization

While "Christianizing the barbarians" might have been the motivation of the colonial era, the leading thought of the 1950s was to Westernize and bring democracy to the losing countries of World War II. It was the era of modernization; development was equated with economic growth. It was a time characterized more by activism than reflection. The approach was simple: "Increase productivity to bring peace and prosperity to all" as espoused by U.S. President Truman in his 1949 Inaugural Address.[3] It was taken for granted that by injecting large amounts of money and technology, rudimentary agrarian societies would become industrialized, and productivity would increase significantly.

The vision of development as modernization coincided not only with the post-war period but also with the process of decolonization and the creation of new states, many of them in very precarious socio-economic conditions. The more or less unconscious assumptions of this approach were derived directly from modernity's linear vision of history and progress and its faith in science and technology. North American economic growth was the model to follow and could be replicated in all other countries. The indicators used to measure progress or development were economic macro-figures, in particular gross national product and per capita income. As Vinay Samuel points out, it was "a non-violent approach to economic change" with the aim of preventing the assisted countries from drifting into the Communist Bloc.[4] Although formulated in later years, Rostow's theory expressed in *The Stages of Economic Growth* represents the quintessence of the modernizing vision.[5]

The principles of modernization were not the exclusive domain of the West, but were also applied in the Communist Bloc, even if they were "eclipsed" by other political and social developments.

---

[3] Harry S. Truman, "Inaugural Address," ed. Gerhard Peters and John T. Wolley (The American Presidency Project, January 20, 1949), http://www.presidency.ucsb.edu/ws/?pid=13282.

[4] Samuel, "Development Movement," 12.

[5] Walt Whitman Rostow, *The Stages of Economic Growth: A Non-Communist Manifesto* (Cambridge: Cambridge University Press, 1960). There is also a third, expanded edition, 1990.

Structuralism

In 1960, the United Nations launched its first Decade of Development and, in 1965, established the United Nations Development Program (UNDP).

While this is not the place to go into details of economic theory, in basic terms, the ideas of economists Adam Smith and David Ricardo prevailed at first, but soon the leaders of key international organizations (the UN, International Monetary Fund, and the World Bank) and their political counterparts turned to Keynesianism,[6] which had borne good fruit after the Great Depression of the 1930s in the United States. Its characteristics were: a high degree of state interventionism, promotion of full employment even at the cost of low wages, promotion of the welfare state for the great masses of the population through subsidies, heavy state indebtedness, and accelerated economic growth. These were short-term politico-economic prescriptions that gave birth – at least in Europe – to an enduring concept and a political party: social democracy.[7]

However, the developmentalist and structuralist process did not bear the expected fruit; by the end of the decade in 1970, it was clear that the increase in macroeconomic growth figures had not reached the population as a whole, as pointed out by Robert McNamara, among many others, at the 1973 annual session of the World Bank.[8]

"Another Development"[9]

The 1970s saw the birth of several critical currents from within official organizations. One of them was the Christian-humanist impulse of Dag Hammarskjöld, second Secretary General of the UN, a fervent Lutheran Christian and posthumous winner of the 1961 Nobel Peace Prize. He was able to mobilize many people and institutions that, fourteen years after his death, gave birth to the 1975 Dag Hammarskjöld Report. This report proposed a very drastic change of course, condensed in ten points, advocating a "New World Order."[10]

It was also the decade in which the American, Denis Goulet, after his time in France and Latin America, laid the foundations for a development ethic. Goulet was also a fervent Christian, a Roman Catholic. However, the thesis that prevailed was the Basic Needs Approach. This was part of Hammarskjöld's

---

[6] Keynesianism is the economic theory that encourages state intervention through economic policy to stimulate demand and encourage consumption. It was proposed by John M. Keynes in response to the Great Depression, which began in 1929.

[7] Peet and Hartwick, *Theories*, 13.

[8] James A. Cogswell, "Relief and development: challenges to mission today," *International Bulletin of Missionary Research* 11, no. 2 (April 1987): 72-76; Peet and Hartwick, *Theories*, chap. 3; Samuel, "Development Movement," 13.

[9] "Another development" is a term applied to an approach that runs counter to earlier, modernist views, as explored in M. Nerfin, ed., *Another Development: Approaches and Strategies* (Uppsala: Dag Hammarskjöld Foundation, 1977).

[10] Dag Hammarskjöld Foundation. *What Now: The 1975 Dag Hammarskjöld Report*, https://www.daghammarskjold.se/publication/now-1975-dag-hammarskjold-report/.

proposals but with a less radical approach. The Basic Needs Approach represented a break with the two previous approaches (modernization and structuralism) and was characterized by its bottom-up, inclusive, people-centered, and self-directed approach. Furthermore, aid was to be distributed as directly as possible, that is, directly to the poor. While the focus on basic needs was concentrated on food, health, and education, its scope was very easily expanded to include other parameters such as security, social justice, employment, and a healthy environment. It also opened the door to other considerations that gained momentum in the following decades including the focus on human rights, indigenous rights, and gender discrimination.

The Basic Needs Approach, although confined to the 1970s in its original form, through renewal and reorientation has persisted to the present. In 1990, under the impulse of Mahbub ul Haq, the first *Human Development Index* (HDI) was released, sponsored by the UNDP but carried out by independent researchers. The HDI is an aggregate index of the three basic dimensions of health, education, and income, assessed through four main indicators: life expectancy at birth, average years of schooling/education, expected years of schooling, and gross national product per capita. The ongoing, annual Human Development Report include many other indicators such as access to justice, comparison between military and educational spending, gender differences, and various measures reflecting inequality, or the Multidimensional Poverty Index.[11]

One of the main ideological supporters of the HDR has been the Indian economist and ethicist Amartya K. Sen (b. 1933), winner of the 1998 Nobel Prize in Economics.[12] His work focused on development as the expansion of human capability and justice have proved to be very influential concepts in current conceptions of this issue. Due to the importance he gives to human freedom and its capacity for self-definition and agency, Sen has been very influential in the new understanding of development that emerged at the end of the twentieth century. In fact, what Sen has introduced are ethical concepts in the midst of economic and political parameters: human individuality and its aspiration to make free choices.

Neo-Neo (Neoliberal and Neoconservative)

As noted above, the Other Development approach was short-lived: it was confined to the 1970s. In the early 1980s, Western governments as well as international organizations increasingly shifted towards neoliberal and neoconservative positions. Several circumstances contributed to this shift. On

---

[11] Pedro Conceição, ed., *Human Development Report 2019: Beyond Income, Beyond Averages, Beyond Today.* (New York: UNDP, 2019). http://hdr.undp.org/sites/default/files/hdr2019.pdf.

[12] Amartya Sen, *The Idea of Justice* (Cambridge: Belknap Press of Harvard University Press, 2011); Amartya Sen, *Development as Freedom* (Oxford: Oxford University Press, 2001).

the one hand, the successive development plans had not been free of charge for Third World countries (as they were called at the time): they had acquired a very high level of debt, up to US$626 billion;[13] in many of them corruption was rampant. On the other hand, in 1973 and 1974 the Arab countries decided to embargo their oil sales to the countries that had supported Israel in the Yom Kippur War, thus provoking the first oil crisis, the effects of which lasted until the end of that decade. The fourfold increase in the price of oil produced enormous profits (petrodollars), which the oil exporting countries deposited in First World banks. In turn, these banks, which had been lending money to the Third World since 1960, increased their operations and the interest at which they lent. In addition, they began to refinance the debt burden, granting new loans to pay off old loans of debtor nations, adding to the problem.

All of this contributed to the so-called debt crisis: developing countries were no longer able to repay their exorbitant debts. Mexico announced its bankruptcy in 1982,[14] followed closely by Argentina, Brazil, Poland, and many others. The political and financial establishment of the First World panicked, fearing a domino effect. The IMF took charge of refinancing the debt at the cost of harsh corrective measures. Structural Adjustment Programs (SAP) were imposed, which invoked a strict Ricardian[15] logic of production and export, as well as stabilization measures (prohibition of strikes, cuts in social spending, and currency devaluation) and adjustment measures (export promotion, reduction of the official/state apparatus, economic liberalization, privatization of public enterprises, and lowering of taxes). "During the period 1980-89, 171 SAPs were introduced in Sub-Saharan Africa; a further 57 had been initiated by the end of 1996."[16]

The power of neo-liberal ideology softened somewhat in the 1990s, but it has remained the general trend. Economic theories inspired by Gunnar Myrdal and Friedrich von Hayeck,[17] Milton Friedman, and most recently Jeffrey Sachs have prevailed over the last twenty-five years. Sachs is also known for being the ideologue of the Millennium Development Goals, signed at the UN Millennium Summit (September 6-8, 2000) by one hundred eighty-nine heads of state or

---

[13] Peet and Hartwick, *Theories*, 89.

[14] The Mexican peso lost half its value in just one week and the State was left carrying a debt of some $20 billion. Peet and Hartwick, *Theories*, 89

[15] From the English economist David Ricardo (1772-1823) who postulated the conditions of profit from trade between states, which ultimately favored only the richer party to the exchange.

[16] David Simon, "Neo-Liberalism, Structural Adjustment and Poverty Reduction Strategies," in *The Companion to Development Studies*, ed. Vandana Desai and Robert B. Potter, 2nd ed. (London and New York: Routledge, 2002), p. 89.

[17] Von Hayeck (1899-1992) was of the Austrian school of economics. He received the 1974 Nobel Prize in Economic Sciences. Margaret Thatcher and Ronald Reagan both depended greatly on his thought.

government. Although the Basic Needs approach and the Millennium Goals[18] are sponsored by the same institution, the UN and UNDP, few realize that their economic and ideological assumptions are contradictory.[19] The former seeks the empowerment and autonomy of the poor, while the latter focuses on the rich investing an infinitesimal part of their wealth in subsidizing the poor, even when the way in which they amass that wealth is seriously detrimental to those same poor people.

2. Alternative Focus

Soon, voices critical of state-sponsored development emerged, views that were supported by governments and official international organizations. Some of these voices remained inside the system while others were expressed in the sphere of development cooperation with the private sector. There is not always a clear distinction between them. We have grouped under this sub-heading four major currents that opposed the official ideology of development or radically questioned it: (1) dependency theory and its later variants, (2) anti-development, (3) the reformulation of development from a postmodern perspective and (4) Appreciative Inquiry.

Dependency

We could say that the theory of dependency emerged in Latin America in several conceptual stages. First, in the 1940s, the Argentine economist Raúl Prebish (1901-1996) questioned the Ricardian model of foreign trade. He argued that the wealth of Europe and the United States was due to the impoverishment of the countries of Latin America (among others), and was growing out of the trade and economic relations between them. In 1970, the Brazilian geographer Teontonio dos Santos described the spatial forms of dependency between the First World, at the center of power, and the Third World countries, on the periphery. A more radical *dependency* position, influenced by the Marxist views in vogue, criticized the policies promoted by Prebish and the Economic Commission for Latin America for ignoring the class struggle and indirectly benefiting the bourgeoisie.[20] But the German-American André Gunder Frank (1925-2005) truly popularized dependency theory by publishing extensively in English. Dependency theory has considerably influenced a current socio-politico-literary current: post-structural post-colonialism.

---

[18] The Millennium Development Goals have been replaced by seventeen Sustainable Development Goals (SDGs). These will be explored in Chap. 15.

[19] Stephen Browne and Thomas George Weiss, eds., *Post-2015 UN Development: Making Change Happen*, Global Institutions 87 (New York: Routledge, 2014).

[20] One of these critics, Fernando H. Cardoso, served as President of Brazil from 1995-2003. His most important work is *Dependency and Development in Latin America* (1979), co-authored with the Chilean Enzo Falleto.

Two of the strengths of dependency theory(/ies) is its ability to strike a balance between reality and utopia, and to be profoundly Latin American in its approaches. Its various currents are combinations of economic structuralism with attempts at self-sufficiency and global trade. As such, dependency theory has fallen into disuse, even if it tried to perpetuate itself in the World-Systems Theory whose main proponent was Immanuel Wallerstein (1930-2019). Unfortunately, after the successive structural adjustments mentioned above, as Colin Clarke observed, today "the vast urban populations in Latin America are currently more marginal from the formal economy than at any time for half a century."[21]

Anti-development

Unlike all other trends, the current that we have called anti-development does not question the descriptions of development, but the very concept of development itself. Perhaps the best-known critique comes from the Colombian anthropologist Arturo Escobar who notes:

> Like "civilization" in the 19th century, "development" is the term that describes not only a value, but also an interpretative or problematic framework through which we understand the impoverished regions of the world. [...] Considering development as an invention also suggests that this invention can be "uninvented" or reinvented in very different ways.[22]

For this writer, the whole concept of the Third World (as he still termed it in his 2012 writing) is a construct, a discourse created from Eurocentric interests.

Although Arturo Escobar offers a profound critique, it is worth noting that he does not totally rule out the possibility that another type of development can be "invented." In fact, in his book *Territories of Difference: Place, Movements, Life, Redes*, he analyzes and praises the style of development carried out on the Colombian Pacific coast by the indigenous organization Proceso de Comunidades Negras [Process of Black Communities].[23]

Some have objected to the virulence of Arturo Escobar, in particular since he writes from the comfort of North American universities. While the same can be said of some of his post-colonialist colleagues, this is not the case of other exponents of anti-development such as Vandana Shiva (India), Wolfgang Sachs

---

[21] Colin Clarke, "The Latin American Structuralists," in *The Companion to Development Studies*, ed. Vandana Desai and Robert B. Potter, 2nd ed. (London and New York: Routledge, 2002). p. 95.

[22] "Antropología y Desarrollo," *Revista Internacional de Ciencias Sociales* 154 (December 1997): 8-9. Trans. D. Greenlee. See also Arturo Escobar, *Encountering Development: The Making and Unmaking of the Third World*, Reprint (Princeton: Princeton University Press, 2012).

[23] Arturo Escobar, *Territories of Difference: Place, Movements, Life, Redes* (Durham: Duke University Press, 2008), https://doi.org/10.1215/9780822389439.

(Germany), Gustavo Esteva (Mexico), Majid Rahema (Iran/France), and Ashish Nandy (India).[24] Nor is it the case of the Swiss Gilbert Rist whose emblematic *The History of Development: From Western Origins to Global Faith*, always places the word "development" in quotation marks.

Mennonite scholar David W. Shenk offers an interesting reflection in his comparison of the different approaches of the world's major religions to development, to progress, and to material well-being and peace:

> Approaches to development [...] are informed by a society's understanding of history. [...] A Hindu or Buddhist worldview considers history a tragic meaningless cycle controlled by fate. An African traditional worldview understands all history to be moving from the present to the past. Both Chinese and Africans have idealized the past. [...] A biblical worldview sees history moving from the garden of Eden [...] to a consummation in the future [...] the fulfillment of the kingdom of God. Biblical faith is permeated with a sense that history has purpose and destiny and movement. In the Muslim perspective, Islam is the primal, middle, and final religion, without innovation or change. The Islamic view is that history is suspended between the creation and the final judgment, [...] [a] doctrine which abhors *bidah* (innovation).[25]

Therefore, from a theological perspective, we must agree – at least in part – that development is a concept with a Christian background and one that is specifically assumed from a Western mentality. Recognizing this has significant implications regarding humility and understanding in the face of anti-development attitudes of any origin, be they Western, Islamic, or Hindu, to mention but a few.

Postmodern

At first glance, it does not appear that development studies and literature show much sympathy for the postmodern movement. Rather, incomprehension seems to prevail between the two, or, more specifically, a complete lexical mismatch: they speak completely different languages.[26] To help us clarify the issue, we note that postmodernity is an essentially European and North American phenomenon, that is to say, of the West. Generally speaking, the rest of the world is globalized, but only postmodern to a small degree.

---

[24] Desai and Potter, *The Companion to Development Studies*, 16-20; Peet and Hartwick, *Theories*, 227-30.

[25] David W. Shenk, *Global Gods: Exploring the Role of Religions in Modern Societies*, 2nd ed. (Scottdale, Penn.: Herald Press, 1999), 314-15.

[26] H. Fernando Bullón, *Transformación de América Latina y Responsabilidad Social*, vol. 3, Misión Cristiana y Responsabilidad Social Series (Buenos Aires: Kairos Ediciones, 2009), 113; Desai and Potter, *Companion*, 123; Bryant L. Myers, "Holistic Mission: New Frontiers," in *Holistic Mission: God's Plan for God's People*, ed. Brian Woolnough and Wonsuk Ma, Regnum Edinburgh 2010 Series (Oxford: Regnum, 2010), 121.

For the postmodern mindset, there is no absolute truth – no recipe for development – that can be applied equally in all situations and circumstances. On the contrary, a plurality of local solutions makes sense to postmodernists. Their favorite topics are culture and power: the relationship between culture understood dynamically (modernity understands culture statically) and development as well as the multiple and complex relationships between the power of developmentalist discourse and its representations of the First, Third, and Fourth Worlds[27] and development. They consider the various ways of perceiving issues of gender, indigeneity, rights and traditions in relation to development and also the *hybridizations* that the interaction of culture, information technology and developments (plural) produce in a constant and changing way.

Postmodernists distrust hierarchies and institutions; they are wary of international organizations, of governments, and of their grand declarations. They are more inclined to accept and collaborate with grassroots structures. They are also very sensitive to all ecological issues. Postmodernity – still in its infancy in terms of its global influence – is sure to bring many surprises in the field of development.

Appreciative Inquiry and Human Scale Development

In this section, we combine two partial approaches that are also alternative approaches to development: Appreciative Inquiry and Human Scale Development. They are relevant and worthy of mention even if they do not fit easily into our other categories.

Appreciative Inquiry marks a radical shift in the basic question that development asks and in the objectives it pursues. Common development approaches ask, "What is the problem?" and seek to improve the living conditions of a given population. In contrast, Appreciative Inquiry asks "What are you proud of? What is your ideal?" and seeks to enhance what is most valuable within the community.

Appreciative Inquiry was developed by the American David Cooperrider, between 1980 and 1986, while he was doing his doctoral research in the US at Case Western Reserve University in Cleveland, Ohio. In 1987, Cooperrider and his thesis advisor, Suresh Srivasta, published *Appreciative Inquiry in Organizational Life*, followed by a steady stream of books, manuals, and videos.[28]

The other alternative approach we briefly mention is Human-Scale Development, mainly promoted by the Chilean economist Arthur Manfred Max-Neef (1932-2019). A connoisseur of the Latin American reality, Max-Neef

---

[27] "Fourth World" refers to settings of urban poverty in the great metropolitan centers of the First World. While not in current use, this terminology was frequently used in the literature of an earlier period.

[28] See their website: https://appreciativeinquiry.case.edu/

proposed a bottom-up, participatory, plural, and diverse approach, articulated by civil society but with the indispensable contribution of the state. One of his most valuable contributions was the matrix of needs. He made a distinction between human needs, which are limited and universal, and the satisfiers of those needs, which are numerous and different for each culture and circumstance.[29]

Human needs, in this approach, are combined in a matrix based on two broad categories. Existential needs (related to human existence) are being, having, doing, and interacting. Axiological needs (related to human values) are subsistence, protection, affection, understanding, participation, idleness, creation, identity, and freedom.[30] Through group work, the community is guided to discover the "negative, positive, and neutral"" satisfiers for its harmonious development. On the other hand, Human-Scale Development, relying on the ideas of E.F. Schumacher,[31] argues that human systems have, in themselves, an optimal or critical dimension, which can only be successfully overcome – in terms of true human development – by multiplying relationships: many small independent but related systems.[32]

Reflection

The description of these different schools or ways of focusing on development is perplexing. It is difficult to assess these approaches in the abstract since the circumstances in which they are applied vary widely. A development focus might be appropriate if it is applied, say, at the national level by a state-sponsored agency, but that same focus might not be helpful when applied in a local project by an NGO.

Further, the mere consideration of material well-being is not by itself a sufficient criterion of evaluation of development and a community's sense of satisfaction. Hence, Amartya Sen (as mentioned above) has included other elements: political participation, civic freedom, and the development of personal and collective capabilities.

Our intention in this chapter, introductory by design, has been to help us understand both the postulates behind the language of development and our need to humbly face critical reflection, recognizing the multiplicity of human,

---

[29] Manfred A Max-Neef, *Human Scale Development: An Option for the Future* (Uppsala, Sweden: CEPAUR, Dag Hammarskjöld Foundation, 1990).

[30] Max-Neef further classified satisfiers into five categories: community-based synergistic satisfiers, ritualized or institutionalized violators, propaganda or pseudo-satisfiers, inhibiting satisfiers, and singular satisfiers.

[31] British economist Ernst Friedrich Schumacher (1911-1977) is the author of E. F. Schumacher, *Small Is Beautiful: Economics as If People Mattered*, Reprint (New York: Harper Perennial, 2010). First published in 1973, it has been considered one of the one hundred most influential books published since World War II.

[32] Manfred Max-Neef, *La Dimensión Perdida: La Deshumanización Del Gigantismo* (Montevideo and Barcelona: Nordan and Icaria, 2007), https://www.max-neef.cl/descargas/Max_Neef-La_dimension_perdida.pdf.

political, economic, and climatic factors involved in the well-being of peoples. Of course, the religious factor cannot be ignored, especially when the vast majority of the world's population professes to be adherents of some religious faith. We turn to this theme in the next chapter.

Questions for Reflection and Discussion

1. Which of the schools or ways of focusing on development have caught your attention? Why?
2. Are you familiar with an NGO involved in development? Are you involved with such an organization? Which of the approaches to development described in this chapter best describe this NGO?

For Further Reading

Conceição, Pedro, ed. *Human Development Report 2019: Beyond Income, Beyond Averages, Beyond Today.* New York: PNUD, 2019. http://hdr.undp.org/sites/default/files/hdr2019.pdf.

Cooperrider, David L, Diana Kaplin Whitney, and Jacqueline M Stavros. *Appreciative Inquiry Handbook: For Leaders of Change*. 2nd ed. San Francisco: Berrett-Koehler, 2008.

Max-Neef, Manfred A. *Human Scale Development: An Option for the Future*. Uppsala, Sweden: CEPAUR, Dag Hammarskjöld Foundation, 1990.

Sen, Amartya K. *Development as Freedom*. Oxford: Oxford University Press, 2001.

4. Roman Catholic Theology of Development

Since its founding, adherents of Christianity have always been involved in addressing human needs. In fact, some of the approaches we have considered in the previous chapter have Christian roots. In this chapter, we explore the specifics of Christian approaches to development in recent years, distinguishing between official Roman Catholic approaches (the so-called Social Doctrine of the Church) and the approaches of Latin American liberation theology. The next chapter will deal with Protestant approaches. Later, we will describe what the Old and New Testament say about the development or collective welfare of peoples.

1. The Official Roman Catholic Focus

The Magisterium of the Church is given normative importance among Roman Catholics. Therefore, in considering Roman Catholic approaches to development, it is essential to consider the various encyclicals and official Catholic documents. Liberation theologies have made considerable contributions to the vision of development and economics. We are aware that an in-depth study should include both the practice of the many missionary orders and the analysis of thinkers. But we will concentrate on offering a synthesis of the first two aspects.

Social Doctrine in the Magisterium of the Church

The first of the encyclicals in this field was *Rerum Novarum*, published by Leo XII on May 15, 1891, with significant contributions in its drafting from the Archbishop of Westminster, Cardinal Henry Edward Manning. This document gave rise to the Social Doctrine of the Church. This increasingly industrial age was a time of growing social inequalities and the rise of socialism. The encyclical dealt with "the situation of the workers" but also included important recommendations for employers and the state. It enshrined the right to property, the obligations of all parties, and the relevance of the Church because of its interest in the moral and religious issues involved. Further, it condemned communism as well as unrestrained capitalism and authorized workers to form unions.

Rerum Novarum has had a very great influence. We could consider it a courageous encyclical that restored to the Roman Catholic Church some of the credibility it had lost among the working classes and eventually led to the formation of the Christian Democracy political movements in Europe.

Forty years after the publication of *Rerum Novarum* it was followed by *Quadragesimo Anno*, published by Pius XI in 1931. This document was markedly conservative, and in many ways a step backward. It forbade strikes, recommending Catholic Action as an alternative, and harshly attacked communism.

On March 26, 1967, Paul VI released *Populorum Progressio*, marked by the broad vision that characterized its author. It was as much concerned with nations as with the person, seeking complete development. In Catholic doctrine, the term "human progress" has been much more frequent than the term "development." Paul VI, known in Milan as the Archbishop of the Workers, called entrepreneurs to a justice-oriented production and distribution of goods and services. He also denounced the worsening imbalance between rich and poor countries (§8, §31), criticized neocolonialism (§52) and affirmed the right of all peoples to well-being (§22). "Development is the new name for peace" (§76) stipulated the document, almost at its conclusion.

John Paul II's pontificate was prolific in producing social documents. In 1981, *Laborem Excersens* dealt with the spirituality of work and the value of the human being as an agent and producer of progress. Further along these lines, *Sollicitudo Rei Socialis*, promulgated six years later, dealt with the value and development of the whole person, while reaffirming the key concepts of *Populorum Progressio*, namely, the excesses of both capitalism and communism/socialism, the value of the person and life (against birth control campaigns), and denouncing the gap between rich and poor. He makes a theological reading of modern problems (§5) and defines what authentic development is. "In trying to achieve true development we must never lose sight of that dimension which is in the specific nature of man," which is at the same time corporal and spiritual. "Man must remain subject to the will of God, who imposes limits upon his use and dominion over things, just as he promises his immortality."[1] Finally, *Centesimus Annus* of 1991 rereads *Rerum Novarum* in the light of the twentieth century, emphasizing solidarity.

Benedict XVI, in his short pontificate, bequeathed us *Caritas in Veritate*, which takes up the themes of *Populorum Progressio*, adapting and commenting on them in the light of the financial crisis of 2007-2008. It was published just prior to the July 2009 G8 summit held in Italy.

---

[1] Juan Pablo II, *Sollicitudo Rei Socialis* (Vatican City: Editrice Vaticana, 1987), par. 29, https://www.vatican.va/content/john-paul-ii/en/encyclicals/documents/hf_jp-ii_enc_30121987_sollicitudo-rei-socialis.html

Up until the time of writing this book, Francis' magisterium has contributed *Laudato Si.* Its title evokes a phrase of Francis of Assisi and is apparently focused on ecology and care for our shared planet.

It also "urges politics to free itself from the yoke of economic power" according to a headline in the international section of Madrid's *El Pais* newspaper.[2] It is an atypical encyclical, first of all, because it is fundamentally addressed by its language and structure to non-believers, that is, to people outside the Roman Catholic Church. It is also atypical in the fact that it quotes many social documents of the regional episcopal conferences of the Global South and relies on the Orthodox Patriarch, Bartholomew I of Constantinople. In any case, the encyclical was harshly criticized by well-known representatives of American conservatives, among them Jeb Bush, brother and son of the two Bush Presidents. It can be said that *Laudato Si* reflects a vision much closer to the Global South on the issues of development, economy, and environment.

2. Liberation Theology

Since its beginnings in the 1960s and 1970s, liberation theology has reflected a great deal on development issues. Over the years, its positions have become more nuanced and diversified, which is why some speak of liberation theologies in the plural. Given the large number of books, articles, and conferences that liberation theologians have produced, we have chosen to concentrate on some of the most representative names and works related to the concepts of development.

Gustavo Gutiérrez, born in Lima, Peru in 1928, is undoubtedly the father of liberation theology. In fact, he is the one who gave us the name for this way of theological understanding. Gutiérrez was one of the consultants of the historic conference of the 1968 Latin American Episcopal Council (CELAM) in Medellín, Colombia; its final document reflects his influence. His thought has been articulated on three axes: the method, the poor and poverty, and the proclamation of the kingdom of God, axes with which almost all liberation theologians concur. Each of these axes has raised its own discussion.

The method of liberation theology has perhaps been the most discussed axis. It was harshly attacked by Cardinal Ratzinger, then Prefect of the Congregation for the Doctrine of the Faith. According to the official Vatican position, this was because of its "totalizing" Marxist influences. But to accuse liberation theology of using the categories of Marxist thought as an ideological corset seems an excessive criticism, given that it clearly criticizes fundamental elements of Marxism itself and of the planned socialist economy as well as its opposites: the capitalist economy and its market system.

For his part, from the Protestant/evangelical side, Samuel Escobar focused his criticism on the vision of history of liberation theology and its hermeneutics.

---

[2] https://internacional.elpais.com/internacional/2015/06/18/actualidad/1434621095_820022.html

Regarding the former, he reproves the revision of the history of liberation theologies (from the Marxist interpretation of history) combined with an optimistic understanding of the evolutionary humanism of Teilhard de Chardin and Vatican II (cf. *Populorum Progressio*). He also challenges it for its utopianism, the eschatological messianism of Marxism that permeates the works of liberationist theologians. Regarding hermeneutics, Escobar argues that liberation theologies see reflection on historical events (which Argentine Jesuit Severino Croatto had referred to as the acts of Latin American liberation) as act one and theology as act two. The Bible is read on the basis of both biblical salvific events and on current events. Therefore, Escobar writes, Croatto "is telling us that there can be new revelation of God in current events, and that these become the key to read the revelation in that which the written Word records."[3] At the same time, with respect to the concept of praxis (closely linked to method) he states:

> Evangelical praxis is Christocentric and is defined on the basis of the gospel. We should not be intimidated by those who, starting from a Marxist conception of praxis and a dialectical materialistic vision of reality and history, only consider praxis what is politically significant from their ideological perspective. Evangelical praxis is to know Jesus Christ and this knowledge is expressed in doing good. Worship and ethics go together in the Old and New Testaments.[4]

As regards the second major axis, the poor and poverty, the characteristic phrase has been *the preferential option for the poor*. The phrase began to be popularized in Medellín (1968) and was consolidated in Puebla (1979). Referring to this well-known expression, Gutiérrez wrote in 2002:

> The phrase emerged in the Christian communities and in the theological reflections of Latin America in the period from Medellín to Puebla, and this last conference took it up and made it widely known. It is very much present today in the magisterium of John Paul II and in that of various episcopates of the universal Church, as well as in texts of various Christian confessions. The preferential option for the poor is a fundamental axis in the proclamation of the Gospel, which, using the well-known biblical metaphor, we commonly call the pastoral task; it is also a fundamental axis in the field of spirituality, that is, in walking in the footsteps of Jesus. And, therefore, it is also an axis in terms of the intelligence of the faith that is made from these two dimensions of Christian life.[5]

---

[3] Samuel Escobar, *La Fe Evangélica y las Teologías de la Liberacíon* (El Paso: Casa Bautista de Publicaciones, 1987), 141. See also J. Severino Croatto, *Biblical Hermeneutics: Toward a Theory of Reading as the Production of Meaning* (Maryknoll: Orbis, 1987).

[4] Escobar, *Fe Evangélica,* 190.

[5] Gustavo Gutiérrez, "Situación y Tareas de la Teología de la Liberación," *Theologica Xaveriana* 143 (2002): 512.

The Brazilian-Korean theologian Jung Mo Sung (born in 1957) understands that this option for the poor represents a fundamental change in the Roman Catholic Church, brought about in the 1960s by the breath of the Holy Spirit in Latin America, that disturbed many, bringing this new awareness of the poor, marginalized and excluded.[6] For many, this is one of the greatest contributions of Latin American theology to the universal Church as a whole,[7] and in fact the concept has been adopted by many churches and authors across the Christian spectrum.

Liberation Theology, Development, and Economy

Although the encyclical *Populorum Progressio* pointed to the word development as "the new name for peace" the term did not go down well with the authors of liberation theology. From the first edition of his classic work, *Liberation Theology: Perspectives*, Gustavo Gutiérrez argued concerning what he called "the critical function of theology with respect to the presence and activity of humankind in history" that "It is my opinion that the term *development* does not well express these profound aspirations. *Liberation*, on the other hand, seems to express them better."[8] There are several factors that led to this semantic change. On the one hand, the clear perception that the push for "development" came from the West and especially from interests close to the government of the United States. On the other hand, the disenchantment with *developmentalism* arose in many Latin American countries, but especially in Brazil. That is why the bishops who gathered in Medellín in 1968 saw the need to add qualifiers to development such as genuine development or integral development and to use it alternatively with the word liberation.

One of the reasons was also to find a word that included messianic expectation and an eschatological dimension, linked to the liberationist vision of history. That is why Gutiérrez goes on to say: "the future does not arrive, it is built."[9]

Liberation theology has had a strong influence on the political and structural as well as economic aspects of social change. These are elements that cannot be left aside when approaching development in an integral manner. In this sense, the evangelical side of Christianity has been much more sparing in reflecting on these dimensions of development and has concentrated on the transformation of people and the micro-transformation of society. Of course, these are generalizations. They represent the most common approaches of both liberation

---

[6] Jung Mo Sung, *Se Deus Existe, Por Qué há Pobreza? A Fe Cristã e os Excluídos*, 3rd ed. (Sao Paulo: Paulinas, 2000), chap. 3.

[7] Now late in his theological career, Gutiérrez has affirmed: "The vision manifested in the formula 'the preferential option for the poor' is the most substantive contribution of the life of the Church in Latin America and of liberation theology to the universal Church." Gutiérrez, "Situación y Tareas," 513.

[8] Gustavo Gutiérrez, *A Theology of Liberation: History, Politics, and Salvation*, trans. Caridad Inda and John Eagleson, Rev. (Maryknoll: Orbis, 1988), xiv.

[9] Gutiérrez, "Situación y Tareas," 505.

theology and the evangelical side. There are always notable exceptions. However, it is worth remembering that:

> All liberation theologians agree that Christian liberation is as much interior and personal as it is structural. It is true that liberation theology has emphasized the political aspect, but [...] *to emphasize one aspect is not to absolutize it*, and in the Latin American reality the political factor is a priority, therefore it must be emphasized in theological reflection, without marginalizing that of the liberation from sin accomplished by Christ.[10]

While liberation theology began by adopting the premises of dependency theory, it soon added other methodological and theoretical paths to the theoretical framework of development. With hindsight, Sung clarifies:

> The path proposed by the theory of dependency was autonomous development, free of dependent relationships. Liberation theologians adopted this theory, introducing other categories, such as that of social classes, as the main instrument of analysis and understanding of social reality.[11]

Regarding the analysis of economic reality, Hugo Assmann, Franz J. Hinkelammert, Jung Mo Sung, and Julio de Santa Ana are among the most prominent authors in the field of liberation theology.

Very early on, Franz Hinkelammert began to write and teach about the fundamental role that the economy plays in the entire development process. Those were the years of Chilean socialism, under the leadership of Salvador Allende: times of political and social effervescence that raised both hopes and detractors, both with equal virulence. In 1970 two titles by Hinkelammert were published: *Dialéctica del Desarrollo Desigual* [Dialectic of Uneven Development] and *Ideologías del Desarrollo y Dialéctica de la Historia* [Ideologies of Development and Dialectics of History]. In both works, the author criticizes the utopia of an unbounded developmentalism (both capitalist and socialist) as well as the aspects in which socialism has erred. He proposes a non-utopian style of Latin American socialism, that is linked to the feasibility of history, of the present.

Almost twenty years later, Hugo Assmann and Hinkelammert wrote an extensive and profound work, with the symbolic title *A Idolatria do Mercado* [The Idolatry of the Market]. Based on Marx's critique of fetishism and the Weberian perception of religion, both authors, step by step, attack the very basis of the capitalist ideology and expose its pseudo-religion character. Indeed, they

---

[10] Segundo Galilea, "Teología de la Liberación: Ensayo de Síntesis," ed. Teodoro Balle, *Selecciones de Teología* 19, no. 76 (December 1980): 5, http://www.seleccionesdeteologia.net/selecciones/llib/vol19/76/076_galilea.pdf. Emphasis added, trans. D. Greenlee.

[11] Jung Mo Sung, "El Pobre Después de la Teología de la Liberación," *Concilium: Revista Internacional de Teología*, no. 361 (2015): 445. Trans. D. Greenlee.

argue, it is not enough to denounce the oppressive logic of the economic systems (both capitalist and communist) on the basis of ethical criteria.

What Assmann and Hinkelammert undertake is to bring to light the silenced, hidden aspects of the idolatrous logic of the hegemonic market; an "effort to identify and bring to light the silenced presuppositions."[12] The authors go a step further in making explicit the sacrificial logic of the system. Totalitarian economic systems (both socialist economics and unfettered capitalism) are incapable of responding to complex systems and of fulfilling the unattainable utopian goals they set forth (messianic happiness for all). Inherent in such incapacity is the need for victims, both of people and of resources and of the ecosystem itself. That is why the economy is profoundly and inherently anti-ecological. A system in which the luxury and pleasure of some is opposed to the anti-pleasure, abstinence, and hard work of others.[13]

The root of liberation theologians' questions does not seem to have changed significantly over the years. Basically, it remains "How do we speak of God in a context of so much injustice?"[14] and "If God exists, why is there poverty?" Sung, however, helps us take a step further into the relationship between poverty, the market system, and exclusion that characterizes the neoliberal hegemonic market of the early twenty-first century. The system advocates that "all are equal" and that "where there is a will there is a way." If the poor cannot purchase, it is because they do not really want to, they lack the will, therefore, they are guilty and deserve to be frustrated and suffer. Likewise, the system stipulates that "only the market is legal," in fact pushing the poor to the parallel market (the market of daily life, the non-speculative market, which has seemingly always been around), more commonly known as the "black economy." The poor, therefore, are doubly blamed.

By means of these two mechanisms, the mass of those excluded from the market and from society increases inexorably. Note the intentional use of "mass." It is the language of depersonification. The consumer is part of society, is a person and a citizen, while the excluded is an amorphous and impersonal mass. The exclusion of many and the greater share of wealth/welfare of some also implies a constant shifting of the balance of power in society, with its attendant struggle.[15]

On the other hand, the total hegemonic market – of neoliberal inspiration – also commodifies religion. "Religion is almost completely subjected to the logic of the market," Sung argues, and competes with other beliefs and religions to

[12] Hugo Assmann and Franz J Hinkelammert, *A Idolatria do Mercado*, Coleção Teologia e libertação. Série V, Desafios da Vida na Sociedade 5 (Petrópolis, Brazil: Vozes, 1989), 120. Trans. C. Giordano.

[13] Assmann and Hinkelammert, *Idolatria*,297.

[14] Gutiérrez, *A Theology of Liberation.*

[15] Jung Mo Sung, "Greed, Desire and Theology," *The Ecumenical Review* 63, no. 3 (October 2011): 261, https://doi.org/10.1111/j.1758-6623.2011.00119.x.

attract followers by offering them more and better services, i.e., religious consumer goods.[16]

On a general level, liberation theology has made an undeniable contribution to the current Christian vision of life, both in its denunciation of the obscene difference in the distribution of wealth and in its essentially theological analysis of poverty and development.

Liberation Theology and Islamia

We should ask ourselves how liberation theology affects Muslim settings and the evangelical missionaries who work in them. We are also interested in pointing out the similarities and differences that characterize the Latin American and Muslim religious contexts. The following considerations are merely a first reflection and should be taken as such.

First, and almost obviously, while injustice and the ever-widening gap between rich and poor is similar in Latin America and in the Muslim world, *Islamia* cannot be categorized as a "continent of poor [Christian] believers" as Gutiérrez claims about Latin America.[17] Liberation theology insists time and again that its appeal is not to the non-believer or the atheist but to the non-person.[18] Meanwhile, at a general level, it could be said that Islam is a fundamentally anti-Christian religion in the sense that it denies doctrines such as the divinity of Jesus Christ, his death on the cross and resurrection, the Trinity, and the authenticity of the Bible. Each of these truths is crucial to Christianity. This implies that the points of contact or convergence between liberation theology and Islam are practically non-existent. In this context, the distinction made by Samuel Escobar between "liberation theology" and "mission theology" comes to mind. The former is based on pastoral presuppositions (defending the faith of the population, which is supposed to be Christian), while the latter arises from a keen sense of mission and evangelization.[19]

Second, liberation theology arises from ethical indignation. In Islam, on the other hand, indignation has nothing to do with an internal revulsion against the condition of poverty of others. Things are the way they are because God has willed it. The poor die of misery because God has willed it. And vice versa: if I am on the side of the rich, it is also because that is God's will. Islam is an immobile and ahistorical system, in stark contrast with liberation theology.

Third, for liberation theology faith must be related to society and is revealed in the acts of history. In the Muslim world, faith and society go together, in a total symbiosis of religion and politics, but Islam is an ahistorical faith, that is to

---

[16] Jung Mo Sung, "Mercado Religioso e Mercado Como Religião," *Horizonte* 12, no. 34 (June 25, 2014): 290-315, https://doi.org/10.5752/P.2175-5841.2014v12n34p290.
[17] Gutiérrez, "Situación y Tareas," 510.
[18] Assmann and Hinkelammert, *Idolatria*; Galilea, "Teología de la Liberación"; Gutiérrez, *Teología de la Liberación*; Sung, *Se Deus Existe*; "El Pobre Después."
[19] Escobar, *Fe Evangélica*, 67.

say, God does not reveal himself in the events of history but in doctrines, in the revelations that Muhammad received, even when these revelations had much to do with the life circumstances of the Prophet. Likewise, there is no possibility of exegesis coupled with critical reflection on the Qur'an or other sacred texts. In Islam, truth is immutable through the centuries.

Fourth, focusing on the narratives described in the second part of this book, we will note a contrast between the practice of the missionaries and projects we will describe and those of liberation theology. As we analyze several of the projects, we will consider the relationships both with the rich and with the poor. Note that this was also a characteristic of the ministry of Jesus Christ: he related to the powerful and wealthy as well as to the needy and excluded.

Questions

At this point, questions arise that help us to see the relationship between the approaches of liberation theology and the projects and missionaries we will discuss:

- To what extent have the fundamental liberationist positions influenced, directly or indirectly, the missionaries and projects studied?
- What should development workers and the related projects we consider learn from their liberationist colleagues who have reflected extensively on issues directly linked to areas such as development, economics, and labor?
- Are there elements of liberation theology's approach to the biblical text that could be applied, directly or with modifications, to the situations of cultural and religious hybridization experienced by Latin American missionaries in Muslim countries?

Questions for Reflection and Discussion

1. Have you read any of the publications of liberation theologians? What did you think about what you read? What lessons did you learn?
2. How do you describe "the preferential option for the poor?" How does it affect the way you live your life as a Christian? Does it affect your church or organization? In what sense?

For Further Reading

Benedict XVI (pope). *Caritas in Veritate*. Vatican City: Editrice Vaticana, 2009. https://www.vatican.va/content/benedict-xvi/en/encyclicals/documents/hf_ben-xvi_enc_20090629_caritas-in-veritate.html.

Francis (pope). *Laudato Si': Encyclical Letter*. Vatican City: Editrice Vatican, 2015 https://www.vatican.va/content/francesco/en/encyclicals/documents/papa-francesco_20150524_enciclica-laudato-si.html.

Galilea, Segundo. *The Beatitudes: To Evangelize as Jesus Did*. Translated by Robert R. Barr. Maryknoll: Orbis, 1987.

Gutiérrez, Gustavo. *A Theology of Liberation: History, Politics, and Salvation*. Translated by Caridad Inda and John Eagleson. Maryknoll: Orbis, 2018.

Scott, Lindy, ed. "Christian Reflections from the Latino South." *Journal of Latin American Theology*. Vol. 15, No. 2, 2020. https://wipfandstock.com/9781725294349/journal-of-latin-american-theology-volume-15-number-2/

Sung, Jung Mo. *Desire, Market and Religion*. London: SCM Press, 2007.

5. Protestant Theology of Development

1. Protestant Focus

Eighteenth and Nineteenth Century Tradition

The relationship between colonialism and mission is far from simple, despite some attempting to simplify the connection by attributing to the latter the simple role of harmful propagator of the former. Yet, as Stephen Neill[1] points out, the benefits of Christian mission in colonial times far outweighed its evils. Neill's text also documents the differences between the various styles of colonial powers and their various relationships both to Christian missions and to local religions.

As far as the relationship with Islam is concerned, the British way of non-interference with the structures of Islam in India or East Africa is quite different from the French way of restricting Islam to the purely religious-cultural sphere in North and West Africa. Another key text for understanding colonialism – especially from the British point of view – is Max Warren's *Social History and Christian Mission.* Regarding the relationship between mission and development, the book highlights that:

> During the last one hundred years the missionary movement has found its predominant 'thrust' in concern for men's material needs – this being seen increasingly as the outcome of a theological insight that *diakonia* is at the very heart of mission.[2]

From a Latin American point of view, Brazilian Valdir Steuernagel has analyzed one element of the colonialist spirit in the person of Gustav Warneck, the "father of missiology." Steuernagel warns us:

> Warneck would have had a hard time imagining that a few decades later some of the younger churches would be sending missionaries to the formerly Christian countries. [...] [B]ut he would agree with the contemporary assertion of many that the mission of the church goes beyond the proclamation of the gospel in its goal of

[1] Stephen Charles Neill (1900-1984), a third-generation missionary to India, was an Anglican missionary, bishop, and scholar. He wrote more than one hundred books and collaborated with the World Council of Churches (1947-54).
[2] Max Warren, *Social History and Christian Mission* (London: SCM Press, 1967), 95.

> redeeming souls. […] The colonialist mentality and the practice of cultural imperialism have not been definitively overcome. Both continue to be a temptation for mission in our days, even in the case of missionary churches in Latin America.[3]

As far as development is concerned, we briefly mention the role played by the churches and missionary agencies in the times of European colonization. It is common knowledge that Protestant missionary initiatives from the time of the early Moravians (the first half of the eighteenth century), through the time of William Carey and his companions in India (first half of the nineteenth century) and through the time of Hudson Taylor in China (second half of the nineteenth century), were always accompanied by important social or development work. Along with many other activities, they built schools, orphanages, and hospitals; fought against slavery and the burning of widows; and promoted literacy and culture.

In Great Britain, in "the second half of the 19th century, three quarters of the voluntary charitable organizations were evangelical in nature and management."[4] Likewise, the birth of the Pentecostal movement had a profound social impact. At the Azuza Street Chapel in Los Angeles, in a movement that began in 1906 under the leadership of William Seymour, the outpouring of the Spirit broke down racial, gender, and class barriers. Everyone sat together – men and women, black and white, rich and poor – and felt like brothers and sisters. In addition, women went from house to house anointing the sick with oil, caring for the needy, and doing housework when necessary. As we consider the American social customs of that time, we must recognize the tremendous social change that took place in that early community.

Large Agencies

In the period following World War II, some of the great Protestant humanitarian aid and development agencies were born and helped set the emerging trend. Among the best known, the United Methodist Committee on Relief (UMCOR) was founded in 1940; Lutheran World Relief in 1945; Christian Aid in 1949; World Vision International in 1950; and Tearfund in 1968. Their work was, at first, relief or emergency aid, but very soon they became specialized in and focused on long-term development work. For example, World Vision, which was founded in Korea to assist orphans, has concentrated its efforts on the children's population sector, although its nearly four thousand employees are involved in many other programs. During those early years of developmental fever between the 1940s and 1970s, as they responded to the needs they perceived, Protestant

---

[3] Valdir Steuernagel, *Obediencia Misionera y Práctica Histórica* (Buenos Aires and Grand Rapids: Nueva Creación and Eerdmans, 1996), 124-25. Trans. D. Greenlee.

[4] H. Fernando Bullón, *Historia de la Iglesia y Responsabilidad Social*, vol. 2, Misión Cristiana y Responsabilidad Social Series (Buenos Aires: Kairos Ediciones, 2009), 140. Trans. D. Greenlee.

churches and organizations uncritically accepted the modernizing approaches and the cultural and political assumptions that went with them.

Bryant Myers' *Walking with the Poor* shows evidence of a deep and well-reasoned theological synthesis, a process spread over four decades. In the first chapter of this seminal book, Myers recounts his own pilgrimage and that of his colleagues in World Vision. In 1975, they participated in courses on how to implement projects given by American government agencies. At the time, some evangelicals argued that preaching was the fundamental task of the church. In the 1980s, Myers and his colleagues "simplistically and incorrectly understood this to mean that Christian witness was something one added to the development program mix to make it complete. [...] The 1990s were a decade of seeking professionalism. Good intentions were no longer enough."[5]

Evangelical Rejection and Recovery

The entire Protestant social tradition had undergone a major polarization, however, especially in the United States and partly in the United Kingdom, at the end of the nineteenth and the first half of the twentieth centuries. While, on the one hand, the historic churches were in favor of the so-called social gospel, on the other hand, the evangelical sector retreated from the world and concentrated on "the spiritual," that is, on the verbal proclamation of the gospel.

The social gospel was a largely postmillennialist current, which sought a "Christianization of the social order" and saw history as a "progressive manifestation of the loving purposes of God."[6] Although their social theology was incipient, they contributed a solid social praxis that late Pietism had neglected. Some of their prominent advocates were Walter Rauschenbusch (1861-1919) and Harry Emerson Fosdick (1878-1970), both Baptist pastors in New York City.

On the other hand, the conservative current lost fifty or sixty years before it began to return to more moderate positions and to concern itself with the needs of the world from a biblical perspective. In Latin America, this return did not begin until the late 1960s.

One event stands as a turning point in the relationship between preaching and social responsibility: the International Congress on World Evangelization held in Lausanne, Switzerland July 16-25, 1974. Convened by the Billy Graham Evangelistic Association, it brought together two thousand three hundred evangelical leaders from one hundred and fifty countries. The congress gave rise to the Lausanne Covenant, which, drafted under the leadership of John R.W. Stott (1921-2011), was the first of its kind. The Covenant has been considered

---

[5] Myers, *Walking with the Poor: Principles and Practices of Transformational Development*, Rev. (Maryknoll: Orbis, 2011), 2.

[6] Johannes Verkuyl, *Contemporary Missiology: An Introduction* (Grand Rapids: Eerdmans, 1978), 194.

the most important and influential evangelical document of the twentieth century. Its fifth paragraph, on Christian social responsibility, makes explicit:

> Because men and women are made in the image of God, every person, regardless of race, religion, colour, culture, class, sex or age, has an intrinsic dignity because of which he or she should be respected and served, not exploited. Here too we express penitence both for our neglect and for having sometimes regarded evangelism and social concern as mutually exclusive. Although reconciliation with other people is not reconciliation with God, nor is social action evangelism, nor is political liberation salvation, nevertheless we affirm that evangelism and socio-political involvement are both part of our Christian duty.[7]

Some of the presentations at the congress also had a deep impact on this topic, especially that of Samuel Escobar, "Evangelization and Man's Search for Freedom, Justice and Fulfillment."[8]

The Lausanne 1974 congress was followed by many subsequent consultations dealing with social issues in general and development in particular. We mention here those we consider to be the most relevant, listing only the global conferences and leaving aside the many held in Latin America, such as CLADE.

- Consultation on Gospel and Culture, Bermuda, 1978, which produced the influential "The Willowbank Report."
- International Consultation on Simple Lifestyle, Hoddesdon, England, 1980.
- Consultation on Theology of Development, Hoddesdon, England, 1980.
- International Consultation on the Relationship between Evangelism and Social Responsibility (CRESR), Grand Rapids, Michigan, USA, 1982.
- Consultation on the Church in Response to the Human Need (CRHN), Wheaton, Illinois, USA 1983.
- Conference on Faith and Economics, Oxford, 1990, which produced the "Oxford Declaration."

With this progress, can we conclude that the issue is closed, that the polarization has been reduced? Unfortunately, not. The Third Lausanne Congress on World Evangelization, held in Cape Town in October 2010, revealed that the "doctrine of primacy"[9] is still very buoyant. In fact, polarization in this regard was one of the relevant aspects of the congress.

---

[7] LCWE, "Lausanne Covenant," 1974, para. 5, https://www.lausanne.org/content/covenant/lausanne-covenant#cov.

[8] James Dixon Douglas, ed., *Let the Earth Hear His Voice: International Congress on World Evangelization, Lausanne, Switzerland: Official Reference Volume: Papers and Responses* (Minneapolis: World Wide Publications, 1975), 319-26, http://www.lausanne.org/lausanne-1974/lausanne-1974-documents.html.

[9] The concept that "evangelism is primary" as expressed in LCWE, "Lausanne Covenant," para. 6.

2. The World Council of Churches and Development

The World Council of Churches (WCC) is a direct heir of the Edinburgh Missionary Conference of 1910. Founded in Amsterdam in 1948, its official birth was delayed until the second half of the twentieth century by the two World Wars. The WCC began as an expression of the union of one hundred forty-seven church bodies together with the fusion of the Faith and Order and the Life and Work movements and, in 1961, the International Missionary Council. Since the 1960s, the WCC has also incorporated most of the Orthodox and Eastern churches as well as indigenous African churches (AIC). Pentecostal churches have also been incorporated since 1990.

Mission and Church

In order to correctly understand the theme of development in the thinking and practice of the historic churches, we must understand the dynamics of the relationship between church and mission that took place in this ecclesial sector during the twentieth century. To summarize, we could say that the first three decades of the twentieth century were characterized – at the missiological and developmental level – by a dissociation between, on the one hand, the churches and the large denominations and, on the other, the missionary work carried out mainly by missionary agencies. In other words, each of these two branches seemed to live in its own world.

At the Edinburgh Missionary Conference in 1910, one of the concerns, as noted by David Bosch, was "the absence of missionary enthusiasm in the churches of the West."[10] Some twenty years later, several leaders on both sides were beginning to feel the need for greater integration. The World Conference on Faith and Order held at Edinburgh in 1937 (which in some ways represented the ecclesiastical side) as well as the Oxford 1937 Life and Work (which was largely concerned with mission and development) both felt the need for "the other side." "Let the Church be Church" stated Life and Work, while the motto of Faith and Order was "Unity of the Church in Christ." The following year, the International Missionary Council (IMC) meeting in Tambaram, India, reached consensus that the relationship between church and mission should be indispensable in practice as well as in theological reflection. It was the first step in the merger of the IMC into the WCC, which was consolidated at the Third Assembly in New Delhi in 1961.

What followed was, on the one hand, very positive: the rediscovery that the church is mission; it is missionary by nature. At the same time, the shifting of the center (the locus) of mission from mission agencies first to the church and then to the world was detrimental to the clarity of the nature of both. As Stephen

[10] David J. Bosch, *Transforming Mission: Paradigm Shifts in Theology of Mission.* (Maryknoll: Orbis, 1991), 369.

Neill often argued, "when everything is mission, nothing is mission."[11] The adoption of the evolving concept of *missio Dei* championed by Johannes Hoekendijk was consolidated at the Fourth Assembly in Uppsala in 1968 and remained in force until the meeting of the Commission on World Mission and Evangelism (CWME) in Bangkok in 1973.

David Bosch interprets this time as a search for renewal within the church, as a way in which the delegates "wished to give expression to their frustration with the bourgeois nature of the church… Uppsala and Bangkok revealed a holy impatience with any complacency on the part of the church."[12] Soon after, the next assembly, held at Nairobi in 1975, began to take up the importance of the church in world mission.

Development

We must understand the developments within the historic Protestant churches and the WCC within the framework of the always ambivalent relationship between the church and mission to the world. We have already noted above the widespread practice of Protestant missions in the nineteenth and twentieth centuries of accompanying preaching with abundant medical, educational, agricultural, and social work. Johan Herman Bavinck, in his classic *An Introduction to the Science of Missions* already expressed his concern about this relationship. He took the notion of a comprehensive approach for granted and quoted the 1928 IMC conference in Jerusalem:

> We are therefore desirous that the program of missionary work among all peoples be sufficiently comprehensive to serve the whole man in every aspect of his life and relationship.

He clarified that "Missions, so it is held, is simultaneously preaching, education, medical care, and social-economic aid" but he argued that the preaching of the gospel is a complicated, complex matter and that missionary aid inevitably entailed the use of modern science, understood as independent (and antagonistic) to God. That is why he advocated an intrinsic union of preaching with the life and spirituality of the missionaries and the emerging church.[13]

After World War II, the churches took the lead in the reconstruction of devastated nations. In fact, at the very founding of the WCC, the issue of "Christian diakonia" was so personally important to Willem Visser't Hooft (first General Secretary of the WCC, serving from 1948-1966) that he made his acceptance of the post of General Secretary conditional on the Council's

---

[11] Stephen Neill, *Creative Tension: The Duff Lectures, 1958.* (London: Edinburgh House Press, 1959), 81.

[12] Bosch, *Transforming*, 385.

[13] Johan Herman Bavinck, *An Introduction to the Science of Missions* (Phillipsburg, N.J.: P & R Publishing, 1960), 107-16.

commitment to demonstrate its ecumenism through a program of mutual aid among the churches.

We have already mentioned the birth of the large Protestant humanitarian aid agencies during this period. The first such agency acting directly on behalf of the churches was the European Central Bureau, formed prior to the birth of the WCC while World War II still raged. In 1945, it was reorganized as the Department of Reconstruction and Inter-Church Aid (DICA) and soon after as the Department of Inter-Church Aid and Service to Refugees (DICASR), because the care of refugees and those displaced by the war and post-war period was seen as a priority.[14]

With regard to the concept and practice of development, the WCC initially expressed views on development similar to those commonly understood at the time, that is, as a modernization movement flowing from the First World outward. That progressive and modernizing approach was challenged at the World Conference on Church and Society held in Geneva in 1966. Shortly afterwards another conference was held in Beirut in 1968, this time in conjunction with the Pontifical Commission for Justice and Peace; the conclusions of this second conference were more in line with the ideas of progress and modernization. Be that as it may, one of the central themes of the WCC Fourth Assembly in Uppsala (1968) was development. "The key word was 'development', and Uppsala was confident that its plans for this and other socio-political enterprises would succeed," Bosch remarks.[15]

The strong weight of Euro-Atlantic theology kept the concepts of development closely linked to technology and modernizing progress despite the fact that these were concepts that society at large was already questioning. However, during this period, the political-theological clamor for an understanding of development as liberation from the dependence of rich and powerful countries was in full swing. The previous year, 1967, Pope Paul VI had referred to "development, the new name for peace."[16] Soon the WCC concept of development began to slowly shift. In Bangkok (1973), the Commission on World Mission and Evangelism (CWME) "confirmed the new emphasis: terms

---

[14] See Esther Hookway and Christopher Francis, *From Inter-Church Aid to Jubilee: A Brief History of Ecumenical Diakonia in the World Council of Churches*, ed. Alexander Belopopsky (Geneva: World Council of Churches Diakonia and Solidarity Team, 2002), http://www.wcc-coe.org/wcc/europe/diakoniahistorybook.pdf; Kjell Nordstokke, "Diakonia and Diaconate in the World Council of Churches," *International Journal for the Study of the Christian Church* 13, no. 4 (November 1, 2013): 286-99, https://doi.org/10.1080/1474225X.2013.867653.

[15] David J. Bosch, *Witness to the World: The Christian Mission in Theological Perspective* (Eugene: Wipf & Stock, 2006), 190.

[16] "*Populorum Progressio* (March 26, 1967) Paul VI," accessed March 23, 2021, https://www.vatican.va/content/paul-vi/en/encyclicals/documents/hf_p-vi_enc_26031967_populorum.html.

like 'salvation' were now translated as 'liberation', 'fellowship' as 'solidarity.'"[17]

At the WCC's fifth Assembly, held in Nairobi in 1975, the change began to become visible. "The dream of a 'theology of development' as key to the solution of the world's problems was shattered."[18] And very soon, in 1980 in Melbourne, the CWME itself adopted the option for the poor as a central hermeneutical concept, a concept that remains present to this day.

Subsequently, with the escalation of global tensions and environmental degradation, the Vancouver Assembly (1983) issued a covenant and a priority program for its member churches summarized in the phrase justice, peace, and the integrity of creation (JPIC). It was soon opened to other churches that were not part of the WCC and reaffirmed at the Canberra (1991) and Harare (1998) assemblies. The theological details of the covenant, which was soon redefined as a worldwide convocation, were established in Seoul in 1990.

Previously, the churches had spoken of bringing their vision of Christian ethics to world affairs. From Vancouver onwards, the WCC would understand its role in the world as a single action expressed in two strands: on the one hand confessing its faith in Christ as the life of the world, and on the other hand exercising "Christian resistance to the powers of death in racism, sexism, caste oppression, economic exploitation, militarism, violations of human rights, and the misuse of science and technology."[19]

On the other hand, the WCC's focus on emergency humanitarian aid situations, very much present from its beginnings, was profoundly reorganized in 1993. Together with the Lutheran World Federation and the various ecumenical development agencies, Action by Churches Together International was formed, with an emphasis on both the church as a unit and on its rapid and professional response to emergencies.[20] Undoubtedly, the fact that "churches" are so clearly included in its name is evidence of the new importance given by the WCC to the church-in-action. It also points to the growing recognition (since the mid-1990s) in the professional and state-sponsored development world of development organizations inspired by religious ideals (known as Faith-based Organizations, FBOs).

The World Council of Churches in Latin America: Development and Church

After this brief review of the history of development within the WCC, it is worth going back a bit to consider Latin American participation in the WCC. The Latin American conciliar (or ecumenical) churches organized the first Latin American

[17] Bosch, *Transforming*, 435.
[18] Bosch, *Witness to the World*, 192.
[19] D. Preman Niles, "Justice, Peace and the Integrity of Creation," in *Dictionary of the Ecumenical Movement*, ed. Nicholas Lossky (World Council of Churches, 2003), http://www.wcc-coe.org/wcc/who/dictionary-article11.html.
[20] Hookway and Francis, *From Inter-Church Aid to Jubilee*.

Evangelical Conference (CELA) in Buenos Aires in 1949. From its second conference, CELA II, held in Lima in 1961, emerged Church and Society in Latin America (ISAL), which was formalized in São Paulo, Brazil in 1962. ISAL would have a decisive influence in articulating its own understanding of development, understood primarily as liberation and partly as revolution.

However, we would like to take this reflection in other directions. First, it is important to realize that Latin American Protestants initially remained aloof and suspicious of the WCC as a consequence of the decision to exclude them from the Edinburgh Missionary Conference of 1910. Generally speaking, it can be said that they kept their distance until the CWME Conference in Mexico in 1963. The tireless work of the Uruguayan Methodist pastor Emilio Castro was a key factor in bringing the historic Latin American churches closer to the WCC. This work took place within UNELAM (Provisional Commission for Latin American Evangelical Unity) (1970-78), which later formally gave birth to CLAI (the Latin American Council of Churches) in 1982. The CLAI is currently the official body that brings together the Latin American conciliar or ecumenical churches.

Second, we highlight the Latin American role in changing the WCC's vision of development. Within the WCC, the participation of Latin Americans such as Emilio Castro, Julio de Santa Ana, and Orlando Fals-Borda in the Geneva Conference of 1966 and a good number of Latin American delegates in Uppsala 1968 would prove decisive in questioning the developmentalist approaches of the Euro-Atlantic churches.[21]

The third insight in and from Latin America that we emphasize is the fact that Latin American theologians brought to the WCC an integral vision of life and the gospel. For them, church, development, evangelism, pastoral care, and theology were intrinsically linked. A simple reading of the contributions that the main Latin American leaders as a whole made to the WCC reflects this integral and integrating understanding. They include the Puerto Rican theologian Orlando Costas; the Methodist bishops Mortimer Arias and Federico Pagura, Uruguayan and Argentinean respectively; Argentinean José Míguez Bonino and the Argentine-American Nancy E. Bedford, who straddles the Baptists and the ecumenical sphere; Brazilians Rubem Alves and Valdir Steuernagel, a Lutheran; the Mexican-Costa Rican biblical scholar Elsa Támez and American-Costa Rican Irene Foulkes, and, the Peruvian Rubén (Tito) Paredes. It is no coincidence that many of these leaders were closely linked to pastoral work.

A fourth aspect that Latin American leaders brought to the WCC was their passion for evangelism, a characteristic of the work of Emilio Castro. In using

---

[21] H. Fernando Bullón, *El Pensamiento Social Protestante y El Debate Latinoamericano Sobre El Desarrollo* (Grand Rapids: Libros Desafío, 2013), 178ss; Bosch, *Transforming*, 434; Jairo Roa Buitrago, *Desarrollo y Liberación: Política, Economía y Religión* (Madrid: Dykinson, 2009), 66ss; Kenneth R Ross et al., eds., *Ecumenical Missiology: Changing Landscapes and New Conceptions of Mission*, Regnum Edinburgh Centenary Series 35 (Oxford: Regnum, 2016), 58.

this term, we must understand its use in its broad sense, as synonymous with mission in the ecumenical literature of the 1950s to 1980s.

A fifth aspect of the Latin American contribution to ecumenical missiology is that, in Latin America, the terms evangelical and Protestant are practically synonymous. Presbyterians and Methodists are considered evangelicals as are, say, Baptists. This self-understanding of Latin American Protestants contributed to leaders and thinkers of both persuasions (ecumenical and evangelical) participating in common theological forums (e.g., the Latin American Theological Fellowship, FTL), and working hard for unity, as in the case of Emilio Castro at the head of UNELAM. Note that "evangelical unity" is even part of UNELAM's name!

The final characteristic that should be emphasized in the Latin American contribution is the sense of joy, of family, of jubilant liturgy and of passion. This is one of the hallmarks of Latin American spirituality: it is capable of transforming every event into a celebration. It is one of the characteristics that struck Johannes Verkuyl (with his Dutch-Indonesian background) about Castro's personality.[22] In the European and academic mentality, it is taken for granted that passion disqualifies one from judging impartially, just the opposite of what Latin Americans take for granted: when forming a commission, or commissioning a task, the person chosen will be the one who shows passion for the matter.

The World Council of Churches and Islam

The WCC has had a long history of dialogue and relations with various world religions, including Islam. Most of the historic and Eastern Christian churches (also known as Eastern Orthodox churches) established in Muslim lands are members of the WCC: the Greek Orthodox Patriarchate of Antioch and all the East, the Syrian Orthodox Patriarchate of Antioch, the Malankara Orthodox Syrian Church, the Holy Apostolic Catholic Assyrian Church of the East, the Church of Pakistan, the Coptic Orthodox Church, the Ecumenical Patriarchate of Constantinople, the Episcopal Church in Jerusalem and the Middle East, the Evangelical Lutheran Church in Jordan and the Holy Land, the Evangelical Presbyterian Church of Iran, and the Indonesian Christian Church (GKI and HKI) are among the best known. Advocacy for these churches, some of which are some two thousand years old, and which experience first-hand the difficulties of carrying out their work in Muslim environments hostile to Christianity, has been one of the major tasks of the WCC.

At the same time, the visibility of the WCC and its media projection make institutional relations one of its strong points in relation to Islam. Thus, the WCC was one of the first to respond to "A Common Word," the appeal launched in October 2007 by one hundred thirty-eight Islamic scholars under the auspices of

---

[22] Johannes Verkuyl et al., "Emilio Castro: Servant of World Mission and Evangelism," *International Review of Mission* 73, no. 289 (January 1984): 106-17, https://doi.org/10.1111/j.1758-6631.1984.tb03257.x.

The Royal Aal al-Bayt Institute for Islamic Thought in Jordan.[23] The call, addressed to the world's top Christian leaders, stressed the need to work together for peace on the grounds that the commandment to love God and neighbor are foundational in both the Qur'an and the Bible.

In the following months, the WCC's office for Interreligious Dialogue and Cooperation responded with a document for all member churches, providing guidelines and a working proposal, as well as acknowledging the differences to be overcome. Likewise, over three hundred Christian leaders responded favorably to the call, in a letter initially prepared by Harold W. Attridge, Miroslav Volf, Joseph Cumming, and Emilie M. Towns, which was first published in the *New York Times* on November 18, 2007.[24]

The WCC also has intentional connection with leaders and scholars of Shi'a Islam. For more than twenty years, regular meetings have taken place in Iran, Geneva, and London.[25]

The journal *Current Dialogue,*[26] published on a roughly biannual basis, is the most accessible reflection of the WCC's dialogue with other religions, including Islam. Of particular interest for our purposes are issues #59: "Religion and Violence" (Dec. 2017); #52: "Christian Self-Understanding in the Context of Islam" (Dec. 2006); #40, which includes a report on WCC dialogue initiatives with Islam (Dec. 2002); and, #36 "Current Dialogue" (Dec. 2000).[27]

On the practical side, since 2007, the WCC has sponsored an interreligious summer school, which brings together young Christian, Jewish, and Muslim students. The six-week program is accredited by the University of Geneva and is held on the grounds of the Château de Bossey.

Another practical program which, although not fully involved in interreligious dialogue is close to it, is the Ecumenical Accompaniment Programme in Palestine and Israel (EAPPI), created in 2002 to accompany the inhabitants of the Palestinian territories in their encounters with Israeli security

---

[23] The Royal Aal al-Bayt Institute for Islamic Thought, "A Common Word between Us and You" (Royal Academy of The Royal Aal al-Bayt Institute for Islamic Thought, October 13, 2007), https://www.acommonword.com/wp-content/uploads/2018/05/ACW-English-Translation.pdf.

[24] Christian had the privilege of discussing the draft of that paper, which was signed by Federico Bertuzzi of PM International (signatory #20) and Juan Carlos Cardenas of IIBET (the Iberoamerican Institute of Cross-Cultural Studies) (signatory #48), my fellow ministers. A list of documents and opinions, some critical, with both documents can be found at: https://answering-islam.org/Letters/common_word.htm.

[25] Mohammad Ali Shomali, "Shi'a Muslims and the World Council of Churches," *Islam Today*, December 25, 2018, online edition, sec. Reports, available at, http://ijtihadnet.com/shia-muslims-and-the-world-council-of-churches/.

[26] Issues are available at https://www.oikoumene.org/resources/publications/current-dialogue/cd-previous-issues.

[27] The WCC has published relatively few books related to Islam. One is Fadi Daou and Nāylā Tabbārah, *Divine Hospitality: A Christian-Muslim Conversation*, trans. Alan J. Amos (Geneva: World Council of Churches, 2017).

forces, as well as to provide eyewitnesses and an international presence in the area. There are generally between twenty-five and thirty people on the ground, who rotate every three months. This presence, as well as the positions taken by the WCC regarding a just peace in Israel and Palestine, has raised much animosity from the Israeli side towards the WCC.

It should be emphasized that the work of dialogue with Islam, for example that carried out by the WCC, should not be confused with the work of daily contact, at street level, that missionaries and Christians in general have with their Muslim neighbors. They are two completely different, complementary, and necessary levels. The first includes an important academic and media component, such as the recent visit of the Secretary General of the Arab League, Dr. Mohammad bin Abdul Karim Al-Issa, to the WCC headquarters in Geneva.[28] Such meetings are often filled with declarations of goodwill. Street-level contact, on the other hand, does not have the pressure of the media spotlight, and seeks other objectives: good neighborliness as well as evangelization and *da'wah* (invitation to convert to Islam) of the other. It is the dialogue that has been most prominently reflected in this work.

3. Integral Mission in Muslim Contexts

The projects we describe later in this book are limited to those carried out in Muslim-majority contexts. The presence of Latin American evangelical missionaries in such lands is noteworthy. An internal report in 2006 estimated the number to be close to eight hundred, and since then it has certainly increased to over one thousand. For this reason, we will devote some space to consider the particularities of Protestant development in Muslim countries.

We have chosen to concentrate on Latin American workers serving in Muslims lands who (1) are dedicated to implementing development or humanitarian service projects of some kind and (2) within that number, those who do so following the parameters of integral mission. The suitability of integral mission postulates for Muslim socio-cultural contexts should be emphasized: they are integrated societies; they do not tolerate compartmentalization and lack of integrality. Hence, integral mission fits well in these cultures.

It is evident that the great majority of Muslim countries do not offer religious freedom, as the term is generally understood. This means that Christian missionary activity is not permitted and that those who wish to enter and/or reside in the country must do so not as religious personnel but under another identity or profession. This seemingly simple fact raises many questions, both theological and practical, on issues related to the personal and family identity of the missionary such as the ethics

[28] Peter Kenny, "Muslim World League Leader Tells World Council of Churches, 'We Must Combat Extremists,'" *Ecumenical News*, November 10, 2017, Online edition, sec. Church, https://www.ecumenicalnews.com/article/muslim-world-league-leader-tells-world-council-of-churches-we-must-combat-extremists/60451.htm.

of lying to the authorities and the need of "entry strategies" that may contain more or less deceptive elements as well as an entire philosophy of ministry. Our focus is on how and why Latino missionaries get involved in development work.

Many missionaries camouflage themselves under disguises such as a business, a development project, or as students. While some workers do these things, and do them well, for others the business, project, or study is simply a platform they stand on, even a necessary evil so that they can do what they really consider priority: evangelism. Good is done through these activities, mostly social service works, but if the worker had freedom and a choice – if the legal, immigration, and political circumstances of the country in question allowed it – they would opt for "pure" evangelism since, for them, it holds priority over other things.

As we think about different ways workers live out this matter, we discern an ascending scale of involvement, supported by theological presuppositions, illustrated in the following table.[29]

Theological Scale of Social Involvement
Development as pre-evangelism
Development as a hook or bridge
Development accompanies evangelism
Development and evangelism are inseparable

Figure 1. Theological Scale of Social Involvement © Ch. Giordano, 2012

But the churches that send, support, and financially contribute to the needs of Latin missionaries to Muslim countries can be described in a different scale of organizational involvement with respect to social work.

	Organizational Scale of Social Involvement
1	The church is spiritual and should not be involved in social work
2	The church itself is occupied with spiritual themes but approves if its members are engaged, as individuals, in social work
3	The church is involved in social service (assisting)
4	The church is involved in social service and social action (combating the causes)
5	The church is involved in social service and social action as well as political action (transforming the circumstances)

Figure 2. Organizational Scale of Social Involvement © Ch. Giordano, 2012

---

[29] Note how the CRESR (Grand Rapids 82) considers social activity as a "consequence [...] bridge [...] and partner" of evangelization but does not reach the fourth rung of our table. Likewise, while not comfortable with primacy, it looks for ways to justify it. LCWE, "Lausanne Covenant," 12–15. For an example, see Bruce Bradshaw, *Bridging the Gap: Evangelism, Development and Shalom*, Innovations in Mission 5 (Monrovia, Calif.: MARC, 1994), 6-7.

Another scale, elaborated by Bryant Myers, describes the various Christian positions regarding poverty, its causes, theological roots, and biblical texts through which the poor are conceptualized, as well as the response that Christians adopt in the face of poverty. It is reproduced here in simplified form.[30]

Christian Views of the Poor		
View of the poor	Why the poor are poor	Christian response
Poor made in the image of God	The poor lack skills, knowledge and opportunity	Give them opportunities
Poor as people in rebellion	They are lazy, they make wrong decisions	Challenge and encourage them to make better choices
Poor as Christ incarnate	The poor lack love	Relieve their suffering as possible
Poor as God's favorites	Poverty is structural	Work for justice, and give voice to the poor
Poor as lost souls	The poor are lost from God	Proclaim the gospel

Figure 3. The Poor: Points of View of Christians © Ch. Giordano, 2012

Note that we have focused on the concept of development and have left aside, for lack of space, the issue of poverty, which is barely brought out in the previous table. Likewise, we have left aside the concept of transformation of the person, structures, culture, and society. Many of the Latin American missionaries in Muslim contexts believe that if a sufficient number of people convert to Christ, this fact alone will be enough to transform their society.

Some attempts to resolve the tensions between social work (or development or projects or business) and evangelization have included versions of tent-making and the more recent Business as Mission (BAM). Both have advantages, but also serious drawbacks. The former only works well when both identities of the tentmaker (for example as a teacher, technician, or trader and also as a missionary) are public, which is rare in Muslim contexts. As for the proponents of BAM, they rarely question the capitalist system itself, but tend to be part of it and uncritically accept the "laws of the market."

---

[30] Myers, *Walking with the Poor*, 2011, 109.

4. Development: Evaluation

In the previous three chapters, we have covered a considerable amount of material, organizing it into three major blocks: secular and state-sponsored approaches, alternative approaches, and both Catholic and Protestant religious approaches. We now focus our evaluation on the ultimate aims of development, on the Protestant synthesis and on the lack of an economic alternative. It should be made clear, however, that any evaluation is subjective, personal, and therefore questionable.

The Aims of Development

An evaluation of development, however cursory, cannot overlook its ultimate purposes, those hidden behind the words. Modernization and structuralism, like the colonization that preceded them, sought first and foremost to implant Western models of society and thought. The underlying theme, "let them be like us," concealed a high degree of ethnocentrism, and relied on the doctrine of manifest destiny.[31] But it went further, seeking to tilt the balance of power toward the West in its struggle against Communism. Development became one of the weapons to consolidate the two great blocs and the Cold War; both blocs – Communist and the West – used it.

Another part of development, both state-sponsored and alternative, has promoted a humanistic worldview. Humans and human well-being are the measure of everything. Human rights are understood mostly as individual rights, and capacity building is aimed at expanding the capabilities of individuals. At the same time, we cannot deny that these approaches to development held a healthy intention to strive for justice and equality. But, as David Bosch has already noted, at the end of the twentieth century, a general unease with regard to development can be observed:

> There is a profound feeling of ambiguity about Western technology and development, indeed, about the very idea of progress itself. Progress, the god of the Enlightenment, proved to be a false god after all.[32]

The whole conglomerate of postmodern visions, including anti-development and Appreciative Inquiry, share a humanistic vision of the world. They also tend to not criticize their own culture while being prone to idealize the culture or sub-culture in which the project is developed or in which the NGO operates. However, they do criticize – sometimes fiercely – the official culture, the state-sponsored way of doing things. An exception to this tendency is Manfred Max-

---

[31] Manifest Destiny: the belief that the United States of America was destined to expand geographically from the Atlantic to the Pacific, and more recently in the U.S. mission to promote and defend democracy.

[32] Bosch, *Transforming*, 188.

Neef's Human-Scale Development, which offers parameters to evaluate one's own culture and distinguish negative *satisfiers* and *pseudo-satisfiers*.

As for non-governmental organizations, their ultimate aims are often laudable in the case of those engaged in direct intervention in the field. The recent tendency to work exclusively through local counterparts often results in a hands-off strategy. Inadvertently, development becomes a commodity, and ultimately the greatest benefits – publicity along with influence and economic benefits – accrues to the Northern NGO.

However, we cannot but denounce the profit motive of a part of development, especially state-sponsored development. Public and private structural loans are nothing more than ways of profiting from the misfortune of others. The foreign debt of one country only swells the accounts of the lending banks in another. The soft loans of Official Development Assistance (ODA) imply the formalization of lucrative contracts with companies and interests of the lending country. In stark contrast, the Bible stipulated, with some exceptions, the prohibition of interest on loans, the cancellation of loans every seven years, and the remission of large debts every fifty years.

Likewise, neoliberal and neoconservative formulas are only intended to benefit the rich countries at the expense of the poor, despite all the rhetoric with which they may be disguised.[33] When governments and international organizations recommend (or impose!) the lifting of customs and tariff barriers, import restrictions, and restrictions on the repatriation of foreign capital, they are recommending or forcing poor countries to do just the opposite of what had made the rich countries wealthy and powerful.[34]

Protestant Synthesis

It is worth asking whether the Protestant and evangelical sector has gone beyond the values of God's kingdom, whether the years and experience have generated a truly Christian conception of development. Our assessment is negative, even though we recognize the progress made in minority sectors. One piece of evidence is the scarcity of publications on the theology of development. In general, what is seen in the field is that most of such writing simply links spiritual work and development projects as "the two wings of a bird that complement each other,"[35] and handle both with different criteria and rationale. We describe this type of development as having a *humanistic foundation varnished with Christianity*. We do not mean by this that there has been no evangelical theological reflection on aspects of development, but we miss a global

---

[33] John Dillon, "The root causes of the current financial crisis," in *Justice not Greed*, ed. Pamela Brubaker and Rogate R. Mshana (Geneva: WCC Publications, 2010), 98.
[34] J.M. Blaut, "Where Was Capitalism Born?," *Antipode* 8, no. 2 (1976): 116, https://doi.org/10.1111/j.1467-8330.1976.tb00633.x; Dillon, "Root Causes," 98.
[35] Bradshaw, *Bridging the Gap*, 2.

articulation, a coherent whole that gives a truly biblical backbone and meaning to development carried out by Christian agents.

Economic Alternative

Although development is not only about material things and the economy, the relationship between development and the economy cannot be overlooked. It is not enough to offer alternatives to development, however laudable and justice-centered they may be, if we leave aside the touchstone on which it is based: the economy.

Achieving – hypothetically, since they have not been achieved – the Millennium Development Goals (or the new Sustainable Development Goals) would not change the global economic system one iota. We believe that no economic alternatives to the neoliberal-neoconservative model have been offered by any of the sectors involved, including Catholics and Protestants. It is true that the validity of the selfish principles of the market has been questioned – liberation theology has excelled in this regard – but no other model has been offered, especially since the fall of the Berlin Wall and the end of state socialism. Especially in Southern Europe, the financial crisis of 2008 led to an economic crisis that swept away the middle class, called into question the "welfare state" and made the already wealthy very rich. In Spain in 2021, twenty-six percent of the population (thirty-nine percent in the Southern region, Andalusia, where we live) is at risk of poverty and social exclusion, while the social gap is one of the largest in the European Union and the poverty and exclusion rate of young people under eighteen reaches thirty-six percent. This social reality has very serious consequences for mental health.[36]

It seems to us that, in order to begin to build an approach to development with a truly Christian foundation, we must call sin by its name and remember the tenth commandment: "You shall not covet your neighbor's house. You shall not covet your neighbor's wife, or his male or female servant, his ox or donkey, or anything that belongs to your neighbor" (Ex. 20:17). In stark contrast, both Adam Smith and Ludwig von Mises, fathers of economics, built their entire economic theory precisely on the opposite principle: "trade is self-interested"[37] and "egoism is the basic law of society."[38]

---

[36] AROPE, (at risk of poverty or social exclusion) is a Eurostat index. Eurostat, "Glossary: At Risk of Poverty or Social Exclusion (AROPE)," Eurostat, June 29, 2021, https://ec.europa.eu/eurostat/statistics-explained/index.php?title=Glossary:At_risk_of_poverty_or_social_exclusion_(AROPE). For the situation in Spain, see: Protestante Digital, "Se Ahonda aún más la Brecha Social en España," *Protestante Digital, AC Press*, March 11, 2016, sec. España, http://protestantedigital.com/espana/38833/Se_ahonda_la_brecha_social_en_Espana, and Enrique Zamorano, "La Pobreza se Agudiza en España Mientras los más Ricos ya se han Recuperado de la Crisis, Según Oxfam Intermón," *El Confidencial*, January 25, 2021, sec. Alma, Corazón y Vida, https://www.elconfidencial.com/alma-corazon-vida/2021-01-25/informe-oxfam-intermon-espana-ricos-social_2921204/.

[37] Adam Smith, 1937:13-14, quoted by Peet and Hartwick, *Theories*, 79.

[38] Ludwig von Mises, 1922:402, quoted by Peet and Hartwick, *Theories*, 79.

The biblical teaching, however, is clear: "Do nothing out of selfish ambition or vain conceit. Rather, in humility value others above yourselves, not looking to your own interests but each of you to the interests of the others" (Phil. 2:3-4).

At the same time, an alternative cannot be limited to written statements on paper. It has to be put into practice. It must be seen in action somewhere, in some community. Jesus' first disciples eradicated poverty from their midst quickly and easily, in a few days or weeks:

> The community of believers was one in heart and mind. None of them would say, "This is mine!" about any of their possessions, but held everything in common. […] There were no needy persons among them. (Acts 4:32,34 CEB)

Today, on the contrary, in the seventy years since World War II and the rise of development of all kinds and styles, poverty continues to grow. Where is the Christian alternative to the perverse world economic system? It seems to us that, except for tiny, socially exclusive community groups, Christians in general have failed to live and demonstrate a viable and credible alternative to the Mammon god, and thus to true development.

Questions for Reflection and Discussion

1. Think about the theological and organizational scales of social involvement discussed in this chapter. Where would you place yourself on these scales? Why? Where would your church fit?
2. "If rich countries donated enough, poverty could be completely eradicated." Do you agree with that statement, or disagree? Why?
3. "If there were enough followers of Jesus in a town or city, that, in itself, would bring about development and social improvement." Do you agree with the statement, or disagree? Why, or how would you qualify the statement?

For Further Reading

Haar, Gerrie ter, ed. *Religion and Development: Ways of Transforming the World*. London: Hurst & Co, 2011.

Holenstein, Anne-Marie. *Role and Significance of Religion and Spirituality in Development Co-Operation: A Reflection and Working Paper*. Translated by Wendy Tyndale. Bern: Swiss Agency for Development and Co-operation SDC, 2005.

Commission on World Mission and Evangelism. "Together towards Life: Mission and Evangelism in Changing Landscapes," January 20, 2012. https://www.oikoumene.org/resources/documents/together-towards-life-mission-and-evangelism-in-changing-landscapes.

Lausanne Movement. "The Cape Town Commitment." LCWE, January 25, 2011. https://www.lausanne.org/content/ctcommitment.

Myers, Bryant L. *Walking with the Poor: Principles and Practices of Transformational Development*. 3rd ed. Maryknoll: Orbis, 2011.

PART TWO

Description of the Contexts and Analysis of Relationships

In this part of the book, we take a descriptive approach, a method we think will appeal to field workers among our readers. We focus on the relationships between development projects and the churches that, directly or indirectly, have arisen as a result. In total, the study covers twelve projects and ten churches.

We have grouped the projects and churches in terms of the primary relationship between the church and the project, whether the relationship is direct or indirect and whether it is geographically close or distant. We also differentiate between settings in terms of the composition of the staff: national, foreign, or mixed.

These chapters will help us to:

- describe and understand the projects and churches we have studied along with their contexts;
- visualize and describe the relationships among them; and,
- begin to draw conclusions as we make comparisons between the projects, churches, and contexts.

6. In the Cities of Africa and Asia

We are looking at the stories of people and the development projects and churches they are part of. In this chapter we examine two very different projects, which nevertheless have much in common. Both projects have been developed in urban environments; both also contributed to the establishment of beautiful churches. The first is found in North Africa, the other in Central Asia.

Merely recounting facts will not enable us to understand the nuances and draw lessons from the stories of these people, projects, and churches, something we will approach in later chapters. We must delve into the relationships between these various players. A description of the facts gives us a snapshot of each element separately. The study of relationships, however, helps us to better understand daily life, interactions, and the reason for the events. A good example of what we have in mind is a drama in a theater. A drama critic who introduces us to the characters might help us learn about the play but watching the players act out the story is far more interesting and brings to light the motivations of each character.

When we refer to "direct relationships" between the projects and churches we mean those that involve organizational links and frequent interactions. On the other hand, we use the term "indirect relationships" to refer to informal links, those without hierarchy or organizational structure.

We have also defined relationships as "close" or "distant" based on geographic proximity, whether they share the same building or are found in the same neighborhood, or perhaps the activities and gatherings take place in nearby locations.

1. Description of the North African Context

Gran Urbe

Gran Urbe (a fictitious name) is a large North African city with more than one million inhabitants. It is a tourist destination as well as the commercial and educational hub of its country's Northern provinces. Gran Urbe is also the spiritual center of the country since its great mosque and university are the site of training for the imams who will serve the thousands of mosques scattered across the country. Sunni Islam, with strong Sufi components, permeates the life of the city. Daily routines are marked by the overlapping calls to prayer, each timed a few seconds apart from its neighbor, sounding from all the minarets in the city. The great bazaar of the old city appears almost deserted on Friday mornings, a phenomenon unthinkable in the rest of the cities of the country. The social pressure to conform to the rituals and precepts of Islam is very strong; dissidents suffer stigmatization and persecution. In fact, a special police force is in charge of religious crimes.

Giving an external appearance of religious freedom, the authorities have permitted the existence of a Catholic parish and a small house used by Protestants as a place of worship. Both are only to be used by foreigners; the secret police keep a constant watch to ensure that nationals do not attend their services. There is no national evangelical church in the city, not even a clandestine one that meets in the houses, although there are some scattered Christians.

A couple of Latin American missionary families settled in the city in 1997. They do not present themselves as missionaries but as professionals involved in various development projects in rural areas in the mountains. They are part of the staff of a non-governmental development organization (NGDO) registered in the country. Little by little, the team is growing, starting projects in the city as well, in collaboration with local associations. They are known in the community; their presence arouses a mixture of curiosity, respect, and suspicion. They have frequent contact and maintain good relations with local authorities and the city's upper and professional classes.

The welding project began in 2001 as a complement to a larger integrated rural development project extended to several villages (water, schools, latrines, and health education). The project is a specialized vocational training program focused on young people in an area with few options for quality employment. It is carried out in collaboration with the local authorities who are providing the premises while the NGDO provides the missionary-trainer and materials. Each student pays a small fee. Some successful trainees have gone further and serve as instructors for the others.

Both the projects and the foreign team that managed them enjoyed high local and official acceptance. Everyone knew that they were followers of *Isa al-Masih*, Jesus the Messiah. In the West, we would say they were committed Christians, but they never used the term Christian because of the strong pejorative associations to that word held by many Muslims. Occasions to bear witness to their faith are plentiful, which they respond to with tact and cultural discernment.

The national church in the capital and the agency PM International (PMI) joined forces in 2001 to see a church planted in the city. The church in the capital city commissioned a young national pastor who, with his wife, formed a team together with the missionary family that was leading the welding project in the rural area. They gathered together some of the long-standing, scattered believers and soon the church was formed.

The group gathered in the house of missionaries, a building that had two entrances, a garden, and a garage and storage room in which they could discreetly gather for their meetings. Baptisms were held in a small swimming pool. Occasionally they made excursions together such as picnics in the countryside. Men and women took part in the services together along with their children. When they gathered, they spoke in the local dialect and not in the form of Arabic used in formal discussion and writing. On holidays such as Easter or Christmas, as many as fifty or sixty gathered together. The wife of the pastor shared in the leadership in a discrete form, for example organizing the singing, plays and dramas, or other activities. The pastor was a member of the national council of pastors and of a network of house churches scattered around the country. But the church, as such, fell apart when persecution grew markedly in 2010.

Integrality and identity. PMI, the agency of the Latin American workers, emphasized as one of its distinctives the concept of integral mission. As soon as workers arrive in the field, they go through a program of deep cultural immersion lasting five months. This includes extensive study of the language, the use of tools from cultural anthropology, time living with national families, and an independent, unaccompanied trip around the country. The rest of the first year is dedicated almost exclusively to gaining a deeper understanding of the culture.

While the agency warmly discourages the workers from testifying about their faith during their first year in the country, this is done with a long-term perspective. This cultural *incarnation* has resulted in many workers being able to communicate fluently in the local language and feeling at home in the culture, and, with that, being able to share their faith with greater clarity and connection to their friends.

At the same time, the approach of the organization has been evolving, helping its members to adopt a transparent and valid *identity* in opposition to the "camouflage" missionary model, which uses a project simply as a pretext to gain residence in the country. This camouflage approach forces workers into a double identity which creates many problems, as Christian has previously described:

> The double identity model is lived out to various degrees and forms. Some argue for a bivocational identity; two identities coexist within the missionary, one public and the other more or less hidden. This model brings with it various important implications, both psychological and spiritual as well as within the family. Missionaries who use this approach find themselves living a double life, almost like being a type of double agent or spy. It becomes difficult for them to maintain their integrity and soon their spiritual life is affected. Even if they are able to obtain a residence visa, this artificial identity is easily seen through by the nationals with whom these workers live, the result being a loss of credibility. Who will believe the message of an imposter?[1]

---

[1] Giordano, Christian in Federico A. Bertuzzi, *Ríos en Tierra Seca: Europeos, Latinos y Exmusulmanes Evangelizando a los Hijos de Ismael en el Viejo Continente* (Granada: Musulmania, 2012), 276, http://musulmania.com/resources/Rios_en_tierra_seca_INTRO.pdf. Trans. D. Greenlee.

In comparison, a true identity, united with an integrated vision of work, has enabled the workers in these rural development and welding projects to be able to freely share their faith in an open, clear way without being accused of proselytism. Their lives are attractive and they provoke many questions from their neighbors and friends as well as from the beneficiaries of the project. Those who are receiving the benefits of the projects, in fact, are those who take the initiative in evangelism as they raise their own questions.

A Replica in Another City

The good results of this model of collaboration between nationals and Latin Americans led to its being replicated in Villa Hermosa, as we will refer to this city located in the South of the country and, at the time, without a church. This rapidly growing port city was a strategic place for opening another welding school.

The missionary who oversaw the project was joined in Villa Hermosa by one of the teachers from the school in Gran Urbe as well as one of the alumni of the course, a young man who excels in his work. Not long after, another missionary couple joined the team. The project, now over eight years old, is housed in an industrial warehouse where about one hundred seventy students are learning the various aspects of industrial welding: electric, acetylene, continuous, and TIG. This self-sufficient project has a waiting list for students because it is the best such school in the country.

The national teacher – who is also a pastor – tried to begin gatherings in his home but one or two of the families who had come to faith in earlier years did not want to take part and remained isolated. Starting in 2010, pressure and threats from the police is very strong, the result being that the church was never truly birthed.

The police pressure continued. Despite the fact that the project and the staff were covered by an international agreement, the authorities did not renew the residence visa for the project leader, resulting in his *de facto* expulsion in the middle of the year 2013.

2. Description of the Asian Context

Tashkent is the capital of Uzbekistan, one of the former Soviet republics of Central Asia. It is a city of about three million inhabitants, its population comprised of many ethnic groups, principally Uzbeks, Kazakhs, Tajiks, and Russians.

The Russian-background population, the majority, has seen their influence in the country significantly decreased. A first step was the change from Cyrillic to a Latin-based alphabet, then the marginalization of the Russian language, and finally their social marginalization. This led to significant social tensions between them and other groups.

After independence in 1991, commercial exchange was permitted on a limited basis with multinationals such as the Korean company Daewoo. Religious activity, though, remained limited. Mosques were allowed, but under supervision. This applied as well to the official Christian entities, principally Russian Orthodox, as well as Baptists and Pentecostals who carried out their services in the Russian language. Other, non-registered churches which carried out their activities in the Uzbek language remained underground, or at least somewhat hidden.

CEDIES, the Center for the Study of the Spanish Language, was a center in Tashkent focused on teaching the Spanish language and Spanish and Iberoamerican culture. It functioned from 1999 through to 2006. The center maintained very good relationships with local universities, various Spanish universities, and foreign embassies in the city. It also acted as a representative of the Cervantes Institute – a non-profit organization created by the Spanish government in 1991 for the promotion of the Spanish language.

The center's high standards attracted many students; it was also a center for cultural activity. Various Latin American missionaries worked as teachers, both in the center as well as in local universities, and served as a point of contact between the universities and foreign projects. Among other things, they edited the first Uzbek-Spanish dictionary. Scholarships and residential study programs were channeled through the project, both for students as well as national professors, in cooperation with the University of Alcalá de Henares in Spain. The formation of the center also provided opportunities for employment in the local community. The project was abruptly closed in 2006 when the government expelled all foreigners, journalists, and NGOs from the country.

The Latin American team consisted of twelve to fifteen members. As professors, they held both a clear identity and high social status. They enjoyed numerous connections, with students and in the community in general, something that provided them with many opportunities to share their faith. Those in the project were cautious not to engage in proselytism even though all those around them knew that they were Christians.

The missionaries associated with CEDIES decided not to try to form a new church, but to spread themselves discreetly among the various churches already existing in the city. This gave them the opportunity to bring to these gatherings their friends from various ethnic backgrounds.

Four single women were invited by a local pastor to help his underground Uzbek church, and in particular to help in discipling leaders of the youth as well as in evangelism. This turned out to be a very positive experience. They met together in homes to study the Bible and answer questions to aid in their spiritual development, meetings in which there was plenty of food on the table and few books in sight – in case the police would show up or a spy was present.

Over time, the group grew to more than forty young people; several marriages among the members resulted. Starting in 2005, restrictions and persecution began to increase. All of the foreigners left the country, and it has been difficult to know what happened to the church. Two of the missionary women who were involved with the group report that some eighty percent of the young people continue in their faith.

3. Analysis of the Relationships

We begin our analysis of the relationships between the churches and projects by noting that there was a similar level of persecution in both of these settings. Despite the evident differences between North Africa and Central Asia, pressure on the Christians was high, sometimes at a level we could call persecution. In both settings Christian churches existed, they were tolerated but faced significant restrictions. Participation was limited to foreigners in the North African case and to those who spoke Russian, a secondary language, in the Central Asia situation. The churches we are considering were made up of local believers who, when they gathered, used the local language. Usually they needed to remain hidden, or at best were minimally tolerated, but only for a short time.

Pressures the believers experienced came principally from their families, but also often included losing employment. At times, they were considered to be traitors or at least non-patriotic. Dramatic police raids on homes or places of work decisively influenced the credibility and the good name of the Christians. They faced threats of being arrested by the police and the possibility of spending long years in jail and even the possibility of losing their own children. Threats made over the telephone were common.

Persecution in these situations in North Africa and Uzbekistan resulted in the sudden closure of projects as well as the expulsion of development workers, most of these devoid of any legal basis or formal accusation. In North Africa, several of the pastors were forced to move from one city to another and there were a few cases of imprisonment.[2] In Uzbekistan, following the mass expulsion of foreigners in 2006, persecution of Christians intensified with heavy fines for possessing a Bible, pastors receiving long prison sentences, and beatings to obtain confessions and names of other Christians.

Second, the relations between the church and the integral rural development and welding projects in Gran Urbe are indirect, that is, there are no organizational links or frequent contacts. They are also geographically distant: they do not share premises or physical space and are developed at a considerable distance. The projects are carried out in rural areas in the mountains and the church gathers in the city. On rare occasions, some local believers have helped the rural development project in health campaigns, but otherwise they have never been involved in the project. One or two of the students in the welding project have

[2] One of the men who was to be baptized in Gran Urbe disappeared without a trace that very day. He may have given into pressure from his family and moved abroad or to a distant city. In the worst-case scenario, it would not be the first case of death at the hands of his relatives, to cleanse the family's honor.

come to faith and joined the church. We assume that the church will have prayed for the projects, for the missionaries who work in them, and for the beneficiaries. Therefore, we can speak of a reciprocal relationship, although of low intensity.

As for Villa Hermosa, the relationship between the project and the church is less evident, primarily because the church never was really birthed, nor did it function as a church. Hypothetically, if this church had been able to function, the relationship would have been equally indirect, both organizationally and geographically distant; it would have been unthinkable to hold religious services or meetings in the project's facilities.

As for the relationship between the project and the church in Tashkent, it was even more indirect and distant. The pastor and other church leaders had no connection with the project.

Third, in all three cases, the church membership was composed of people outside the project. That is, the beneficiaries of the projects and the focus audience of the church were different. Occasionally, one of the beneficiaries might come to hear the gospel and join the church, but this was not the norm. In fact, in the case of Tashkent, some who came to faith in Jesus through the team were not of Uzbek background, and so were incorporated into Russian-speaking churches. This implies that the missionary team worked on two fronts: in making the project work with excellence and in the growth of disciples.

In the case of Tashkent, the *intentionality* of establishing churches has shifted to the intentionality of supporting the existing church in evangelism and disciple-making. The Latin American missionary team consciously decided not to establish a new church of their own.

We have analyzed, in fourth place, the relationship between the missionaries and the project and the church. In the three cases analyzed, the missionaries are both directors of the projects and project workers. In some cases, they have Muslim employees who work as welding instructors or Spanish language teachers. Some of these workers have developed a very close relationship with the missionaries and their families. They know practically everything about their lives, their motivations, and their faith. They also share in the important decisions of the project. A few have become followers of Jesus, but not all of them.

As far as the church is concerned, the missionaries support but do not lead the church. This is especially clear in Gran Urbe and Tashkent. We imagine that the missionaries played a much more prominent role in the intentional efforts to establish the church in Villa Hermosa, although to no avail. But in all three cases, the pastor is national; the role of foreigners is secondary, in some cases as support or advisor to the pastor, or as a resource to disciple young people. In all three cases, the missionaries are seen by the church and its leadership as resources for spiritual input, as mature believers, as examples to imitate, and even as leaders of some kind, but not with the responsibility of leading the church.

The cooperation between nationals and foreigners in the sphere of the church is noteworthy. As far as North Africa is concerned, the case of Gran Urbe set a precedent as the first experience of collaboration between the organized national church in that country and a foreign missionary agency.[3] Previously, the national church did not allow foreigners to attend its services, partly because of the unwanted visibility that would be associated with the participation of foreigners and partly because of mistrust. The initiative in Gran Urbe was a lovely experience of teamwork between a national pastor and a missionary family.

Another facet of the relationship between missionaries and the church was the willingness of the latter to offer their homes for the use of the church. An attitude of service was evident when, week after week, they received a large group in their home, and all the more so doing this as guests in a society in which every meeting included abundant food and concepts of privacy that were far different from in the missionaries' home settings.

In the three cases analyzed, few or none of the missionary team attended the national church. In the case of Gran Urbe, it was the family of the welding teacher who also provided their home: an Argentinean couple with two children of eight and ten years of age at the time they began taking part in the group. As for Tashkent, the missionaries normally did not attend the worship gatherings, although occasionally the leader of the missionary team did, with much discretion.

A fifth aspect to consider is the relationship of the church and of the missionaries with the culture, that is, the degree of contextualization. Although we do not have sufficient data to make an in-depth evaluation, the accounts collected indicate a moderately high degree of contextualization. In the case of the church of Gran Urbe, the country as a whole wants to resemble or come closer to the West. This has influenced the worship and the identity of the church, which has a tendency towards more Westernized worship formats. However, we can affirm that there are clear signs of theological appropriation of the culture.

For years, the church in the country has been composing its own music in the local Arabic dialect and incorporating typical instruments. This has contributed significantly to the indigenousness of the liturgy and of evangelism. They produced numerous CDs, some in classical Arabic, but most in the distinct Arabic dialects of each North African country. A step forward has been the creation of groups of Christian musicians who entertain at weddings and parties with appropriate, indigenous Christian music.

Likewise, the use of the local Arabic dialect is a clear sign of contextualization. We need to explain that the entire population of the region is multilingual. In the mosque and for public speaking classical Arabic (*al-fusha*) is used, while newspapers and TV news are expressed in Modern Standard Arabic, very similar to Egyptian Arabic. In normal life – in the market, in the street, in the house – the country's dialect is spoken, dialects that are generally unwritten. In addition to understanding (at least to some extent) classical Arabic and, Modern Standard Arabic along with their local dialect, all those who have

[3] The fact that the missionary agency was from the Global South, undoubtedly contributed to building trust and the establishment of this collaboration.

gone to school speak French. For many, their mother tongue (or at least grandparents' tongue) may be one of the Berber languages. All of this is a real challenge for those from the outside with a monolingual mentality!

Previously, the Bible was translated into classical Arabic for two reasons: first, because that is the usual language for discussing religious topics and, second, it is the official written language. Recently, versions of the Bible have appeared in Moroccan, Tunisian, and Algerian dialects of Arabic as well as in some of the Berber languages.

In this context, the choice of the local Arabic dialect for worship, evangelism, and music is particularly relevant. On the one hand, it brings the gospel closer to the culture, giving it an indigenous flavor. On the other hand, though, it has the disadvantage of trivializing it, since the dialects tend to be banal, mundane, and everyday as opposed to the spirituality of classical Arabic. Hence, North Africans who have been Christians from some twenty years ago or more have usually preferred to read the Bible and pray in classical Arabic. When national leaders choose to use their local dialect in their gatherings and in their witness, it is a sign of their conscious decision to bring the gospel closer to their fellow citizens.

Another indication of contextualization is the use of Islamic religious vocabulary adapted to a biblical meaning. An example is the use by Christians of Gran Urbe of the Arabic term *al-ijwan* (the brotherhood) as one of the ways of referring to the congregation, to the group of believers. This expression is used by radical Muslim groups, notably as part of the official name of the Muslim Brotherhood. In contrast, the term *al-ijwan* is to our knowledge never used by Egyptian Christians as a proper term. They prefer the more common Arabic alternative, *jamaat* (congregation).

These North African church leaders also frequently reinterpret social holidays, such as weddings, circumcisions, and anniversaries, by giving them a Christian meaning. To a lesser extent, they also do so with the fasting of Ramadan.

As far as the missionaries are concerned, we have not carried out a rigorous measurement of their degree of *contextualization*. We can only offer some indications from the interviews and our own observations. The missionary team in Gran Urbe included several families with a more than acceptable language level for a foreigner, above level four on a scale of one to five.[4] In the specific case of the missionary who participated in the establishment of the church, he was able to preach, disciple, and fluently converse on abstract topics in Arabic dialect. His family in general felt at ease in the neighborhoods: they had many friends, and their children went to the public school and played in the street with the neighborhood children. Their house, externally and internally, was very similar to that of any national of the neighborhood; all of the family remembers

---

[4] Larry D. Pate, *Misionología: Nuestro Cometido Transcultural* (Miami: Vida, 1987), 415-22.

those times with nostalgia. As for the Tashkent team, they all lived in common, middle-class neighborhoods and apartments (not in residential areas for foreigners). The local language level of the missionary team was medium-high, while that of the four female missionaries was high, according to the scale referenced above. The spirit in which they frequently offered hospitality is also of great significance, making use of local customs and cuisine to provide a relaxed and suitable environment for the exchange with the students.

Sixth, we consider the issues of *identity*, *proselytism*, and *integrality*. The identity of the missionaries was, in all cases, genuine and transparent. Their professions were not a camouflage to obtain a visa and thus be able to dedicate themselves to evangelism. They were really what they said they were: a professional welder, engineer, health technician, teacher, or linguist. Moreover, they considered their project work as an integral part of their vocation and ministry. They did not hide their motivations: to bless the country and its inhabitants in the name of *Isa al-Masih*, Jesus the Messiah. Nor did they hide the origin of their salary: they were supported by a group of Christian friends from their respective countries in order to be able to be there doing that work. In some cases, they received a minimum salary from the university where they taught.

In other words, we can describe them as integral: their life, their actions, and their message coincided.

As far as proselytizing was concerned, they carefully avoided handing out pamphlets or Bibles, making distinctions between Christians and Muslims in their projects, or trying to recruit people to their religion. They never criticized Islam and spoke of the Prophet Muhammad with respect. But they were all very clear in sharing their faith, their testimony, in offering prayer for the needy or the sick, and in answering questions. In fact, in the case of the community development project near Gran Urbe, the question, "Why are you doing this for us?" was commonly raised, with the observation by the one posing the question, "I would never do something like this for an infidel."

The North African national church chose to redefine its *identity* with respect to the previous generation of Christians. They made use of every possible means to affirm their citizenship, their loyalty to the nation and the rulers, and their desire to do good for society. "We are from here, though we are followers of the Messiah," they would say. They also set aside the anti-Muslim sentiment that had characterized the previous generation, reaffirming Muslim cultural values such as using common names for their children, not eating pork or drinking alcohol, practicing circumcision, loving folk and traditional music, and fasting. The church knew itself to be part of a national network of other churches, whose pastors met regularly, as opposed to the isolated believers or disjointed clusters of earlier times.

Finally, it is worth asking why the church was not successfully planted in Villa Hermosa. We can only make conjectures, but we venture to offer our insights, and in particular to offer ideas we have earlier considered with our colleagues who participated in this effort.

One of the reasons was the timing, the coincidence of the launch of the project and the rise of persecution. The missionaries and the project were just gaining trust and the right to speak when pressure from police became heavy. However, this factor, despite being very evident, should not be considered the first in importance.

Another reason may be due to the personality of the national pastor and the way he was appointed. He did not succeed in gaining the friendship and trust of the few older believers in the city. He was not commissioned by the national church, neither in the capital nor in Gran Urbe. To understand this better, it would be interesting to know whether the first attempts at meetings were sufficiently supported by the national church leaders. North African culture teaches distrust of anyone outside the extended family, a deep-rooted and widespread sentiment. From a young age, people are inculcated with the idea that sensible people relate only to their extended family. To do otherwise is, they insist, to invite unnecessary trouble. In fact, one of the pastoral problems facing all churches of Arab background is the need to emphasize and nurture the feeling of trust among church members: fellowship is not spontaneous but quite the opposite. Perhaps that first handful of Christians had no ties with the pastor or the national leaders who visited them. Or perhaps the pioneer team did not sufficiently explore the family and spiritual ties they could have drawn on to gain the trust of these older believers. But it could also be that the older believers simply did not want to meet. They were comfortable as secret believers and may not have wanted to change their status or become more committed.

However, one reason we see as significant is the absence of a new, fresh nucleus of those who had recently become followers of Jesus. In Gran Urbe, before the group started, the missionary was visiting and discipling a small group of people who had expressed their interest in response to Bible correspondence courses, radio broadcasts, and satellite TV; a slow, discreet, and individual work. As each one of them individually began to mature in the faith, the missionary gathered them informally, and only after that, the church was brought together. From the reports we obtained, it seems that there was no nucleus of new believers in Villa Hermosa, the "fresh sap" to make a new plant sprout with strength.

Questions for Reflection and Discussion

1. How are the concepts of integrality, proselytism, and identity applied and lived out in your setting?
2. If you live, or have lived for a long period of time in a large urban setting, which of the elements of society and of the church that we described in this chapter are familiar to you? Which are not? How would you compare the characteristics of these urban churches we described with your urban church?
3. Are you familiar with an NGO or community development project carried out by Christians? Try to describe the relationships between the workers, the project, and those who receive the benefits of the project, along with a description of the effect of the project. Can you make a diagram to show these links?

For Further Reading

Marsh, Charles R. *Too Hard for God?* Carlisle: OM, 2000.

Yoder, Richard A., Calvin W. Redekop, and Vernont E. Jantzi. *Development to a Different Drummer: Anabaptist/Mennonite Experiences and Perspectives*. Intercourse: Good Books, 2005.

Greenlee, David. "Growing Churches in Resistant Areas." *Evangelical Missions Quarterly*, 38, no. 4 (October 2002), 456-462.

Greenlee, David. *One Cross, One Way, Many Journeys: Thinking Again about Conversion*. Atlanta: Authentic, 2007.

7. Rural Experiences

We return now to consider two projects and two churches in North Africa as well as a third church in the interior of Senegal, all in rural settings. National believers are clearly the leaders of each of these churches.

1. Description of the North African Setting

The City called La Joya

A mountainous region in a North African country is inhabited by a Berber ethnic group known for its indomitable, individualistic character. This community has been able to continue in this isolated setting in the North of the country in part due to its own character and in part because of the marginalization with which the government has treated them in reprisal for their lack of affection for the regime. In fact, foreigners were not even allowed to visit this region, the police controlling all points of entry and exit.

In 2002, God miraculously opened the door for a teaching project, principally for women, developed together with a local organization. With backing from a high official, the local foundation made a large building available to the project. The missionary-related NGO was able to place both personnel and equipment in the principal city of the region, beginning its work with literacy classes, computer skills, and Spanish language courses.

La Joya, as we will call it, is a smaller city with about one hundred thousand inhabitants, dependent on agriculture and domestic tourism. La Joya has maintained its rural mentality and, it seems, everyone in town still knows each other. The presence of foreigners in such a place did not go unnoticed.

The project made an important contribution to the formation of a transparent, honorable identity of the missionaries: they were teachers. Furthermore, they were greatly appreciated because they teach a disadvantaged group (the illiteracy rate of women in this zone is significantly higher than the rate in the rest of the country), and the way they treat their students is quite different from other schools: the teachers neither strike nor insult the students.

In the beginning of the year 2004, a terrible earthquake devastated the region leaving more than six hundred dead and many buildings destroyed. The damage was much greater in the villages, where houses often were of flimsy construction quality. In the middle of a harsh winter, missionaries both of PM International (PMI) and other agencies worked together to provide emergency aid in some of the villages that had been ignored by the government. In the city, at the same time, the population in general and the authorities saw how the foreign teachers stretched themselves beyond their means to take care of the victims, and that was compared to the inaction of the government. Even in rural parts of the community characterized by a distrustful nature, this attitude of the teachers opened many doors.

Even so, the church arose from an individual initiative. After the rush of emergency aid, in one of the villages a missionary who lived in La Joya approached a family head offering to help him rebuild his house. He personally repeated the offer, one after another, to several families. It was a low-profile initiative, offered individually and privately but known to all. (In the villages everything is known!) This close contact, extended in time, incarnational in nature, and offered in the midst of the arduous work of reconstruction led to some men and a few women becoming followers of Jesus.

Due to the cultural forces at work here, the church was made up of a majority of men, about a dozen. Men and women gathered separately, rotating from house to house to avoid drawing attention to themselves. Leadership was exercised by one person, but he was supported by two or three men, each of them national believers.

The church continues functioning despite the persecution against the believers and the expulsions in 2010 of many foreigner Christians. In fact, the church has functioned based on its own resources; the missionary typically visited the leader about once a month.

Another Rural Church

In the capital of one of the North African countries, a computer-assisted cognitive skills development project for children living with disabilities was initiated. It was a delightful project, carried out in collaboration with a local institution. The missionary NGO provided the missionary-technician and the computer equipment. The project had no direct relationship with the emergence of the church in the nearby rural area, except through the involvement of the missionary. However, it provided the credibility necessary for the missionary to remain in the area.

The rural church in the area near Grand Ville, as we will call it, was born out of family ties. A man became a follower of Jesus in the South of the country and his life was transformed. Previously, he was a drunkard, foul-mouthed, and violent, but the extraordinary change in him drew his wife and children to also follow Jesus.

After some time, the man traveled several hours to the home of his relatives in the Grand Ville area, spoke to them about the Lord Jesus, and connected them with a missionary he had met. This missionary had led the project for handicapped children in Grand Ville. He and his family also hosted the meetings of groups of believers from the capital city and nearby villages, who met there on a rotating basis. Since the persecution started in 2010, however, those from the villages have tended to meet in their rural area, which is more discreet than gathering in an apartment block in the city.

In 2012, when the church was seven years old, it was composed of about a dozen people perceived by the local society to be of low social status, rural men and women living with their animals on small plots of land.

Family and neighborhood relationships were the basis of growth. An approximately equal number of men and women meet together, although they quite naturally sit on opposite sides of the room. One of the group exercises leadership; he is supervised by a national pastor from the capital. The teaching is mostly spoken (rather than read); it is both practical and informal and responds to emerging needs. Through July 2012, the missionary and his wife had been visiting and discipling the group weekly or biweekly.

2. Description of the Senegalese Context

The Senegalese church in the villages of Fatick province began, tentatively, in 1995, through the family ties of members of the Open Brethren Assembly in the capital, Dakar. The members and surrounding community are part of the Serere ethnic group, Muslims with an animist background. Islam arrived only recently, some 200 years ago; villagers remember who among their community was first to convert to Islam. Roman Catholics also have a presence within this community.

The villages are in a semi-desert area of the interior of the country. A worker well-informed about the situation told us that the Serere "originally lived in the North [of the country]. They fled to Dakar and to the coast when the Muslims arrived, and then to the interior, always fleeing from Islamization; trying to maintain their identity while not receiving that which was strange and foreign."

A subsistence economy characterizes the village with cultivation of millet and peanuts along with herding a small number of animals, mainly goats and sheep. Many of the men temporarily migrate to the city in order to survive, alternating the cycles of planting and harvesting with these temporary jobs.

Starting in the year 2007, the church experienced a period of exceptional growth. At that time, the church asked a missionary to take over the work. For over a year, he traveled every week by public transportation to the villages so that he could support the six main leaders. This was no small commitment. By public transportation, the initial part of the journey can take between five and eight hours. At a junction, where the dirt road leading to the village meets the paved highway, he would take a horse cart for another hour or two. The total journey took at least seven hours, often much longer. By comparison, a driver in a 4x4 vehicle could make the journey in about three hours.

Part of the agreement between the church and the missionary was that he would pay for the trip. In turn, the church would provide him with food and water during his visits.

By the year 2013, the church had more than three hundred fifty adults and more than five hundred children. They gathered for worship in three buildings they had built, as well as meeting in houses. All of their organization was indigenous, and the leadership was in the hands of believers from the villages.

The villagers' abundant evangelistic zeal and missionary vision was carried out in the following way: first they would go to a neighboring village where the gospel was not yet known, making calls on the community leaders (elders, imam, and Catholic priest if there was one) to meet them, introduce themselves, and ask permission to greet each family. On a second visit, they would greet each family announcing that they have an important message. On the third visit, they showed the "Jesus" film in the Serere language. On the fourth visit, they would go to each house and take the time to ask what the people thought about the film, answer questions, respond to doubts, and explain their message. Out of this, they were able to bring together interested families.

These followers of Jesus benefited from having the entire Bible in the Serere language. Entire families participated in their services: men, women, and children. Opposition was generally mild since they began their connection with the village by first requesting permission of the village leaders.

Analysis of the setting shows a high degree of contextualization and integrality. The villagers applied the gospel to all aspects of life and organized their worship gatherings according to their customs. They decided not to participate in animist ceremonies, but they do participate in community festivals such as weddings, baptisms, and other celebrations. When they gather in houses to pray, before concluding, they go outside the door to pray publicly for the other houses and families of the village.

There is no development project as such in these villages (foreign or associated with an NGO). Instead, we find that the church has taken specific initiatives committed to the welfare of their villages. They have collaborated in bringing water sources to villages, in building a millet mill, in taking care of the fields of the elderly and those who are ill, assisting widows, and mediating in conflicts. One year after the period in which the missionary had assisted them, they celebrated the baptism of fifty-eight individuals, the biggest baptism the country had ever seen. The believers invited the pastors representing the various denominations and the evangelical federation of the country to join in the baptism ceremony. Deferring to the local leaders, when invited to baptize the first new believer the missionary insisted that the local pastor be the first to descend into the water and officiate. Note how this fact breaks with the preeminence typically given in African societies to foreigners or the person from the city, a mindset that is a direct result of their recent colonial past.

3. Analysis of the Relationship

Because the context of these three churches is significantly different, analysis of the relationships of these three rural churches must be thoughtfully differentiated.

The church in La Joya, North Africa, came about in a special situation: following an earthquake. The same time, the rural church in Grand Ville reflects a somewhat normal situation, typical of the countryside near the large capital cities of North Africa. On the other hand, the churches in the villages of Senegal's interior did not suffer official persecution but pressure on individuals. These churches are all found in societies marked by an ancient culture of consensus. Nevertheless, the similarities that we will be pointing out allow us to group them together in a single chapter.

First, we note what many consider to be *divine intervention* in all three settings. The Berber area in the North of the first country was closed to foreigners. No visas were granted, all access roads had police checkpoints. And then, unplanned and unforeseen by the team, God opened a door for a project through the sponsorship of a high-ranking personality. The organization linked to PMI received a direct invitation to work on that project. Soon after, a very strong earthquake struck the area, allowing for emergency assistance from several Christian organizations. The delay and inaction of the government exacerbated the rebellious and independent spirit of the people and, in turn, made them even more open to receive reconstruction aid. While police pressure decreased, communities that earlier had been reluctant to engage with foreigners opened up completely as socially isolated and remote families and villages cautiously began to welcome them.

In the rural zones of Grand Ville, as we mentioned before, the miraculous conversion and change of a single person and his resulting testimony opened doors to an entire social network of relatives who lived both near and far.

In the Fatick villages in the interior of Senegal, the testimony of the church had been known since 1995. There were a few conversions and a very slow rate of growth. In 2005, two families in one village had a dispute that neither they nor the village elders were able to resolve. They decided to ask the Christians for advice. Receiving wisdom from God, the Christians proposed a solution that satisfied both parties and impressed the whole village. Soon the missionary appointed by the church in the capital arrived: a white man who spoke Wolof perfectly and who traveled for hours by bus and horse-drawn cart, something unheard of! As of our last contact with the church several years later, its growth has been accompanied by miracles of various kinds.

God intervenes, and a rigorous missiological analysis cannot overlook these combinations of events that are difficult to explain in any other way.

Secondly, the most significant characteristic common to all three cases is the *national leadership*, and with it the complementary role of the foreigners. In the church in La Joya, the missionary husband and wife started from scratch, discipling the families that were coming to faith. He spent time with the husband and she with the wife and small children. Soon, one of the new believers was appointed as the leader of the small community while the missionaries remained as counselors. In fact, the missionaries left the place relatively soon, within a couple of years, moving to another city several hours away by car and in a different country. The missionary continued to visit the pastor, usually once a month. According to the missionary's words, he has refocused his ministry: "I no longer work with the people; I dedicate myself to disciple the pastors."

The process in the rural zone of Grand Ville has been different. The point of reference or the "spiritual father" of these believers is the man who came to faith in the South of the country and experienced a radical change in his life. He is the one who brought his relatives to faith in Christ. Living about twelve hours away by car, he visits them about once per year. He is also the one who requested the missionary to come and disciple the small group of believers. Initially the missionary objected, stating that there were more appropriate individuals, but the national believer insisted: God had spoken to him through dreams and had indicated that this person in particular was the one.

One of the believers in the group serves as its leader. They have a connection with the national church in the capital, not far away, and maintain a strong even if distant relationship with their "spiritual father." The missionary and his wife have helped a small group with weekly visits, discipling, teaching, and simply being examples. They left the country at the end of 2012 due to health reasons. The church has continued functioning normally.

The churches in the villages of Fatick in Senegal have an ordained national pastor as well as several who help in various ways including evangelism. All of them were born and lived in these villages. They have had freedom to do things in their own way, according to their culture and customs. They have discussed with the missionary their problems and matters that arise, exploring the pros and cons, and examining the Scriptures together and praying. The role of the missionary is that of a counselor or more experienced brother, but the decisions are made by the local pastor. Above, we described their approach in evangelism. They would also get together to sing on Fridays and Saturdays, composing their own songs or adapting others as they desired. The people of the villages like to hear them sing and many attend their practice sessions. It is the Senegalese themselves who have decided which guidelines to establish with respect to animism and to the society.

In the three cases mentioned in this chapter, it is clearly the nationals who hold the reins of the church while the missionaries serve in a supporting role.

In third place, the relationships between the development project and the church are indirect, if any exist, but they are different in each case. The church had something of a *reciprocal* relationship with the teaching and women's empowerment project in La Joya, although it was an *indirect, distant relationship directed toward different beneficiaries*. We remember that the project was developed in the city while the church developed in the villages.

Some of the female students in the project occasionally helped as volunteers in the reconstruction of houses, for example, caring for and teaching children as the men worked. They also helped in the process of evangelism and discipleship in this oral cultural setting, translating into the Berber language and making audio recordings of Bible materials for children and women.

The relationship of the reconstruction project with the church was also *indirect*, but it was *close*, and *directed to the beneficiaries themselves*. It was a completely incarnational relationship because the missionary participated in the hard construction work, was involved with the family, and spent many hours with each family nucleus. It was a *non-proselytizing* relationship, because those who were interested in the gospel were helped as well as those who were not. Likewise, it was a relationship of discipleship, of transference of values. Work, evangelization, and discipleship were integrated, without compartmentalization. In the case of families who decided to accept the gospel message, discipleship and Christian growth came very easily. But those who showed no interest in following Jesus Christ still learned Christian values: solidarity, work well done, compassion, and generosity, as well as tolerance towards the Christian faith.

The project and the church did not have a direct, formal, organizational relationship, and in fact the project as such had a relatively short life, a couple of years, but it had continuity in its impact. The whole village, but especially the Christians, had learned to help each other, in a traditionally individualistic and independent culture, and have continued to do so as needs arise. In other words, it was a *relationship of discipleship.*

In contrast, the rural church near Grand Ville has never been linked to a project. The missionary was previously part of a project in the capital city with children living with disabilities. That project allowed him to remain in the city, to have an honorable identity, and to relate in natural ways with his neighbors, the church, and society. If anything, we could speak of an *indirect and distant* relationship.

As far as the Senegalese case study is concerned, there is no project as such run by an organization. Instead, the situation we have observed is entirely about the church. Therefore, there is no relationship between the project and the church, although, as we have pointed out, the church is actively involved in the welfare of its community.

Fourth, the relationships of the project and the church *with the culture* are equally interesting. The case of the project in La Joya is important in terms of gender relations. Society in the Northern part of the country is strongly segregated, even more so than in the rest of the territory. Men and women do not mix or have meaningful relationships. In this context, the women's education project established changes. First, it addressed women and attacked the causes of their marginalization: lack of education and self-esteem. It not only provided literacy, computer literacy and other professional skills, but also gave them visibility and status. "Women are important and deserve to be empowered" was the wordless message that the project as a whole conveyed to the entire population. Moreover, it did so with respect, with dignity. The teachers did not strike students or insult them but were patient and treated the female students as equals, behavior that was completely new in that context, where teachers are superior, very directive, and unfriendly.

The church, on the other hand, has not made as much progress on gender issues. Once again, we recall that it is located in a rural area. Worship services are held separately, women in one place and men in another; each follows a completely separate path. Rarely does a husband talk to his wife about weighty issues. Therefore, it would be unrealistic to expect Christian husbands to lead their wives or daughters to the gospel or to pass on to them what they were learning from the Bible. The church is made up of about ten men and two or three women. Why such a disparity in numbers? Why haven't more women become followers of Jesus? We don't yet have the answer. The women had as much exposure to the gospel or more than the men. They lived through the same experiences – the earthquake – and received both emergency and reconstruction assistance. In fact, the rebuilding involved two women missionaries (a wife and a single woman) while only one Christian man worked with the men. One would expect a more equal number of conversions, but this was not the case. We can only wonder if, for these Berber women, the gospel was indeed really "good news." However, we dare not judge from the outside, as distant observers. It is a situation, though, that many who are close to the setting have noted, a missiological quandary that requires further reflection and experimentation.

The relationships between the church in the countryside near Grand Ville and its culture can help us understand some of the patterns we have observed. First, as previously mentioned, the church grew up along family social networks, a deeply cultural characteristic.

In terms of gender issues, it would be reasonable to think that its proximity to the capital city – where worship services are mixed, attended by both men and women – would have influenced its behavior. In fact, in the early days, before the persecution of 2010, worship services alternated between meeting in the rural area and the capital, where missionaries were lived and hosted the gatherings. So, the first model of church that these rural North African believers observed was urban and mixed in terms of gender. As is natural in that culture, the men sit on one side of the room and the women on the other. With children also present, the atmosphere is like an extended family gathering. Everyone is present during the time of worship; everyone prays, reads, sings, and partakes of the Lord's Supper together with the others. Sometimes, when there are young children, they are taken to another room either to play or to teach them at their level.

Another aspect in which the church near Grand Ville has learned to relate to its culture has been in the ceremonies linked to funerals. It is customary to have a feast forty days after the burial. That was the moment chosen by the believers to present to their relatives their hope in Jesus the Messiah.

The relationship of the church in Fatick, in the interior of Senegal, to its culture demonstrates a high degree of contextualization, probably the highest of the three analyzed in this chapter. This is not surprising given the age of the church and the leading role of the local believers in the church. In this very animistic context, the church has decided in which ceremonies and community festivals they will participate and in which they do not. So, for example, Christians do not participate in ceremonies to ensure the fertility of the fields, rites in which people pour milk on the land and make charms in order to have good crops. Instead, at the time of sowing seed, Christians gather to pray for the harvest.

However, they have decided to participate in feasts and celebrations related to weddings, births, anniversaries, and circumcision. Men and women worship together with freedom for all to participate with testimonies, prayers, and other participation. The availability of the complete Bible in the Serere language has played an important role in the process of contextualization. There are many indications that the church reads the Bible with Serere eyes, and the believers discover in it answers to their problems, many of them related to the spirit world and the spiritual struggle.

In fifth place, let us consider the relationship of the *missionaries with the church*. We have already highlighted the incarnational relationship of the reconstruction project in the rural North African zone of La Joya. But we need to highlight the high degree of personal involvement of the missionaries first in the emergency and in the following weeks, and also in the months of reconstruction. While all the volunteers who participated in the emergency relief were dedicated above and beyond what would normally be expected, they were visitors, people who came from other cities, or who made the trip intentionally. But in the case of the missionaries who lived in the city, their high degree of involvement was of another kind. They went through the trauma of the earthquake just like the rest of the community, but their neighbors saw them caring for others beyond what could normally be expected. They saw them put their car, their time, and even their own family's livelihood at the disposal of those in need. And when outside assistance fell short, they went to the supermarket or the building materials supplier to buy in bulk, bargaining for a better price because their money was not enough, appealing to community solidarity, and finding ways to involve their neighbors in emergency relief as well. These foreigners were involved even beyond what one would expect from close family!

As far as the villages in the Fatick region of the interior of Senegal, the relationships of the missionary with the church and with the culture were, from the beginning, completely different from what one would expect from a foreigner. We have mentioned that initially, for a little more than a year, the missionary traveled every week to the villages by public transportation. This allowed him to be in the village for about three or four hours. Although these travel conditions were common for everyone some years ago, nowadays foreigners rarely travel in public transportation, for such a long time, and on a regular basis. Therefore, the conduct and persistence of this missionary favorably impressed the population of these poor villages.

Furthermore, from the first day, the missionary placed himself in a position of dependence. He told them: "I will pay for the trip and you will give me food and drink; I will eat and drink what you offer me." It is not common for foreigners to drink village water. They may eat what is offered to them when it is cooked but drinking from the contaminated water of rural wells is another matter. On the other hand, the missionary is very well-adapted to the culture in terms of his perception of time, his way of eating, and in matters of organization and values. He feels completely at ease in that culture. In this sense, the previous thirteen years in which he was involved in a project in the capital have served him to forge his cultural identity: he is no longer a Brazilian; he is a Brazilian-Senegalese, a symbiosis of the two cultures.

Thus, in both La Joya and Fatick, the incarnational and culturally integrated way of life of the Latin American missionaries has resulted in a mutual relationship of great openness, of true appreciation, and has been decisive for the emergence and growth of both churches.

Finally, let us comment on questions of *integrality*, *identity*, and *proselytism* in the three cases we are considering. Integrality is much more than joining together "proclamation" with "works."

The Christian faith has come to La Joya in a non-compartmentalized way. Naturally, it has affected work, solidarity, mutual aid, and family while also touching both material and spiritual things. At the same time, since integrality is a journey, an ideal never achieved, a social transformation that affects the structures of the rural village has yet to materialize. Christians are known to all. They live their faith discreetly so as not to attract unnecessary problems, but they have endured police pressures without giving up their faith. In contrast, in the rural church near Grand Ville, the gospel has transformed people, it has begun to make a difference with cultural customs, but it has not reached the community or social level; believers still live their faith clandestinely; they are secret believers. The situation is quite different in the Senegalese hinterland where the gospel is beginning to produce initial signs of social change. Believers are not only known but prominent. The church is actively involved in the transformation of families, the community, and individuals, in this order of priority. Note that the transformation of individuals comes last, just the opposite of what is happening in Western churches.

In each of the cases, the identity of both the missionaries and the Christians is clear and transparent. In La Joya, the missionary introduced himself as a follower of *Isa al-Masih*, and everyone knew that he was the informal leader of the house church. Soon the leadership passed to one of the local national believers, and although he does not use the title "pastor" everyone in the village knows that he is "the head" (*rais*, a common Arabic term) of the little house group. The situation in the Fatick villages is at the opposite extreme in terms of circumstances. The Brazilian-Senegalese missionary openly presents himself as a pastor. His role is to support the local pastor and to teach the young leaders. Everyone in the villages knows that. The social context of Senegal allows a degree of religious tolerance that is reflected in the vocabulary. But the transparency with which they handle their identity in the two very different situations is the same. In fact, even the role played by the leaders (national and foreign) is very similar: they support the local leader/pastor and provide leadership training. Witnessing to their faith in daily circumstances goes hand in hand with their more formal witness in the church and is thus reflected in their identity. There is no contradiction, no ambiguity, but transparency, which is one of the manifestations of integrality.

In the first and third cases (La Joya and Fatick) proselytizing – in its negative sense – clearly did not take place. The followers of the Messiah have demonstrated no differentiation or favoritism between those who believe as they do and those who do not, even while openly spreading the good news of Jesus.

Integrality and evangelization have been supported by a clear, well-known, transparent, and well-appreciated religious identity. Christians enjoy the esteem of the population. Likewise, missionaries have a clear and transparent identity, perceived as genuine by their neighbors and society in general. These are key aspects on which the rest of life and ministry are based: if the neighbors do not believe that you are who you say you are, or they harbor doubts about your motivations, how are they going to believe in the new message that you bring?

Questions for Reflection and Discussion

1. If you live, or have lived, in a rural setting for an extended time, which of the elements of culture and of church that we have mentioned are familiar to you? How would you compare the characteristics of your rural church with those we have described?
2. How did your church get started? Is there a written history or an archive available? Interview an older person who knows the history of the church. Consider recording or writing down this narrative.
3. Do more women or men come to faith in your church? Why does this happen? Thinking from your own perspective, what do you find attractive about the gospel? In your church, what (if anything) is distinct about what women and men find attractive about the gospel? What conclusions can you draw?

For Further Reading

Bedford, Nancy E. "'The World Palpitates': Globalization and the Religious Faith and Practices of Latin American Women." In *The Oxford Handbook of Feminist Theology*, edited by Sheila Briggs and Mary McClintock Fulkerson. Oxford: Oxford University Press, 2011. https://doi.org/10.1093/oxfordhb/9780199273881.003.0008.

Mallouhi, Christine. *Waging Peace on Islam*. Downers Grove: InterVarsity, 2000.

Mernissi, Fatima. *Dreams of Trespass: Tales of a Harem Girlhood.* Reading, Mass.: Perseus, 1995.

Nelson, Ronald W. "Some Crucial Dimensions of Ministry to Fulbe." *Missiology* 11, no. 2 (April 1, 1983): 201-18.

Shenk, David W. *Christian, Muslim, Friend: Twelve Paths to Real Relationship*. The Christians Meeting Muslims. Harrisonburg, Vir.: Herald Press, 2014.

8. Mission and Medicine

During a period of over twenty years, going back to 1994, Christian had the privilege of following the progress of three teams of Latin American missionaries in Dakar, Senegal. In this chapter, we look at projects related to those teams, comparing two medical projects in the greater Dakar region. Both are associated with a church, but each holds a distinct methodology, has differences in personnel as well as distinct results. Comparing these two projects casts much light on the relationships between churches and development projects.

1. Description of the Context: Këru Yakaar and Keur Jamm

Këru Yakaar (The House of Hope) is a clinic sponsored by Youth With A Mission (YWAM), located in the densely populated neighborhood of Urbam in Dakar, Senegal. In 1994, on the occasion of the visit of the ship *Anastasis*,[1] the government donated a large piece of land on which the clinic was built. Këru Yakaar provides medical care (consultations and an outpatient clinic), dental care, child nutrition services, and counseling for pregnant mothers. Hallmarks of the clinic are its quality care and warm, personalized attention. The clinic is probably the largest private clinic in the city, providing care to more than one hundred fifty patients daily at the clinic, about sixty or seventy at the dentist's office, and about two hundred malnourished children per year. One of the major attractions of the project is its inexpensive pharmacy, the best stocked pharmacy in the city, because they are authorized to buy from the National Pharmacy and because of their stock management. They also sell medicines to other projects, the medicines being relatively inexpensive for the patients. The project is virtually self-sustaining financially and the administration has now been handed over to national staff.

While ninety percent of the beneficiaries of the clinic are Muslim (along with many poor Christians), all the clinic's staff are Christians, members of the various churches in the city. They are expected to witness to patients during

[1] From 1978-2007 the ship *Anastasis* was a mobile hospital ship, housing three state-of-the-art operating rooms, a 40-bed hospital ward, a dental clinic, a laboratory, an X-ray unit, and three cargo holds.

consultations – prayer with the patients is offered and Christian literature made available – but medical care takes precedence over spiritual care. Establishing a church has not been an aim of the project, but instead they point interested persons to the church closest to their home. However, in the first years of the project, one of the missionaries conducted Bible studies in his home, gatherings marked by a steady increase in attendance. After several years, though, the project team decided to form a church, Keur Jamm (House of Peace), which has maintained a relationship with YWAM.

The Keur Jamm church was born out of the work of a YWAM missionary in Dakar in 1984 who gathered a group in his house to study the Bible. As the group grew, they decided to become a church and called Adoniram Pires to be their pastor, a Brazilian Baptist missionary with pastoral experience who was based in the country. After four years of growth, YWAM felt it was better to have a pastor with a Pentecostal orientation and entered into an agreement with the Nigerian mission CAPRO. Eloi Dogue, a Senegalese of Serere origin, became pastor in 2006 and served in that role until 2013.

Between 1994 and 2005, the congregation changed its rented meeting place seven times due to pressure on the owners from neighboring Muslim leaders. They finally bought a piece of land in 2005 and have settled in Grand Yoff, a large district of the city with some five hundred thousand inhabitants. Many immigrants from Senegal's inland villages come to live in this district, noted for its strong Muslim roots and fifty-four mosques.

The church now gathers in the beautiful three-story building the members built, dedicated on March 25, 2006. The congregation is comprised of about three hundred and fifty people from almost all the ethnic groups of the country except Wolofs. The membership of the other churches, some of them larger than Keur Jamm, is composed mostly of Africans from other nations with a Christian background who worship in French, as well as other foreigners such as the Korean church. Thus, Keur Jamm is the most Senegalese church in the city because its membership is Senegalese rather than African in general. However, the fact that there are no Wolof in the congregation, the dominant and nationally symbolic ethnic group, is a major drawback to its national identity.

The Keur Jamm church worships together in French and Wolof. It has a strong integral orientation, expressed both in the neighborhood and in the surrounding villages. The members want to reach out to the neighborhood and serve them in many ways. They have an extensive ministry to the children, who swarm the streets late at night because they disturb the others with whom they live in their one-room houses. They also reach out to women, the real pillars of the often-polygamous households. They have opened several daughter churches in villages in the interior and in the South of the country.

2. Description of the Context: Keru Barkeel

The city of Pikine[2] is a satellite settlement of Dakar, on the Dakar-Rufisque-Thies road. With over one million inhabitants, it is the second most populated city in the country. Growth has been very rapid, disorderly, and partially illegal, with major water and electricity supply problems. Part of the city has been built on the Niayes riverbed, one of the cultivated areas that once produced most of the vegetables consumed in the capital. In the rainy season, entire areas may be flooded by half a meter of sewage and stagnant water. Four major asphalt roads crisscross the city, while most of the other roads are sandy. The unemployment rate is very high. The population, coming from the villages or from forced relocations from neighborhoods in the capital, is mainly composed of Wolofs, although all the country's ethnic groups are, to a greater or lesser extent, represented in the city.

The Wolofs form one of the most representative and influential ethnic groups in Senegal. They constitute approximately forty percent of the total population of some fourteen million. Their language is Wolof, written with either Latin or Arabic characters, and referred to as the Wolofal script. However, since they are the dominant ethnic group of the country with a strong sense of class, many people of other ethnicities assimilate into Wolof culture in order to promote themselves in society. Together, they are the Wolofons, the French term for all those who speak Wolof, a group that may well reach sixty or even seventy percent of the population. The Wolofs are Muslims deeply rooted in the Sufism of the city of Touba, the Murid brotherhood led by Baye Fall, successor of Amadou Bamba. Early socialization in Qur'anic schools, strong social cohesion, *talibé-murid* (disciple-teacher) devotion, and economic ties form a murid (*talibé*) into a disciple for life.

The Wolof are the ethnic group least impacted by the gospel. In fact, in the early 2000s, only fifty Wolof Christians were known in the whole country, and the figure has apparently changed very little since.

The *Keru Barkeel* project (House of Blessing) project is a comprehensive care center in the city of Pikine, sponsored by PM International (PMI) and with origins in 1994.[3] It provides medical consultation, clinical analysis, nutrition services, a pharmacy, training for women in sewing, literacy, and cooking, a catering labor cooperative, and a church.

Keru Barkeel began as a simple project to teach sewing to women, also offering room for reading and study and a room used for evangelism. The main room was multi-purpose: on Sundays, the sewing machines were put away and the chairs were rearranged for worship services. With the arrival of a doctor as part of the Latin American missionary team, a small clinic was started in 2000

---

[2] http://fr.wikipedia.org/wiki/Pikine

[3] Familia Rocha No Senegal, "Centro Medico Social Keru Barkeel: Paredes Do Térreo Levantadas!!," *Centro Medico Social Keru Barkeel* (blog), August 19, 2013, http://centrosocialdakar.blogspot.com/2013/08/paredes-do-terreo-levantadas.html.

and gradually expanded. The center moved to a two-storey building on one of the main avenues that had better facilities for both the clinic and the women's literacy and sewing training programs. One room was set aside as a church and prayer room. Eventually, the project staff began to serve some remote villages through biweekly medical visits and speaking of the good news of Jesus.

The medical aspect of the project included attention to malnourished children, nursing, clinical analysis, and a low-cost pharmacy. Training scholarships for health-related studies were made available to several Senegalese, while a second doctor and nurse joined the team. The women's area also grew to incorporate a cooking and baking class. The clinic served about six hundred patients per month and the women's training trained about fifty women during the school year.

With this growth, the project moved to a third location, this time to a three-storey building. A dispensary was built and equipped in the village of Ndouxoura, some thirty miles, or fifty kilometers, away.

The women's area was restructured in 2006. The teaching of sewing has decreased, mainly due to the increase in the level of education in the neighborhood and in the increasing number of similar training opportunities available to the women. The kitchen and catering department, however, saw significant growth. As they began to prepare orders for parties, this program was turned into a catering cooperative and has contributed not only to providing income for the women involved but dignity, and personal value.

The whole project is staffed by several missionaries and by Senegalese personnel. An integral mindset, which does not separate the spiritual from the material and social, is one of its characteristics. The project, though, is not self-sufficient and has faced cutbacks and dismissals of personnel, which have negatively affected the project as a whole and the church. The project also is seen as being in competition with pharmacies and private clinics, whose services are offered at much higher prices.

Focused from the beginning on the Wolof ethnic group, the church has gone through different stages but has never grown or become independent from the supervision of the missionaries. It first began as a small meeting place for conferences and evangelism. The entire missionary team of four or five families attended, plus a few Senegalese. One of the missionaries was the pastor.

The services, as we have mentioned, were held in the same place where classes were held during the week. This fact clashes with the Muslim concept that a place of worship is a sacred physical space, reserved exclusively for religious rites. When they realized the importance of this issue, the team decided to set aside a room for prayer and worship. It was a small room on the second floor, which they painted and arranged with care. They put a carpet in the room and took off their shoes to enter, sitting on the floor, with men and women on opposite sides of the room. During the times of worship, they spoke mainly Wolof.

For reasons we have not fully understood, the team decided not to continue these practices, adding chairs and a pulpit to the room. One of the missionaries was the pastor. Later, in 2006, differences within the team led to the dismissal of the pastor-missionary and the departure of some members. On our visit in January 2013, the attendance was very low: three or four Senegalese plus three adult missionaries. The worship was conducted mostly in French and was led by one of the older believers, an employee of the project. At the entrance, a few Bibles in French, stacked and used, were available. The general impression was one of decline.

3. Analysis of the Relationships

There are many parallels between these two projects. Both are urban, medical projects, both operate inexpensive pharmacies (the only ones in Dakar), both have mixed foreign and national staff, and both do an excellent job in terms of medical quality standards. As for the two churches, both have intentionally focused on the Wolof and Senegalese population, but that is where their similarities end. The projects' relationships with the churches are quite different. These facts allow for a very nuanced analysis. To avoid jumping repeatedly from one case to the other, we will describe all the relationships of each project or church, in order.

The Këru Yakaar Clinic

First, let us examine the degree of *integrality*. In this respect, we would describe the Këru Yakaar clinic as holistic but not integral. Certainly, the friendly treatment of patients is one of its strengths. The fact that the staff is Christian contributes to the good atmosphere. Këru Yakaar's stated aim is to present the gospel and provide quality medical care to poor people. At present, however, the medical side clearly has priority.

It seems that there used to be an evangelist present and the "Jesus" film in Wolof was shown every day. On our visit in January 2013, we were introduced to the entire staff of the center but no one with that responsibility was identified, nor did it appear that the film was shown daily. Staff are expected to witness to their faith and offer prayer as the opportunity arises, which we have no doubt they do, but their emphasis seems to be on medical care. Perhaps that balance is reversed in the program for unwed mothers, as more emphasis is placed on psychological support and helping the women come to terms with an unwanted pregnancy.

We define *holism* as the practice of uniting preaching (or evangelism in general) with doing good works in the name of Christ. It is uniting the two aspects, but without mixing them completely. It is a partial manifestation of integrality. In contrast, perhaps one of the reasons for the compartmentalization of work and evangelism is that neither the clinic nor the YWAM team has the goal of establishing or starting a church through the project. That is to say, *intentionality* is null or very low; forming a church is the work of others. The clinic limits itself to referring people interested in the gospel to the church closest to the patient's neighborhood, or, if a closer relationship has arisen between the patient and staff, to the church attended by the medical personnel who have spoken to them. Evangelistic contact is necessarily brief, as long as a visit lasts. It can be repeated in successive visits if medical treatment requires it, but the system does not allow patients with spiritual interest to return to the clinic solely for the purpose of deepening their knowledge of the gospel. They must go elsewhere and usually to someone else. In making these observations, we are not making a value judgment but simply clarifying that the system is set up that way.

Second, the Këru Yakaar clinic has focused on *the poor*; they are its intended audience, and the project has been able to successfully link this focus with the low-cost pharmacy. Public health care in the country is not of poor quality; although facilities tend to be poorly equipped, doctors in general are good professionals. The problem for economically deprived patients is that they cannot afford to pay the price of prescribed drugs. Helping them overcome this stumbling through the low-cost pharmacy run by the clinic is a fundamental part of the success of the project.

At the same time, its focus on the poor is to the detriment of another audience. A waiting room, and patients waiting in line, is a part of the Këru Yakaar system. The queue begins to form early in the morning. Many pastors and people from the middle class, however, generally do not want to stand in line for hours. In African society, elders and people in authority have priority. It is a deep-rooted principle, but one that is not respected in Këru Yakaar. Earlier, one of the senior foreign doctors found a way to marry clinic procedures with social custom. He would schedule the pastors and people in authority for appointments late in the day. This way, they did not have to wait in a line.

The clinic's relationship with the neighborhood is passive. The clinic offers a service; patients must take the initiative to come. At the institutional level, the clinic maintains close and constant relations with the government hospital in Dakar but does not seem to seek relations with the authorities and the neighborhood.

Thirdly, regarding the *relationship with the churches*, the Keur Jamm church was born, in a way, from the initiative of a YWAM missionary and it has maintained a relationship with the clinic. However, it is an *indirect, informal, and distant* relationship (they are in different neighborhoods). We have mentioned that all the staff members are Christians, something difficult to attain in Senegal given the small evangelical population, less than one percent. In fact, the clinic maintains relationships with many churches and projects that provide staff members. They are cared for and pastored in their churches, so that they can not only do their work well but also witness whenever the opportunity arises. The churches also pray for the ministry of the clinic and its staff, and when they have members needing medical attention, they refer them to the clinic. In turn, the clinic refers people with an interest in the gospel to the churches.

The clinic also supplies the pharmacies of other smaller Christian projects and provides assistance and expertise to start-up projects. For example, it has recently provided practical training to a professional whose Lutheran church wants to start a dispensary in the interior of the country. So, we can speak of *multiple, complex, and reciprocal* relationships. However, the clinic administrator told us that they have the feeling that they give much more than they receive; it could be that the reciprocal part of the relationship is unbalanced.

Finally, as far as *identity* is concerned, the clinic is clearly a Christian project but is respectful of and non-proselytizing toward the Muslims who are ninety percent of the clinic's patients. People popularly call it "the American clinic" even though for years no Americans have been involved in the project.

The Keur Jamm Church

First of all, for the Keur Jamm church the concept of *integrality* is relatively new; it was introduced by Pastor Dogue when he joined the church in mid-2006. He had worked for a few years with World Vision and learned the idea from them. They seem to apply it most consistently in the villages, where integral community development goes hand-in-hand with preaching. There, they apply a progressive five-fold approach: first education, then clean water, health, food security, and finally economic development. The church's interest in the community opens doors for evangelism. When the time comes to evangelize, the approach is one of saturation, carried out three or four days in a row, with movies, songs, preaching, and so on. As mentioned earlier, they have opened two or three rural churches in this way.

The church is also involved in providing wheelchairs for the association of people living with disabilities in their district of the city. They hold a Christmas party and provide a tree with presents for the children, which they complement with shoeboxes from Samaritan's Purse "Operation Christmas Child" project. For Christmas 2013, they expected to receive ninety thousand shoeboxes for the same number of children within the district. For the majority of the children of Grand Yoff, this would be the first gift that they have ever received.

Note that evangelism (in terms of speaking of the good news) is an additional element of what they do, not something at cross purposes. That is to say, evangelism "goes with" but is not an integral part of what they do. Samaritan's Purse, on the other hand, includes Christian evangelistic material in every gift box. That fact is very offensive to Muslim societies, but Samaritan's Purse intentionally takes advantage of the power asymmetry between the donor and the needy child. Note also that community aid in villages "opens doors" for evangelism, and that gifts to children "open the hearts of parents." In each case, the project is a hook, a bridge to proclamation.

Referring to the Theological Scale of Social Involvement presented in Chapter 5, the Këru Yakaar clinic considers the project as pre-evangelism. The Keur Jamm church goes one step further, and understands the project as hook or bridge, which we still qualify as holism. The next two levels on the scale, "development accompanies evangelism" and "development and evangelism are inseparable," correspond better to an integral (or integrated) understanding.

However, it would not be correct to say that the Keur Jamm church is holistic. Other data point to a more integral concept. It is the church as such, not the individual members, that is involved in the needs of the neighborhood. Likewise, Keur Jamm's approach is not merely relief, but aims at the causes, at the root of social problems and works for a social transformation of the neighborhood through the gospel. This is clearly integral. So, it is probably more accurate to conclude that Keur Jamm manifests *integrality in development*. The fundamentals are there, and we trust that, with time and practice, they will grow in consistency.[4]

Second, let us consider the *identity* of the church as well as its *relationship to the culture*. Keur Jamm has opted for a Christian cultural model, that is to say its identity is linked to the Western worship and evangelistic forms. The architecture of the building as well as the interior arrangement of pews and pulpit are typically Western, as are the musical instruments they use. However, they are located in a very Muslim neighborhood that they want to win over and influence; that is why they use Wolof as their language along with French. When asked about Muslim festivals and customs the pastor distanced himself from them: the church has chosen to ignore the Muslim-animist festivals, customs and culture that characterize their neighborhood and instead emphasize Westernized Christian festivals and culture. In other words, the contextualization of ecclesiology and evangelism is poor. The teaching the members receive is anti-Muslim. In fact, the church feels at war with the "Muslim sea" that surrounds it.

Another fact that clarifies the identity of the church is its commitment to *the poor*, the lower and lower-middle economic class. It is a conscious choice. That is why they are located in this neighborhood, lacking in many social, employment, and civic services. Perhaps this option has been influenced by the pastor's background with World Vision. This focus on the lower and lower-middle class means that people of higher social status probably do not feel comfortable in Keur Jamm. Aware of this, the church frequently refers potential members to other churches whose membership is made up of people from the sectors of society perceived to hold higher status.

In order to understand the identity of Keur Jamm Church, we should mention that it is a *missionary* church, focused on growth, and with a high *intentionality* in starting new churches. At the same time, it is a solid church organizationally, in the sense that it does not depend on a celebrity pastor. There is a council of elders, a team of deacons, and an extended team that includes those responsible for all the ministries; they meet quarterly to evaluate and decide the future course of the church.

---

[4] In July 2013, Pastor Eloi Dogue was promoted to a senior position in his organization, CAPRO, and moved to Lagos, Nigeria. The church has been left under the care of the council of elders and deacons. It remains to be seen how this change affects the development of the church as well as its integrality.

Third, and closely related to the above, let us consider Keur Jamm's relationship with its *neighborhood*. The church's Christian cultural identity and limited contextualization coupled with the use of social work as an evangelistic hook inevitably led to a relationship of hostility from the neighborhood. "They don't want them there. If they could, they would throw them out," a veteran pastor told us. However, this need not be the case. The church brings something positive to the table that would probably be valued had the church constructed its identity differently. The fact that most church members live in the neighborhood contributes to the relationship with the neighborhood.

The church and some of the mosques share relations at an institutional level. These are still emerging but, even so, are very significant. For example, invitations are issued to attend joint events and functions. The church is also collaborating with the civil authorities, especially in the care of children and women.

Considering the church's relationships with the *beneficiaries* of its extensive social and community work, we realize that, in the city, the beneficiaries of Keur Jamm's projects are not the directly-intended audience that the church seeks as its members. That is, the beneficiaries and those considered to be potential new believers only partially overlap. At the same time, in the villages, the project beneficiaries are also the focus of the evangelistic efforts.

Finally, let us note that Keur Jamm is a very important church in Senegal because it is the most Senegalese church (in the ethnic sense, not for its ecclesiology or contextualization). It is a sort of advance guard, a first step towards the integration of Christian communities into the structure and social fabric of the capital. This fact becomes even more relevant when we consider that *there is not a single Wolof church in the whole country*. What does a Wolof church look like culturally? No one yet has the answer to that important question, simply because there is no such thing. That is why it is important to appreciate Keur Jamm: it is the church that has taken the most steps on the road to consolidating a Wolof Christian cultural identity. There have been some attempts that have so far been unsuccessful.

The Keru Barkeel Project

In this section, we intend to separate the project and the church to better understand the various relationships. This will not be easy because the church and the project are inseparable in some respects.

First of all, the project claims to be *integral*; the word forms part of its name, the Keru Barkeel Integral Center. And, in fact, it has developed many different branches: health, nutrition education, care for mothers and malnourished children, skills training for women, a business cooperative, and the church. For many years, the project included a chaplain, a Latin American missionary, who visited the beneficiaries in their homes, offering prayer and spiritual guidance. This is to say that the project has tried to attend to the various needs of the needy population, those that are common in the satellite town of Pikine.

At the same time, as a regular practice, staff take the initiative of offering prayer for the beneficiaries, something that occurs with great frequency. The symbiosis of medical care and assistance or training with prayer is a demonstration of integrality, growing out of an integrated worldview, and for that reason is a combination that is well-received by the public, as befits animistic societies. Divine answers to prayer are frequent and remarkable.

The relationship with the culture seems satisfactory. Many of the procedures used in the project are well-adapted to the culture of the beneficiaries: the form in which medical prescriptions are dispensed, explanations about nutrition, the style of training for women, or the health education and medical campaigns in the villages. All is done in the Wolof language and in an oral rather than literary style.

On the other hand, the project has made few steps toward passing responsibility and ownership of the project to the Senegalese. The presence and oversight of the Latin American missionaries is still very clear. On the other hand, the project has granted scholarships to various Senegalese to enable them to develop skills in laboratory analysis, nursing, and pharmacy services. The catering cooperative is perhaps the effort showing the most local ownership. The women who have been trained take most of the responsibility although they still largely depend on the Latin American missionary women to obtain the bulk of the catering requests (for example, catering for events at the Brazilian embassy) that enables them to succeed economically.

In second place, the *identity* of the project is clearly Christian. Most of the staff are Christians. Even so, the nature of the project is not linked to Western and Christian cultural forms. This is seen in practice by comparing Keru Barkeel with projects in this district that are Muslim in origin and identity: they differ little in their way of doing things.

In third place, there is a *passive relationship* between the project and the district, just as in its counterpart Këru Yakaar. They offer a service and wait for the beneficiaries, patients, and women, to come. There has been no relationship developed with the political, civic, religious, or other authorities of the district. Probably contributing to this distancing is the fact that the majority of the Latin American missionaries live outside this city, in the capital. Only one nurse from the team lives in Pikine. She knows various neighborhood leaders and is herself known; for this reason, she has been able to mediate in various conflict situations. However, several of the hired staff are based in Pikine.

Occasionally a nearby pharmacy has complained, sensing that the low-cost Keru Barkeel pharmacy has offered unfair competition. The situation has been ably resolved by the doctor of the missionary team, noting the areas in which neighborhood pharmacy and the project find mutual benefit.

We note that the *primary audience* of the project and that of the church only overlap in part: the beneficiaries of the project. Even so, the perspective of the church goes beyond this since it is looking not just at those who receive benefits directly from the project but to their neighbors in general who see the high quality of work they are doing. However, the lack of active relationships between the Latin American missionary team and the people of the district beyond the project means that the goal of the church – reaching those who are not beneficiaries – is not very realistic. In this sense, we could describe the project as having low intentionality toward establishing a church, especially the medical area of the project.

We cannot say, as is the case with Këru Yakaar, that they are waiting for others to establish a church but, equally, the medical and assistance work takes priority over the planting of the church. As the doctor of the team stated: "I am a medical missionary not a missionary doctor."

However, the impact of the project on its surroundings is undeniable, as evidenced by the testimony of one of the neighbors. At the project's previous location, the neighbor next door could see from his backyard almost everything that was going on at the Keru Barkeel Center. He was an old man, a polygamist, a Muslim, and one of the respected men in the neighborhood. After seeing the conduct and testimony of the project staff, he began to spread the following message in the neighborhood: "These people are better and more honest than the best of the Muslims."

Fourth, the project's relations *with its staff* have deteriorated over the past two years. One of the reasons is that the project has failed to become self-financing. This has had a negative impact on the handover of power to the Senegalese: it is impossible to hand over to them something that cannot be sustained financially. On the other hand, there has been pressure from PMI, the mission that sponsors the project, both in the direction of self-sustainability and to see people coming to faith in Jesus. Another reason is that it is always difficult to be a patron and a pastor at the same time. The relationships of the missionary team with the project and with the church have been direct and very close, which perhaps has not helped.

Two of the notable differences between Këru Yakaar and Keru Barkeel lie precisely in self-sustainability and the handover to nationals. Perhaps the key lies in the fact that the director of the former has been, from the outset, a good administrator, while the key figure in the latter is a doctor. Nevertheless, a comparison of the two projects cannot ignore the fact that, first, Këru Yakaar is located in the capital, on a large plot of land of its own, which allows for a large volume of patients per day. However, they have recently had to raise their fees in order to cover their costs. Keru Barkeel, in contrast, works in a less wealthy city, in a rented building that does not meet the required conditions. The prices of its services must necessarily be very low, while its expenses are high. Secondly, the city of Pikine is ethnically dominated by *Wolofons* (those who speak Wolof regardless of their ethnicity), Islam is much more deeply rooted, and the pressures exerted by the mosques against the project are considerably greater than in the capital.

The Keru Barkeel Church

As we turn our consideration to the Keru Barkeel church, the first point we draw out is, of necessity, the relationship *between the project and the church.* As we have indicated previously, the church has always been closely linked to the project. Both share the same building, the Latin American missionary team is the leading player in both, and their primary audience is the same. It is correct, therefore, to say that the relationships between the two are *direct and close*.

Moreover, they are *reciprocal* since there are many interactions in both directions. The church prays for the project, pastors its expatriate and national staff, and constitutes one of the founding purposes of the project: to establish a church among the Wolof people. In the opposite sense, the project is the main avenue for bringing members into the church. It also provides a salary and offers dignity to the hired staff.

The project also provides a layer of protection for the church in a militant Muslim environment; the neighborhood would hardly consent to the presence of a church if it were not "protected" or justified by a project of obvious community benefit. In fact, the neighborhood of the city where the center is located is twinned with one of the neighborhoods of the city of Mecca in Saudi Arabia, something that contributes to expressions of Muslim fundamentalism. Further, there is only one other Christian church in Pikine, an apostolic church, on the border with the city of Guedwaye, which was started a few years ago.

On the other hand, the visibility of the church is overshadowed by the project. The church meets in a small room on the second floor of the project building. There is also disproportion in scale: the project is open every day and serves many more people, while the church reached an attendance of about fifteen people in its best days.

Second, let us consider the *identity* of the church and its relationships with *other churches*. The Keru Barkeel church has, since its inception, wanted to be a Wolof church, to reach Wolofs and to be culturally Wolof. This is a praiseworthy desire since, as mentioned above, there is no other Wolof church in the whole country. Barely fifty Wolof believers were known at the time of our research among the country's evangelical believers, almost none of them in leadership positions, with the exception of one pastor in Saint Louis, in Northern Senegal. Starting a Wolof church is obviously a challenge since there is no model; no one knows what a Wolof church looks like. So, Keru Barkeel's attempt must be appreciated, even if its success is questionable, after almost twenty years of operation.

The identity of the church has changed over the years. In the early days, experimentation and the search for a Wolof cultural model was, as far as we know, more active. We have already recounted above the attempt of the "holy room" for worship. In the early years, the preacher dressed appropriately for a teacher of spiritual subjects, wearing a traditional *boubou*, a large robe, flowing down to the feet. Worship was conducted in Wolof. But the holy room experiment was relatively short-lived. Chairs and a pulpit were introduced. Lately, the French language has displaced Wolof. Having a few Bibles piled up for public use may seem very normal to a Western Christian but, to a Muslim, it constitutes a very great lack of respect for a holy book. These stacked Bibles, moreover, are French, which underlines the predominance of that language over Wolof, considering that the New Testament is available in Wolof and much of the Old Testament.

According to Muslim beliefs, a holy book, and especially the Qur'an, is not to be touched with dirty hands; it is always in the place of honor, and when it is stored, it is wrapped in a clean cloth to protect it; it is never placed on the floor or held lower than the waist. To leave it on a chair on which one has previously rested one's bottom – with its bad smell – is a serious offense. Moreover, Muslims understand that since the Word is holy, it should not have illustrations on the cover or inside. The cover itself should be elegant, never black or paper (it should be hardcover, *cartoné* or leather). The interior should not be printed on white paper but should be off-white. The text of the Scripture should be surrounded by a frame, and introductions, titles, notes and references should be printed outside the frame. To do otherwise automatically implies that the book in question is not considered holy.

A change of identity probably reflects the different understandings the team members have of what a church is and how it should function. This impression is confirmed by the strong internal disagreements within the team, which led in 2006 to the dismissal of the missionary who served as pastor. To the best of our knowledge, the team never produced a written document reflecting their philosophy of ministry, what kind of church they wanted to see formed. Many consider this sort of memorandum of understanding to be fundamental to the smooth running of a pioneering interdenominational (and often international) team.

As for relations with other churches, Keru Barkeel is a member of the Fraternité Évangélique du Sénégal (the Senegal Evangelical Alliance), although in practice it is the missionaries who attend the meetings; that is to say that the church itself does not feel part of the larger entity. It depends only on itself.

Thirdly, we mention the relationship between the church and *the neighborhood*. Although relations are not very intense, they are polarized: on the one hand, the beneficiaries and near neighbors speak favorably of the project and include the church in those views; on the other hand, the leaders of some mosques have complained about the presence of a church and have accused the clinic of proselytizing. One of those *imams* went to the clinic and had a long talk with the doctor. Within a few months, the police called the project manager to investigate accusations of proselytizing, which were resolved favorably. Other than that, the church keeps a relatively low profile, limited to its worship services.

Finally, the general impression we have gained from our visit and interviews is that the Keru Barkeel church has passed through various phases of growth and the missionary team is informally looking for other options in terms of structure and practice of the church. Almost all of them think that, if they were to start again, they would physically separate the church from the project. Some speak of partnering with a church or national denomination that wants to sponsor a Wolof church. The problem is to find such a church or pastor; it is not an easy task in the current Senegalese evangelical landscape.

Update: Since our visit in 2013, the project has closed in Pikine; they purchased land in a newly developed area on the outskirts of Dakar, and with a generous donation from a Brazilian businessman have built a clinic. Today, after only a few years, the clinic is self-sufficient, led by a local Christian doctor, and a church has been established in a nearby neighborhood facility, led by a national pastor. The situation has in every way been completely turned around. We look forward to visiting them as soon as we have the opportunity.

Questions for Reflection and Discussion

1. What about the Keur Jamm church caught your attention? In what ways is it the same, or different, from your own church?
2. Thinking of the relationships these two churches have with their neighborhood, what is the relationship of your own church with its neighborhood and community? Sketch out a diagram of these relationships, a "conceptual map," and how they are put into practice.
3. What does "proselytism" mean for you? How is it different from evangelism?

For Further Reading

Coulon, Christian. "The Grand Magal in Touba: A Religious Festival of the Mouride Brotherhood of Senegal." *African Affairs* 98, no. 391 (April 1, 1999): 195-210. https://doi.org/10.1093/oxfordjournals.afraf.a008007.

Dowsett, Rose, ed. *Global Mission: Reflections and Case Studies in Contextualization for the Whole Church.* Globalization of Mission series. Pasadena: William Carey Library, 2011. Chap. 12.

Sanneh, Lamin. *The Crown and the Turban: Muslims and West African Pluralism.* Boulder: Westview Press, 1997.

Simon Schwall, Travel tips for Dakar, Senegal, Video | Youtube (Dakar, 2017), https://www.youtube.com/watch?v=Q_5TdcaTbuw.

9. A Missionary Business

Business has accompanied missionary work for many centuries. So it was when the Apostle Paul and his companions Priscilla and Aquila manufactured tents. So it was with the Nestorian Christian merchants who carried the gospel along the Silk Road from the fifth to the thirteenth centuries. Following that example, a Brazilian missionary family of the Missão Betania (Bethany Mission) started a business in Dakar. In this chapter, we focus on the relationship between that missionary business and the churches that the project has given birth to in the Dakar area of Senegal.

1. A Description of the Context: the Steakhouse

The project, a typical Brazilian steakhouse or *churrascaría*, is located in Dakar. It was developed in response to the need to give employment and a socio-professional future to a small group of new believers among the *talibés* (street children) fleeing from the mistreatment of their *Mouride* (a prominent Sufi brotherhood) teachers. The timing of the project's founding was also coupled with the reduction in funds from abroad that the missionaries received when the currency of their home country, the Brazilian real, was devalued.

The Bethany Mission team had been working in Senegal since 1995 but had seen very little response to their efforts. Then, in 1999, they began working with street children and saw some of them come to faith and be baptized. The missionaries experienced persecution[1] and had few opportunities or options to help bring about change in the boys' lives. How could they help them and, in particular, develop both employable skills and character?

Eventually, they came upon the idea of opening a *churrascaría*, a typical Brazilian steakhouse. At first, it only served food to other missionaries, but later it opened daily to the public. The restaurant had a slow start; the missionaries had little capital and no experience running a restaurant. Over time, some of them dropped out of the project; they did not understand that making money could be appropiate for missionaries.

[1] In fact, at the time of our January 2013 visit to the project, two Brazilian missionaries were in prison, accused of proselytizing children, the *talibés*. They were held in prison for five months.

Currently, the business – the only one of its kind in the city – produces profits that have been used to support and help start three churches: two in the city and one in a rural area. Training the staff has taken a long time because the street children are survivors; they are focused on today, with no sense of responsibility, no schooling, and no work experience. Years of patience and love and the obvious work of the Holy Spirit have brought about a spectacular change in many of these children who now run the restaurant, pastor one of the churches, and hold various other positions of responsibility.

The church that was formed in the rural Lac Rose area came about through the initiative of one of the new believers. They have replicated in a rural area the model of the churrascaría and the associated church, following their own cultural forms. The village had no school, so they started a small educational project in a rented room with a local teacher. It soon grew and, with a donation from some foreigners, a piece of land was purchased. The school is typically Senegalese in its facilities and its management. It is self-financed, although Bethany Mission has promoted a sponsorship program to supplement other needs of the students: clothing, food, books, and further studies. The school room was also used to start worship services led by a Sengalese lady and her mother. Today, it has grown larger in attendance than the church associated with the churrascaría in the capital.

2. Analysis of Relationships

First, we will deal with the *objective of the project*, which in two ways is different from the cases we have analyzed so far. The *churrascaría* is a project whose main objective is to provide benefits to the believers. It is also different in that it is a business, as opposed to other charitable and non-profit projects. Some of the projects we have studied included the component of training or helping believers, but it was not their central focus. In this case, it has been the motivation which led to the founding of this business and guides all of its activities.

There are two beneficiaries of the project: firstly, street children who are new believers, who have no job or livelihood, and who would otherwise be permanently dependent on the charity of their hosts. The project provides them with training, income, independence, and dignity. But the project also sought to supplement the livelihood of the Brazilian missionaries themselves, whose currency had devalued considerably. Today, due in part to the revitalization of the Brazilian economy and in part to the success of the project, supplementing the livelihood that the missionaries receive from their country of origin is no longer as necessary: the Brazilian real has appreciated and offerings to the missionaries have increased, mainly from Christian Brazilian businessmen who are supportive of this missionary model.

Secondly, the relationships between the *project and the church* are varied and complex. They are *direct* relationships in that they are institutional, frequent, and clear. The leadership of the church and of the project coincide. The missionary oversees everything, although the team has initiated an important process of delegation and transfer of authority. In addition, two of the churches depend financially on the business.

They are also *indirect* relationships that are especially visible with the new project and rural church in the area of Lac Rose. The goal is for all three churches to be autonomous, and indeed this latest rural project is largely self-managed and self-supporting. The project takes the initiative to request what it thinks it needs and the business responds to the best of its ability.

The relationships are also *reciprocal*; the churches pray for the business project and provide the labor. Conversely, the business trains people who will later serve as leaders in key positions in the church. Likewise, everyone feels part of something greater, of a great common missionary outreach project for their country. On the other hand, the relationship between employees and employer has not always been clear, because the employer is the main missionary, who at the same time is the "father" of the children, character development trainer, and pastor. Little by little they are looking for ways to separate these roles.

One of the boys who, early in the project, was a new believer has taken over the pastorate of the church in the capital city, and the business is looking for a manager. Therefore, the senior missionary is planning to move into a new role, overseeing things from a distance, alternating his time between Brazil and Senegal. When this process is completed, the business and the churches will have truly become national, and a very important step in the indigenization of the project will have been taken.

For the business, choosing to train street children has been costly; it has been a long process of character formation and maturation through work. It would have been much easier to hire staff with previous work experience in the restaurant industry.

The members of the missionary team take turns participating in the leadership of the business. This brings us to a third aspect: the relationship of the project with the Bethany Mission and its supporters. We have mentioned above that some missionaries dropped out of the project; they were reluctant to transform a charitable missionary initiative into a business. In addition, foreign customers of the churrascaría requested wine to accompany their meals, as well as *caipirinha*, the national cocktail of Brazil. Both of these issues theologically complicated the missionaries' relationships with each other and with the mission. In the end, Bethany Mission aligned itself with the views of the developers of the *churrascaría*. The process has been costly: they have lost four missionary families over these issues.

The other very important aspect concerns the perceptions regarding the transformation of the project into a business held by Brazilian churches and individuals who provided financial support to the missionaries and the project. Would they decide to withdraw their support, considering it no longer necessary?

We should note that the *churrascaría* pays the national personnel, but not the missionaries. At the same time, the business began with plates, cutlery, pot, and pans – and even the very space for the restaurant – that belonged to the missionary couple who had conceived the idea. That is, the missionaries themselves had been investing their personal resources in the project, especially in the initial years, until it generated sufficient returns that this was not needed. Most of the Brazilian supporters, some ninety-five percent, in fact, opted to continue supporting the missionaries, although it should be emphasized that this has required significant commitment from the missionaries to keep up with the communication as well as promoting understanding. That is, the missionaries have had a double field of work: in Senegal and among their churches of origin.

Fourth, let us consider the *identity* of the project. The promoters define it as a missionary business. While some of their former mission partners saw business as incompatible with missionary work as such, the initiators have anchored their theology of work and mission with an integral understanding. They have made a symbiosis of both. The example of the Apostle Paul was decisive for them through this text: "You yourselves know that these hands of mine have supplied my own needs and the needs of my companions. In everything I did, I showed you that by this kind of hard work we must help the weak"(Acts 20:34-35a). That is to say, the project demonstrates *integrality* in this aspect.

On the other hand, related to i*ntegrality, proselytism, and culture*, it does not seem that the missionaries analyzed or considered the causes of the persecution that they experienced, evidently arising due to their way of evangelism and baptizing the new believers. Has their approach to evangelism and proselytism changed? Neither our insights from our interview with these workers nor the other data we have available have given us evidence of a change in this sense but we have not had the opportunity to verify this directly, since we did not have the opportunity to visit the churches.

The missionary identity of the business is linked to the identity of the main missionary. The missionary was expected to take a back seat during 2014, when a business manager was to be installed. Reflection on progress since that time would help us see how this identity is transmitted and maintained.

Fifth, the relationship of the *missionaries with the nationals* is another important point to consider. The missionaries have been able to reflect on their home country and the way in which North American and British missions passed the baton to the Brazilian churches in the mid-twentieth century. They have decided to pursue smooth transitions, as soon as the national church can assume leadership and sustain its own institutions.

One of the boys from the first group of new believers has assumed the role of pastor of the church in the capital and would be ordained. A national pastor who completed his theological training has been ordained to head the urban church in Thies, a city in the interior, and two Senegalese women have assumed leadership of the project and the rural church in Lac Rose. The missionary identity of the business has served to forge the identity of the church, which has understood mission as an inherent part of its responsibility.

When foreigners are around, the dominant mentality among Senegalese is that they themselves are poor and that foreigners must provide for the development or implementation of any ministry. Senegalese evangelical churches that support their pastors are rare. Running counter to this majority feeling, Bethany Mission has been able to change this mentality. The leaders and members of the churches founded by the mission in Senegal have taken the responsibility of spreading the gospel in their country and sending missionaries to start other churches.

Finally, the relationship of the missionaries with *the culture* has not always been easy. In fact, in the first five years, the culture shock they experienced was so strong that it led to depression. It was their first experience in a Muslim country. In their own words, they brought a "Brazilian head" in terms of ministry and church planting. They had to "learn many things and unlearn many more." Although they had prior experience serving and helping plant churches in Brazil, their previous experience in church planting was quite different from the way that same process is carried out in a Muslim context in general and in West Africa in particular. In other words, their pre-field training was valuable in the long run and for them personally, but it had not provided them with the training needed to help them adapt to the new culture in which they found themselves. This is a pattern of training too often repeated. On the one hand, training for the field is of little practical use, and on the other, expectations of quick results, by Latin American standards, are not met.

In summary, this case has shown us a successful, although not always easy, relationship model between project and church, which will probably continue with other businesses. It is a model of Business as Mission that is gaining relevance in missiological circles.

Questions for Reflection and Discussion

1. What insights and questions has this narrative brought to your mind?
2. Are "missionary businesses" appropriate in all contexts, or only in "mission fields"? Why?
3. Are you acquainted with a "missionary business" or a business built on social services in your area? What are its characteristics?

For Further Reading

Befus, David R. *Kingdom Business: The Ministry of Promoting Economic Activity*. Miami: Latin America Mission, 2002.

Evans, Alex, Richard Gower, and Tearfund. "The Restorative Economy: Completing Our Unfinished Millenium Jubilee." Tearfund, 2015. https://learn.tearfund.org/~/media/files/tilz/research/tearfund_therestorativeeconomy_summary.pdf.

Hickel, Jason, and Martin Kirk. "Are You Ready To Consider That Capitalism Is The Real Problem?" *Fast Company* (blog), July 11, 2017. https://www.fastcompany.com/40439316/are-you-ready-to-consider-that-capitalism-is-the-real-problem.

Johnson, C. Neal. *Business as Mission: A Comprehensive Guide to Theory and Practice*. Downers Grove: InterVarsity, 2011.

Suter, Heinz, and Marco Gmür. *Business Power for God's Purpose: Partnership with the Unreached.* Greng-Murten, Switzerland: VKG (Verlag für kulturbezogenen Gemeindebau), 1997.

10. The Churches in *Islamia*

A small group of North African Christians gather on the premises of a Protestant church in the capital city of their country. They enter the building through a discreet side door, cross a courtyard, and greet each other warmly in a simple room, sheltered from prying eyes. Together as a couple, we have had the privilege of meeting them. A visit by outsiders is not a frequent occurrence and few foreigners have any real understanding of their situation.

The reality of this country, straddling Africa and Europe, is complex and is precariously balanced. On one side, European businessmen come and go freely to formalize and manage important businesses, because the country enjoys special treatment with the European Union. Culturally, the country's level of education is very high; illiteracy has been practically eradicated from the country. The arts and literature flourish. Freedom of the press is practically total: the media themselves treat with courtesy the subjects they know to be sensitive. The public health care service is probably the best in North Africa, yet in this seemingly advanced and open society, people cannot change their religion. Ceasing to be a Muslim is a very complex social, professional, economic, and legal adventure.

The many foreigners residing in the country can freely attend two or three Protestant and Catholic churches in the capital. These authorized churches have beautiful places of worship on some of the main streets or squares of the city. This is the case of the Protestant church where we attended this semi-clandestine meeting. Of course, the police and intelligence services know that a handful of national Christians meet here as well, with the knowledge of those in charge of the Protestant church. Their attending is not legally permitted but both sides, the authorities and the pastors, make it look like nothing is happening. The authorities do not want religious intolerance to be public, and the pastors do not want to stop supporting the national Christians, although they do it very discreetly. For both sides, it is important not to lose face, not to have to deal with both the pressures of the European Union and of the foreigners who control important portions of the economy, and, not to snub the Islamic groups increasingly present in society and in parliament.

In the midst of this fragile balance, the national Christians sing, pray, and study the Bible with a mixture of joy and caution. Their songs are beautiful; some they have composed themselves, others were written by Christians from a neighboring country and adapted to the local Arabic.

One of the songs they sang on the day of our visit, known throughout North Africa, speaks of the joy of the Holy Spirit, joy that permeates all of life. I remember that many years ago, the melody of these songs made me very nervous. They are built on tonic and subdominant musical chords, and I would get frustrated waiting for the dominant chord, which in Western musical patterns resolves the melody. Now, after almost thirty years, I have learned to enjoy the rhythm, the harmony, and the essence of these melodies of my North African sisters and brothers, and to accompany them with my guitar.

Women and men participated equally in the service, although men were the leaders. A group of three middle-aged men, one of them linked to the university, served as leaders of the group. In fact, within a few months, these three leaders launched an international prayer campaign for their country that has borne abundant fruit, both in new conversions and baptisms and in appreciation for their beautiful land. All of them had heard of the great Christian figures of the past who excelled in these lands: Augustine, Tertullian, and the martyrs Perpetua and Felicia. But for centuries there was negligible Christian presence in all of North Africa. Here, there is no such thing as the religious minorities of Egypt or Lebanon with their ancient roots. Here being Muslim is tantamount to being a national of the country, and the opposite is synonymous with betrayal of all patriotic and religious values.

At one point in that simple service, I noticed that the attendees sang with more enthusiasm, marked by more clapping and greater volume. In the main hall of the church, African Christians from the various Christian background nations of the continent were singing and praising to the din of keyboards, tambourines, drums, clapping, and dancing. My local sisters and brothers took advantage of the African's increased volume to raise their own voices and give vent to the many emotions they carried in their chests: a mixture of caution and joy, pain and hope, and sighs both of repression and of freedom.

What are the churches in *Islamia* like, what are their characteristics and how can we classify them or consider them in groups? These are the questions that, in a general way, we will try to answer in this chapter. In contrast, the following chapter will provide a detailed description and comparison of the churches.

1. Six Large Regions in *Islamia* and Their Varying Characteristics

Once again, it is important to emphasize the great diversity within the Muslim world. Conscious that any generalization is susceptible to oversimplification, to help us understand the churches in *Islamia*, we will refer to six major regions within the Muslim world. In discussing them, we will consider five factors in particular: the existence or absence of religious pluralism, the conditions of religious freedom or tolerance, the acceptance or rejection of development projects, the admiration or rejection of the West, and the missiological conditions related to the churches (for example, how Christian mission is carried out: formal, unconventional, etc.).

The major zones are the Middle East, North Africa, the Arabian Peninsula, the Sahel, "exclusivist" Asia, and "pluralist" Asia.

The **Middle East** is made up of Egypt, Jordan, Lebanon, Iraq, Syria, Palestine, and Turkey. These are countries in which Christian minorities have existed for centuries and, with their churches and rituals, have contributed to making religious pluralism normal. Some of these minorities have singularly contributed to the progress and identity of the country. In general, there is religious tolerance more or less sanctioned by law. It is always difficult to leave Islam, but it is not impossible. In general, the people of the Middle East look favorably on cultural initiatives, community development and promotion of disadvantaged groups (handicapped, women, those on the margins of society, etc.), although they are reluctant to receive "Christian" emergency aid, that is, aid perceived to be coming from supposedly Christian countries. Turkey is an exception: there are few charitable associations, practically no NGOs, and little social work that is not state- or party-related. Turkey considers itself to be a developed country. Middle Eastern societies have admiration for some of the social and economic achievements of the West (freedom, economic welfare, health care, etc.) and Western TV programs have a wide following. In many of these countries, the Christian missionary presence goes back many centuries, although evangelical initiatives are recent and often exclusivist, ignoring the ancient Christian churches of the region.

In **North Africa**, once the cradle of Christianity, Christian presence was gradually and systematically eradicated; it was not until recent European colonization that missionary initiatives resumed. In these countries – Mauritania, Morocco, Algeria, Libya, and Tunisia – there are no Christian minorities continuing from ancient times, and therefore no religious pluralism. Religious tolerance is low. Indeed, to be North African is to be Muslim: this is society's unanimous opinion. Despite this attitude, these countries often seem to imitate Europe, as seen, for example, in the status of French as a second official language in most of these countries. Rooftops are covered with satellite television dishes (many houses have two or three) that capture sports, news, and European television magazines. They welcome Western development agencies but, at the same time, will only accept European or Western emergency aid in truly extreme situations. Further, these countries reject all visible or known missionary work. Being a missionary, pastor, or Christian theologian or holding a similar role is not only highly questioned, but it also brings social stigma.

The **Arabian Peninsula** countries of Saudi Arabia, the United Arab Emirates, Kuwait, Eritrea, and Yemen together with Sudan represent the hard core of Islamism. Iran can be included, for our classification, in the same group, although it represents a competing version of Islam: Shi'ism. Religious pluralism and tolerance are at an all-time low. They reject all humanitarian aid and development initiatives that do not come from Muslim sources. They consider the activities of development agencies (even secular or atheist ones) as forms of propaganda and covert proselytism. They do not want to resemble the West in any way, but are in conflict with it, trying to demonstrate their economic, cultural, architectural, and other expressions of superiority.

In these countries, there are reports of many becoming followers of Jesus the Messiah and of much spiritual thirst, but all of this is expressed very discreetly. Missionary presence is non-conventional and unplanned, mainly in the form of Asian and African workers. (We say "unplanned" in the sense that many of these workers went first for economic reasons, with missionary activity coming as a result of being there, not the reason for being there.) Although a high proportion of these workers receive very low wages and live in conditions of semi-slavery, their testimony is powerful, and God honors them with many miracles and signs.

The strip of Africa South of the Sahara extending from the Atlantic to the Indian Ocean is known as the **Sahel**. For purpose of our categorization, it includes Senegal, Mali, Niger, Chad, and Ethiopia. The expression of Islam in this region could be called African Islam. It is a relatively late African contextualization of Islam, which prioritizes consensus and community welfare over orthodoxy. The laws of these countries typically provide for religious freedom and a high degree of religious tolerance, although their practical application is not uniform. Christian presence, both Catholic and Protestant, is spread widely, often along ethnic lines. The pluralism present in the Sahel is not so much a relationship between Islam and Christianity, but between Islam and practices of African traditional religions. This pluralism, although syncretistic, is a precedent that favors the acceptance of Christian minorities.

Further, the introduction of Islam in the Sahel is quite recent. In many ethnic groups, such as the Soninke of Senegal and Mali, oral tradition keeps alive the memory of the first member of their tribe who embraced Islam three centuries ago. While they welcome all humanitarian, emergency, and development aid, these societies do not want to resemble the West. That is perhaps a reality that seems too utopian for them, but many still dream of emigrating to the West, or helping a relative emigrate, someone who could send money back to their extended family back home.

In these countries, Christian missionaries are often accepted and held in high regard. When Christian was traveling through the interior of Senegal, he stopped in a small village whose brand-new mosque and the square in front of it were, quite literally, bigger than the entire village. A young man told Christian that the Saudi Arabians had paid for the mosque, and after chatting a bit, remarked that "Christian missionaries build schools and hospitals instead of huge churches, so missionaries are welcome!"

In considering Asia, we have attempted a division according to the rigor of Islam. Some countries or zones of countries are more exclusivist, that is, less favorable to religious pluralism and less tolerant in terms of religious freedom. Among what we refer to as the **exclusivist Asian** countries are Northern India, Pakistan, parts of Indonesia, parts of Malaysia, and Brunei, as well as the

Comoros and Maldives. Most Central Asian countries, including Afghanistan, Uzbekistan, Tajikistan, Turkmenistan, and Kyrgyzstan, are also exclusivist. They do not want to resemble the West or copy its socio-cultural models. They are not very receptive or even totally reluctant to external development initiatives or non-Muslim humanitarian aid. Missionary work in these areas requires a great deal of creativity and a high degree of cultural adaptation.

In contrast, the rest of Asia tends to be very accustomed to religious pluralism, the coexistence of followers of Hinduism, Buddhism, Shintoism, Christianity, and Islam. Practice varies between tolerance and almost total religious freedom. These countries tend to welcome development projects and agencies but do not want to resemble the West, with few exceptions. Missionary presence is tolerated with varying degrees of acceptance. Among this group of **pluralistic Asian countries** or areas we include Southern India, Sri Lanka, Thailand, parts of Indonesia, the Philippines, Bangladesh, and Kazakhstan as well as the approximately twenty-three million Chinese Muslims.

1. A Typology of Churches

One purpose of this chapter is to propose a typology of churches arising with a Muslim background. Some sort of classification is necessary, or at least useful even if the shortcomings of such a classification may outweigh its benefits. There is no existing comprehensive and intrinsic classification of churches in *Islamia* although some of the many typologies may be more or less useful. Instead of returning to those, we will focus on several aspects of these churches that help us to understand them and classify or distinguish between them, both the churches and the settings in which they are found.

Combining and comparing these types of churches and their contexts gives rise to a simple matrix. The indicators used to form it are subject only to limited personal interpretation. These markers include the presence of historical minorities; whether the context is rural, semi-rural or urban; the degree of religious tolerance; whether the expression of Islam is predominantly Sunni, Shi'ite or Sufi; the age of the church; whether it is growing, stagnant, or surviving; whether its membership is gender segregated, integrated, or in an intermediate stage; whether it is dependent on foreign aid and leadership, semi-dependent, or independent; its degree of contextualization following John Travis' C-Scale;[1] and whether its leadership is individual or a team. A simplified matrix such as this would offer two hundred ninety-nine combinations (23x13), but more divisions and concepts could easily be added.

Using this matrix could help us analyze, for example, several urban churches in Shi'ite and semi-tolerant areas. This could shed much light on this cluster of

---

[1] John Travis, "Must All Muslims Leave 'Islam' to Follow Jesus?," *Evangelical Missions Quarterly*, October 1998, https://missionexus.org/must-all-muslims-leave-islam-to-follow-jesus/.

churches and might help us discern factors that we had otherwise overlooked, factors that are significant in terms of their differences or similarities. Of course, such a matrix is useful for handling quantitative data; an in-depth study intended to help understand the churches should be complemented by qualitative data, particularly regarding those previously hidden factors that the matrix has brought to light.

Typology of Churches		Historical Minorities		City			Tolerance			Islam			Religious Pluralism	
		Yes	No	Rural	Semi	City	Tolerance	Semi	Persecution	Suni	Chii	Sufi	Yes	No
Vitality	Growing													
	Stagnant													
	Surviving													
Age	≤ 5 years													
	≤ 10 years													
	10+ years													
Gender	Segregated													
	Semi													
	Integrated													
Organization / Visibility	Public													
	House													
	Network													
Contextual-ization	C1													
	C2													
	C3													
	C4													
	C5													
	Another													
Dependence	Dependent													
	Semi													
	Independent													
Leadership	Individual													
	Team													

Figure 4. Typology of Churches © Ch. Giordano, 2012

In any case, we will use the categories of this typology to analyze each of the projects individually and comparatively. In the following sections, we comment on some of the categories, according to the relevance they bring to our general understanding of the situation of the churches in Muslim-majority social contexts.

Vitality

Vitality is an intrinsic characteristic of a church. In his study of twelve North African churches, David Greenlee classified them as vigorous, plateau, or struggling.[2] There is no doubt that many factors contribute to the vigor of a church, and the same factors cannot be applied to all of them. For example, the humanitarian aid and development project carried out by Latin American missionaries in Kurdistan in the 1980s and 1990s contributed significantly to the formation and growth of the church; however, in neighboring Turkey, Protestant humanitarian aid in the wake of the 1999 earthquake delayed church growth by about ten years according to an experienced Iberoamerican worker there. Recent persecution in Morocco virtually disrupted the house churches in the capital. On the one hand, house churches meeting in the homes of foreign missionaries have always been more vulnerable due to the mobility of the missionaries who tend to change cities or move between countries much more frequently than the national members of these fellowships.

The composition of the membership is an important factor in the vitality and sustainability of a church. Those made up mostly of single men find it difficult to meet in a safe place, but on the other hand, they have more freedom of movement. However, groups of several families who are not relatives are more obvious, a disadvantage if they want to be discreet. Yet, such a group may have several houses available for their gatherings and the members bring a wide range of gifts to the church.[3]

Although there are still no exhaustive studies to assess the situation, the Arab Spring seems to have been a wake-up call for both the Coptic Church and the Egyptian evangelical communities. Throughout North Africa, evangelical churches are experiencing a strengthening from the Arab Spring onwards.[4] What

---

[2] David Greenlee, "Growing Churches in Resistant Areas," in *Envisioning Effective Ministry: Evangelism in a Muslim Context*, ed. Laurie Fortunak Nichols and Gary R. Corwin (Wheaton: Evangelism and Missions Information Service, 2010), 259-64. Originally published in *Evangelical Missions Quarterly* 38, no. 4 (October 2002).

[3] Muslim societies give priority to relationships with relatives, the extended family, and discourage relationships with "outsiders".

[4] This is the case of the small, semi-clandestine communities of Jesus's followers in Tunisia and Morocco, as well as Algeria where the evangelical churches have greater visibility and seniority, especially among the population of Kabylia. We do not have contrasting data from the churches in the Gulf. Reports from Turkey point to a clear

seems very clear is the positive and very important role in spreading the gospel in North Africa and the Middle East, as well as in consolidating the churches, played by radio programs, Bible correspondence courses, the wide availability of Christian resources on the Internet, and especially satellite television.

Contextualization

Another possible classification can be made on the basis of foreign influence and control. A distinction can be made between churches founded or influenced by foreigners, those that are in the process of becoming indigenous, and those that are perceived to be very indigenous in their expressions and life.

The influence of satellite television and the Internet contribute greatly to the spread of "standard" models of worship, inspired by Western formats: contemporary or pop-style worship music led by a worship band with one or more singers, followed by a sermon. The boundaries of what is indigenous and what is not have blurred. Sometimes we find Hillsong or similar music translated into languages spoken mostly by Muslims, which is a contradiction in itself. How can the rhythms, harmony, theological themes, and cultural background of the songs make sense, even if "translated"?

These are models that perhaps gain some isolated converts, extracting them from their familiar environment, but in the long run they contribute nothing to their society, they do not represent a model that is attractive or beneficial to the population as a whole. The "standard-globalized" worship and liturgy model may be attractive to some members of societies that are looking to the West as a model, as is the case in Morocco, Iran, or Turkey, but in the long run it does not bear lasting fruit. In the case of societies that define their identity as Muslim, such as Indonesia, Malaysia, Iraq, or Tunisia, the practice of "standard-globalized" liturgy is still a major barrier in their approach to the gospel. This is the case of the church in the Tunisian capital. For several years, the Protestant church has been following this "standard-globalized" model, in French, addressed mainly to European foreigners and Sub-Saharan Africans from Christian countries. Many Muslim nationals enter, listen, perhaps attend a few weeks, but do not stay. In comparison, it is interesting to note how Moroccan churches have recently composed their own songs, use religious vocabulary commonly understood by their compatriots, wear specific festive dress for religious festivals, and refer to the church as "the brotherhood" (according to a common Sufi term), in a form of spontaneous contextualization.

One way of classifying or describing churches according to their expression of contextualization has been the "C-Scale" proposed by John Travis.[5] Its five levels, C1-C6, represent five models of Christ-centered communities, each level described in terms of the adaptation to and identification with the culture of the

growth and strengthening, even with the opposition – bordering on persecution – of the Islamist governmental apparatus of President Erdogan.

[5] Travis, "Must All Muslims".

people. C6 is a designation for secret Christians, those who do not meet together or publicly manifest their faith. The "insider movement," which in recent years has given rise to conflicting opinions, is in fact nothing new, and we should not put the emphasis on judging it from the outside, as David Greenlee rightly points out.[6]

One of our friends mentioned some churches in Southeast Asia which have adopted the format of a *turuq* (Arabic, pl. *tariqah* or *tarikat* in Turkish), a Sufi brotherhood. They begin with a word of blessing, read Scripture as if chanting, then have a time of silent meditation, after which each one shares what they each have learned or received from God. They then take authority over evil and the Evil One and conclude by perhaps chanting a psalm. All this is carried out barefoot with mats on the floor and prostrating themselves for prayer. Mike Brislen relates the mosque, *tariqah* and *ummah* to their Christian equivalents. He notes:

> Influenced by functional anthropology, discussions of contextualization, at least in evangelical circles, center primarily on worship forms. We must reach deeper, beyond the surface-level phenomena of forms.[7]
>
> Joining the Muslim-culture church is joining the *tariqa* of Isa, committing oneself to follow Isa. It is to accept him as Lord and Savior. The new-creation Muslims must recognize that the Muslim-culture church requires a commitment equal to or surpassing that of a Muslim *tariqa*. Practices such as special dress for worship time may help to communicate this level of commitment. A distinction between seekers and committed believers will probably become apparent. As in many Muslim *tariqas*, the *tariqa* of Isa would want to share its faith, the good news that it has received.
>
> [...] The Muslim-culture church will celebrate its life in Jesus. Goats will be slaughtered, coke and tea will be drunk, meals will be eaten, songs will be sung, stories will be told, poems will be recited, and memories will be made. The church will celebrate the birth of Isa, his death and resurrection, the coming of the Spirit, etc. The *Ids* of the Muslim calendar could be celebrated with new meanings – events in the life of Christ or the relevant history of the church. The families of the believers may even celebrate together with the believers and gain a real taste of celebration of Isa and experience Christian worship.[8]

Personally, we are very interested in learning more about these Sufi-inspired forms of church life that represent an alternative to Western evangelical spirituality: a spirituality with mystical and revivalist Muslim roots. Since its beginnings in the eighth century, Sufism has been a mystical current, seeking

---

[6] David Greenlee, *One Cross, One Way, Many Journeys: Thinking Again about Conversion* (Tyrone, Ga.: Authentic, 2007), chap. 6.

[7] Mike Brislen, "A Model for a Muslim-Culture Church," *Missiology* XXIV, no. 3 (July 1996): 358.

[8] Brislen, "Model," 365.

direct contact with the Divine, based on community learning groups guided by a master ("discipleship," according to evangelical jargon), with a strong revivalist component in relation to mainstream Islam, and healthy proselytizing (often through music). The points of contact with modern evangelical spirituality are very clear.

Questions for Reflection and Discussion

1. Make a list of things you have learned while reading this chapter or ideas that have caught your attention.
2. What reaction or response does your society or community give to church activities demonstrating social solidarity or to Christian NGOs?
3. Are you aware of a church in your vicinity made up of believers who were brought up as Muslims? Have you ever visited them? If yes, did anything catch your attention about the way they express themselves in fellowship and worship?

For Further Reading

Baumer, Christoph. *The Church of the East: An Illustrated History of Assyrian Christianity*. London; New York: I.B. Tauris, 2006.

Raheb, Mitri. "Sailing Through Troubled Waters: Palestinian Christians in the Holy Land." *Dialog* 41, no. 2 (2002): 97-102. https://doi.org/10.1111/1540-6385.00105.

Jenkins, Philip. *The Lost History of Christianity: The Thousand-Year Golden Age of the Church in the Middle East, Africa, and Asia – and How It Died.* New York: Harper One, 2008.

McCurry, Don. *Tales That Teach.* Colorado Springs: Ministries to Muslims, 2009.

Chapman, Colin. "Christians in the Middle East – Past, Present and Future." *Transformation* 29, no. 2 (April 1, 2012): 91-110. https://meec.org.uk/wp-content/uploads/2017/10/Christians_in_the_ME.pdf

11. Initial Insights

In the previous chapters, we have focused on a group of people, development projects, and churches. Their descriptions have been at the center of the story, each in its own context.

Now, let's take a step back to consider the big picture so that we can reflect as a whole on these stories and the insights we have gained. We hope to highlight important relationships as well as other significant aspects we discover in the stories of these people, projects, and churches. In this chapter, we as researchers and authors will take the center stage; our own reflection will now be at the center of our writing.

What do the stories and circumstances, the unique features of these Muslim contexts suggest to us as we compare them with our own? What initial lessons do we draw? Of course, we must examine other people's lives with great humility, with reverence even, considering the work of God in people who have lived in circumstances that are different from our own.

We wrote this chapter after having taken a glimpse during a brief period into the lives of the people whose stories we have told. We enjoyed discussing those stories at length. Later, we spent hours comparing our notes; evaluating options, explanations, and lessons; and reviewing photographs, interviews, and our impressions. And now, with what we intend to be a good mixture of bold humility, we venture to put in writing our insights and the lessons that we ourselves have drawn from observing the life and work of these colleagues in God's mission. We encourage you, dear reader, to draw your own lessons and conclusions, since reading is always an interaction, a dialogue from three standpoints and perspectives: the reader's own and that of the writer and researcher, both of whom encounter the facts as they have been narrated.

We have grouped our reflections in no particular order, perhaps because the whole is as important as the parts that make it up.

1. Various Types of Relationships

When I, Christian, began this book, I took it for granted that integrality would be the key element of our analysis and that an empirical measurement of the level of implementation of integral mission would be a decisive factor in our effort to evaluate projects, churches, and even individuals. Yes, we still adhere somewhat to that idea (which will be confirmed near the end of the book), but together Charo and I have realized that mission is not mission without incarnation, without being involved in and interwoven with relationships. For this reason, we will first deal with relationships, a fundamental theme for an integral understanding of the Iberoamerican mission in *Islamia*, as well as in other contexts of Christian mission.

Multiple Relationships

Our reflection has shown that the relationship between projects and churches is complex. It is too simplistic to ask, "How many new believers have been converted through the project?" We have identified direct, indirect, mixed, close, distant, multiple, and reciprocal relationships. These relationships are established not only between the project and the church, but also with the workers, the society, the missionary agency, the national church structures, and the missionary's sending churches in their country of origin. Our comments here refer to the projects and churches described, but readers will easily apply them to almost all of the geographical and social contexts in which the mission of the church is carried out today.

Five Models

Andrés Guzmán distinguishes five types of relationships between a project and the establishment of a pioneer church.[1] We have adapted and expanded his classification, having found it very helpful to understand that there are at least five types of such relationships or approaches. We also note that we may find very high-quality projects that follow any of these five approaches. Each of the approaches has its value; choosing which to follow will depend on many context-dependent factors.

We have denominated the first model: *single audience*. The missionaries live incarnationally among the beneficiaries of the project, who are also the people among whom they want to see a church established. That is, those who become followers of Jesus and form the church are among those who have been direct beneficiaries of the project. People see the quality of the work or of the help, but they are especially attracted by the quality of life of the missionaries. Generally, after a certain time, they ask, "Why are you doing this?" and want to know about the faith of the missionaries. They have reached the point of deciding communally to listen to the gospel. There are many examples of this model. One of the keys is that it is the community, or a substantial part of it, that asks and wants to hear the gospel with all its consequences. The community leaders must be aware, officially or informally, of this desire to listen to the faith of the missionaries. That is, the community must give its assent, tacit or expressed, to

---

[1] Andrés Guzmán, "Ourselves as Servants," in *Perspectives on the World Christian Movement: A Reader*, 4th ed. (Pasadena: William Carey Library, 2009), 700-702.

the formation of a church. Otherwise, group pressure will make it difficult for a viable church to emerge, with possibilities for the future.

What we call the *two audiences* model separates church formation from the project. In this model, any impression of proselytism is avoided. It is very clear that becoming a Christian believer does not imply receiving greater benefits or advantages in terms of the project or other aid. While this model is incarnational, the missionaries incarnate themselves in another stratum of society that differs from the one that receives the help. They live and identify themselves more with professionals, with those of the middle class, and probably with people of the city, of the government, and of the neighborhood where they live. That is, they identify themselves with "those who watch" (to use Andrés Guzmán's phrase) as they carry out the project. These are the people among whom they want to establish the church.

We want to clarify that the missionary team is very intentional, very focused, in testifying about their faith, discipling, and grouping disciples among the public "that watches." They are very intentional in establishing friendships with them, relationships that will provide opportunities to share about the Messiah and what it means to follow him. This does not mean that they shy away from witnessing to project beneficiaries or employees the project may have hired. However, they have decided not to take advantage of the power differential between giver and receiver of aid and have chosen another way for that audience to hear about *Isa al Masih* and join the church. They open the door for them to ask. They are intentional in creating channels and opportunities for communication, although the initiative has to lie with the recipients, and they make it clear to them – again – that becoming a Christian will not bring them any benefits or advantages from the project. Everyone receives the same treatment and benefits from the project; there is no discrimination on the basis of faith.

Another characteristic of this approach is that every effort is made to ensure that local people are in charge of the church from the beginning. The missionaries are disciple-makers and disciple-gatherers, but they adopt a secondary role in the formation, leadership, format, and style of the church.

Single task is the term we apply to the third approach, the model of those who insist that good works do not need justification, that they have value in themselves. It is the approach of professionals who understand that their calling is to serve with their profession and that others are going to plant churches. They are those who consider themselves to be missionaries even while their public role and work is that of doctors, teachers, engineers, therapists, and work in other capacities. They do not shy away from speaking about their faith, of course; in fact, they take advantage of every opportunity to speak about the Lord, offer prayer, or give someone a portion of the *Injil*. This is a perfectly valid model, but the expectations must be clear to all the project stakeholders.

Despite otherwise good intentions, this is the model of those missionaries who are not intentional enough in the formation of the church. They have what

Guzmán privately described to us as the "illusion of intentionality." They probably manage the project with great skill but may never have been taught how to establish a church. They may have realized that the steps they followed to help start churches in their homeland is very different from the approach needed in the country where they serve. They want to see a church formed, they would be very happy if that came about, but their intentionality is limited or misguided. The reality is that a church does not just happen, it does not arise on its own.

We call the fourth model the *right to hear* relationship between church and project, although we could also call it the "rice plus leaflet" model. It is the approach of those who say that "everyone has a right to hear." Those who follow this model intentionally takes advantage of the asymmetry of power between donor (or powerful) and needy. They do not consider whether or not the beneficiary wants to hear the gospel; they impose it upon them. Receiving the leaflet, watching the video, and hearing the propaganda or presentation is a *sine qua non* to benefit from the project and related aid. In reality, it is not the right to *hear* but the right to *speak* that is being used (or abused): "We have the right to speak of our faith." Although this model may be useful at some times and in some other parts of the world, in Muslim contexts, this model is usually only linked to humanitarian aid in cases of catastrophes, because in other circumstances it would provoke a frontal and possibly violent rejection. It is a model that tends to bear apparently good fruit in the short term, even if its long-term effect is negative.

There is a fifth model of relationship between projects and churches that we have called *benefits to Christians*. Projects described by this model focus on a selective public and do not equally benefit the whole of society. Examples of such projects include a micro-credit project associated with the church or professional training for believers. These are projects that seek to empower church members, perhaps to help them emerge from a situation of marginalization. A well-known example is one that helps Coptic children living and working in Cairo's garbage dumps. This model assumes that there is already a church or group of believers to benefit. This model can be very beneficial, although it can also produce or foster dependency, rice Christians. Its value is undeniable in the short and long term, as long as the access requirements are clear with respect to the rest of society.

The Golden Relationship

An analysis of the multiple relationships between the projects and the churches led us to realize a danger: the confusion of which is the priority relationship. We have called it the *golden relationship*. A project should have a balanced relationship with its competitors, with those working on the project (local workers, missionaries, and other partners), with the church with which it is (or will be) linked, with the other churches in the area, with the pastors and leaders of those churches, with donors, with the agency or organization it is part of, with the neighborhood and community in which it is located, with the corresponding local and regional authorities, and of course with its beneficiaries.

Figure 5. Relationships of a Project

In the same way, the church should cultivate harmonious relationships. Obviously, this begins with its own members and includes the church's own pastor(s) and those of nearby churches. It extends to relationships with other churches in the area, with the missionaries and workers that are involved with the church, with donors from outside the church (a frequent circumstance in pioneer periods), with the projects with which the church is involved regularly or occasionally, with its enemies (frequently this dimension is not taken into account), with an association of churches or missions with which it is linked, with the neighborhood and community in which the church is located, and with the authorities.

The problem is that, too often, the project seems to exist mainly and primarily for its beneficiaries and the church for its members (the simple thick line in the diagrams). The energy that is left – always limited – is consumed by the many other demands that the other necessary relationships claim. And the main relationship, the *golden relationship*, comes last.

The main reason for the existence of a project and of a church is the world and, by proximity, its community. The church exists for the world. The project exists for the world. As Dietrich Bonhoeffer rightly pointed out: "The Church is only the Church when it exists for others."[2] And, as Andrew Kirk wrote, "The Church is by nature missionary to the extent that, if it ceases to be missionary, it has not just failed in one of its tasks, it has ceased being Church."[3]

A diagram will help to illustrate these relationships. The double thick line indicating the golden relationship can be seen in the diagram. Considering the valid demands of the other relationships, especially those of the beneficiaries, it is easy to see how the many competing demands can distract from the real goal. Note that the beneficiaries, the donors, and the agency or organization may "scream" a lot, vocalize their demands very loudly, while the community will not come calling.

Figure 6. Relationships of a Church

In the case of the church, on the other hand, it is the relationship with the members (and perhaps with the projects or "ministries" that the church carries out) that demands more attention, to the detriment of service and involvement in the community. Too easily the church exists with an inward orientation rather than being fundamentally for the world.

In both cases, the relationship represented in the diagram by the thick lines is the one that catches the attention, to the detriment of the relationship indicated by the double line representing the fundamental relationship.

---

[2] Dietrich Bonhoeffer, *Letters and Papers from Prison*, ed. Eberhard Bethge et al. (Minneapolis, MN: Fortress, 2010). "Outline of a book".

[3] J. Andrew Kirk, *What is Mission?* (Minneapolis: Augsburg Fortress Publishers, 2000), 30.

2. Proselytism

Self-Conscious Society

The first conclusion that struck us is that of a society that has a problem in its self-consciousness, a society that seems to be frightened by the advance of the gospel. Perhaps this is not the impression that an observer has at first glance, because Islam seems very belligerent, aggressive, and jealous of its faith. Islamic countries promote laws against "religious intolerance" – what a paradox! – and blasphemy, seeking to impose their biased view on bodies such as the United Nations. Cases of assaults and attacks against churches and Christians are frequent in Muslim countries. All this, if one looks below the surface, could denote a great deal of insecurity and fear. On the contrary, those who feel secure do not need to attack their intended rivals.

A church in Paris, made up of followers of Jesus who were raised as Muslims, captured this characteristic of Islam and its societies well. Said Oujibou, its pastor, declared during the 1999 CLAME II meeting in Malaga, Spain (attended by Christians): "We are not afraid of Islam; it has nothing to offer compared to Jesus and the Gospel, nothing." The same feeling is conveyed by the symbols, apologetics, and evangelism of the Straightway Christian Chapel movement of Ghana, formed by former Muslims, who testify openly of Christ unhindered by complexes and fear.[4]

It would seem the persecution and aggressiveness experienced in Muslim societies have managed to transmit the idea among Western Christians that Islam is a fierce lion. While maintaining our respect for Islam as a religion, and for the people who profess it, is it correct to suggest that the anti-conversion belligerence directed outward from Islam is a product of an unhealthy fear that is an element of some aspects of Muslim societies?

It's All about Perception

Strictly speaking, proselytism involves the right of every person to share their opinions and to want to convince others. But this right is understood differently in different settings. Muslims tend to assume that only the truth (as manifested in the Qur'an and Islamic beliefs) has rights and, consequently, lies (all other beliefs and religions) only have obligations and no rights. Note that this is taken for granted; it is a largely unconscious assumption. This means that if the missionary is perceived as a proselytizer, as wanting to convince his counterpart, trust is immediately broken, the conversation is strained, and any understanding is virtually impossible.

The issue of proselytism is complex, especially because both sides handle different definitions of it, and change them according to the circumstances. At least in a general sense, any attempt to convert a Muslim to any other faith is

[4] Elom Dovlo and Alfred Ofosu Asante, "Reinterpreting the Straight Path: Ghanian Muslim Converts in Mission to Muslims," *Exchange* 32, no. 3 (January 2003): 214-38.

seen, from the ranks of Muhammad's followers, as proselytizing (even if their attempts to convert others are favorably referred to as *da'wah*). Does that mean that there is no way to present the gospel to the Muslim faithful? Nothing could be further from the truth! A large proportion of Muslims have spiritual concerns, sincerely seek to please God, and are happy to engage in conversations about spiritual matters. Christian has had occasion to monitor over one hundred Iberoamerican "followers of the Messiah" in six Muslim countries over twelve years, women and men who have been actively sharing their faith. While a few were accused of proselytizing, most were not.

We believe the key lies in how we are perceived. First, we must earn the right to speak. In a culture of honor and shame, the honor of the messenger is key. Second, relationships are critical. We are talking about cultures, Latin and Muslim, where relationships come before theoretical definitions. Third, pressure, both individual and social, must be avoided. In this understanding, the King's messenger presents the Truth, with capital letters. Unlike what happens in the West, for the Muslim, the truth is not relative but absolute and worthy of being followed, even unto death.

We repeat, it is a matter of perception, of how one is perceived, of what feelings the messenger awakens in *them*. It is a matter of tact, if you will, on the part of God-fearing people, who not only take care of what they say or do but pay close attention to how they do it and under what circumstances. Properly witnessing for Christ in a Muslim society while minimizing unnecessary cultural offense is definitely an art that is learned and cultivated.

Language of Conquest

Closely related to the proselytizing attitude, military language of conquest has become very popular on the lips of Iberoamerican missionaries. It is associated with the concept of spiritual warfare. Can we imagine how an average Muslim citizen, a normal and peaceful father or mother of a family, feels when hearing expressions like *war*, *armies of the Lord*, *resist*, *rebuke*, *conquer the earth*, and *defeat the strong man*? How can that father or mother distinguish that symbolic language used by evangelicals from the language of the modern crusades and wars in Palestine or Syria, to name but a few?

Unfortunately, some go a step beyond language, associating Islam as the enemy to be defeated. Marcos Amado, synthesizing Christine Mallouhi's ideas, warns us:

> Many Christians paint Islam as the great antichrist, the enemy to conquer. […] For this group of Christians, the battle is seen as a strategic and necessary ingredient for there to be a victorious witness.
>
> In this way of functioning, prayer becomes a strategic weapon, Islam is presented as the villain of history, and the conversion of Muslims is simply a strategy of

> conquest. The consequences of this school [of thought] are very similar to those brought about by the medieval church.[5]

Commenting on attitudes toward spiritual warfare and territorial spirits, Samuel Escobar wrote:

> A thin line has been crossed when nationalism and patriotism lead us to demonize peoples and nations as enemies of our own nation. My suspicion is reinforced when I see this militaristic view of the world expressed also in worship and music that use almost exclusively the warlike language of the Old Testament.[6]

A small group of missionary leaders, gathered in Pasadena in the year 2000, issued a statement regarding "Mission Language and Metaphors,"[7] which, unfortunately, has gone completely unnoticed in the Iberoamerican missionary environment.

The Effects of Persecution

We include the issue of persecution under the heading of proselytizing because one of the main grounds for persecution is proselytism. In describing the six major geographic zones that make up the Muslim world, we linked tolerance and persecution to the existence or lack of religious pluralism. In some places, persecution is cyclical, flaring up every eight to ten years and then easing off. Here, we focus on the effects or consequences of persecution.

The cases studied show distinct, in fact polar differences. On the one hand, some people and churches have chosen to conform, to adopt a more discreet profile, to keep their evangelism to a minimum, and to live their faith on an individual or private level. They do not deny their faith, but they live it very discreetly. This has been the case for many churches in North Africa; approximately one third of the established churches in one country ceased to function following the persecution that began in 2010 and has continued until the time of writing this edition in 2021. On the opposite pole, others have chosen not to change, to continue with their visible profile, to continue evangelism openly and to continue worshipping as before. They have been – and continue to be – put under a great deal of police pressure, but the authorities have preferred not to resort to extreme measures, such as trials and imprisonment. In the specific cases we have studied in North Africa, the churches that have opted for the second option have continued to grow.

---

[5] Marcos Amado, "Declarando Paz al Islam," PM Internacional, 2001. Trans. D. Greenlee; an edited copy is available at https://misionestransculturales.org/declaremos-paz-a-los-musulmanes

[6] Samuel Escobar, *The New Global Mission: The Gospel from Everywhere to Everyone* (Downers Grove: InterVarsity Press, 2003), 60.

[7] "Consultation on Mission Language and Metaphors" (Pasadena: Fuller Theological Seminary, June 1, 2000), http://www.ad2000.org/re00620.htm.

Obviously, we do not intend to judge the situation from the comfort we experience in Europe. There are valid reasons for both positions, however a long-term study of the repression exercised by Muslims toward Christians sheds much light: yielding to pressures only results in the detriment of the church.

3. Comparison of Three Churches in North Africa

Since they share a similar setting, a comparison between the three North African churches can shed light on the situation. They are the churches in Gran Urbe and those in the vicinity of La Joya and Grand Ville; the former urban and the latter two rural. Further, we will draw on the parameters of the matrix proposed in Chapter 10 to describe our key terms: vitality, age of the church, matters related to gender, organization and visibility, contextualization, outside dependence, leadership, persecution, and the expression of Islam.

Vitality, Visibility, Organization, and Age of the Church

The three churches analyzed were formed in the decade following the year 2000. They are house churches, in situations of what at best was semi-tolerance. They needed to be very discreet so as not to trigger a denunciation by neighbors resulting in action by the police. In honor-shame societies strongly dominated by relationships, semi-tolerance means that both the police and those concerned pretend that they do not know what is going on. If Christians keep quiet and do not draw attention to themselves, the police may temporarily ignore them or act through individual pressure. This fragile balance is broken when there is a complaint: the police are forced to act publicly on pain of losing face, which makes them very uncomfortable because the government does not want to be criticized by foreign governments. In an honor-shame society, which includes Mediterranean and Latin American societies, shaming the other or making others feel uncomfortable is always the last resort.

In their early years, the vitality of the three churches could be described by several standards as vigorous: they grew in membership and structure, developed their own leadership, and projected themselves more or less visibly into their respective communities. In particular, from 2006 to 2009, the church in Gran Urbe was brimming with optimism and gathered about twenty to thirty people weekly and up to twice as many for Easter or Christmas celebrations. The other two churches were rural and had fewer members (approximately a dozen). The church in La Joya was known throughout the town, met on a rotating basis in several houses, and, although its leader suffered a lot of pressure and police harassment, the church was more or less tolerated *de facto*. The church in Grand Ville was practically clandestine; it was "under the radar," and only a few family members know of its existence, although that small circle was slowly expanding. So, we are faced with three churches that have opted for three models or degrees of visibility: almost visible, *de facto* invisible, and completely invisible; or in other words, almost public, semi-tolerated, and clandestine.

The persecution that began in early 2010 led to the closure of the church in Gran Urbe and the dispersion of its members. Several of them, including the leadership, moved to other cities. However, some believers chose to attend the international church and make themselves publicly known as followers of the Messiah.

The city's international Protestant church, one of three authorized throughout the country, conducts services in French and English. Only foreigners are officially allowed to attend. However, as these and several other national believers began to attend, the church has recently begun holding services in Arabic. This is an experimental move. There is no precedent for the government to tolerate worship services in Arabic in buildings authorized to house foreign churches; we will have to see how the situation evolves.

In the same situation of persecution, the rural church in La Joya chose to resist the pressures and continue its gatherings. They count on the unspoken backing of the local population who have given their tacit assent to the formation of a discreet church, this is coupled with the fact that the citizens do not look favorably on the police.

In contrast, the church in the countryside near Grand Ville has opted to be quasi-clandestine or invisible. Their isolation in scattered villages in the countryside facilitates that choice. Before the persecution, they met alternately in the countryside and in the missionaries' apartment in the city, they sang, they celebrated baptisms in an inflatable pool, and they joined with other congregations for parties and special occasions. In this new phase, their growth is oriented to family networks.

The church in Gran Urbe was able to continue for only nine years. The churches in La Joya and Grand Ville have continued since 2005 until today.

Leadership, Gender, and Organization

The three churches we are considering have all had shared leadership, although it is not truly collegial. That is, there has been a plurality of leaders, although not all of them serving at the same level. In Gran Urbe, the national network of churches ordained a national pastor, who teamed up with a Latin American missionary who advised and supported him while remaining in the background. Some women, likewise, exercised discreet leadership. In La Joya and Grand Ville, the leadership has been assumed by a single person, although with two or three others supporting or advising him, all of them male.

The churches in Gran Urbe and Grand Ville have always felt that they are part of a network of national churches and are supported by pastors recognized or prominent in that network. In comparison, the church in La Joya, although it knows of the existence of other churches and pastors, does not feel the need for communion with them, perhaps because of the legendary independence and isolationism of its ethnic group. The founding missionary visits the church leader once a month to mentor him, and at the same time is a link with the outside world.

The church in La Joya is completely segregated in terms of gender. Men meet in one house and women in another. As we noted earlier, in that culture, a man rarely talks to his wife about weighty issues. By contrast, the church in the countryside of Grand Ville is mixed gender: men, women, and children share worship, prayers, the Lord's Supper, and so on. Men and women sit on opposite sides of the same room as is customary in family gatherings. The church in Gran Urbe, perhaps because it was completely urban, was the most gender integrated.

Expression of Islam

In all three cases, the community follows the Sunni form of Islam with widespread observance of popular Islam. There is also an orientation toward Sufi expressions of Islam. Marabout tombs abound and are places of popular veneration. Until the 1920s, throughout North Africa, most males belonged to some Sufi brotherhood. After a period of decline, Sufism in general and the brotherhoods in particular have experienced a remarkable revival in the latter part of the twentieth century.

Recently, a group of experts defined five types of Islam: mystical and popular Islam, missionary and polemical Islam, ideological and political Islam, militant and violent Islam, and progressive and liberal Islam.[8] These are often present, often overlapping, in all Muslim societies. In the case of North Africa, popular/mystical Islam constitutes the basic substratum of the population. At the same time, there is a significant proportion of people who would fit under the heading of progressive/liberal. Society is generally tolerant, as long as the religion or the Prophet is not directly attacked. Cycles of persecution usually come hand in hand with the pressures that the political/ideological sector exerts on parliament, government, and local police officers. The latter sector has been growing in recent years due, in part, to the polarization between the West and Islam, as well as the dissatisfaction of the masses with the inaction of their politicians.

4. Comparison of Four Churches in Senegal

We now compare the three churches in Senegal, plus the mother church of one of them. These are the churches of Keru Barkeel and Keur Jamm, the church in the Fatick villages, and the Brethren assembly in Dakar that sponsored the work in the villages.

Vitality, Visibility, and Age

Both the Keur Jamm and the village churches are vigorous and growing churches, with a solid leadership base and sufficient space of their own for

[8] Lausanne Global Consultation on Islam, "Five Faces of Islam" (Lausanne Global Consultation on Islam, April 2014), https://www.lausanne.org/news-releases/global-consultation-on-islam.

development. The Brethren assembly in Dakar is also vigorous, although its growth is a bit slower than the two other churches. In contrast, Keru Barkeel is in decline, struggling to maintain itself. The visibility of these churches is very different; the first two are highly visible, known by the whole community, while Keru Barkeel and the Brethren assembly are barely visible.

We already mentioned that Keru Barkeel is hidden in a room on the second floor of the health project. It has no outside indication of its presence, and although the community knows that there is a church there none (or very, very few) of them have ever attended a service; they do not know what is done there or who its members are.

The Brethren assembly meets in a first-floor apartment and the courtyard of a block of apartments, accessed through a back alley. It has no outward indication of its presence; you would not find the place, even if you were given directions, unless someone took you there. Some forty to fifty people congregate, more than a third of whom are young, of various African ethnicities and some Westerners. They are saving money to buy their own land on which to build a temple.

The Brethren assembly is the oldest church of those we are considering, having been founded some thirty or forty years ago. Keru Barkeel, Keur Jamm, and the village church are about the same age, about twenty years old. If we were to order them by size, from largest to smallest, we would name the village churches with several hundred attendees, then Keur Jamm (three hundred fifty), the Brethren (fifty) and Keru Barkeel (a dozen).

Leadership, Gender, and Organization

The church in the villages has a pastor and several associates. The associates serve as evangelists and are responsible for the various church meeting places. Keur Jamm has a pastor, a council of elders, a council of deacons, and an extended church council, which includes all departmental heads. The Brethren assembly has three elders who serve in a pastoral role. Keru Barkeel currently has no pastor and is partially led by a Senegalese believer and a missionary, the medical director of the clinic.

All four churches are undergoing changes, of varying degrees, in their leadership. The pastor of Keur Jamm at the time of our research was later promoted by his mission and has moved to Nigeria to take up a leadership position. One of the three Brethren elders – who himself was the advisor or overseer of the church in the villages – has returned to Brazil due to family issues, while another of their leaders has serious marital problems. In other words, two of the churches we are considering lost one of their leaders, and another is in question.

It is difficult to predict how these leadership changes would affect these four churches, although we can suppose that the least affected will be the churches in the villages, which had significant ties with but little dependence on the supervising missionary. Likewise, we can assume that the broad, mid-level leadership of Keur Jamm would be able to sustain the church while they find another pastor who connects with the congregation and the neighborhood and will be able to take the church forward. In our view, it is likely that the Brethren assembly would go through a time of stagnation while they renew or reorganize their leadership. As for Keru Barkeel, any mid- to long-term solution will involve profound changes.

In terms of gender, none of the four churches fully accepts the ministry of women as equal to that of men. For theological reasons, Keur Jamm and the Brethren assembly limit leadership to men. The Brethren extend that limitation to all aspects of church life while, in Keur Jamm, women can have responsibility beyond teaching and preaching and women do in fact lead several departments. The church in the villages is part of the Brethren fellowship. We think that the limitations placed on women there are because of a mix of both theological and cultural reasons, although we do not rule out that gender issues may be handled differently, since the church is in a strong growth process.

The four churches are part of the Fraternité Evangélique du Sénégal (Evangelical Fellowship of Senegal), which groups together all the evangelical and Protestant churches in the country. In turn, Keur Jamm is part of the denomination linked to CAPRO, the Nigerian missions agency, while the churches in the villages and the Dakar assembly are part of the Plymouth Brethren. On the other hand, Keru Barkeel, although part of the Fraternité, feels alone because it is not part of any denomination or ecclesial grouping.

Islam, Integrality, and Proselytism

Senegalese Islam is unique because of the influence of the Mouride brotherhood centered on the city of Touba. While Sufism permeates society throughout West Africa, nowhere are the brotherhoods as powerful as in Senegal. One of the main reasons is the alliance that Sufism of Touba has forged between religion and wealth production through labor, politics, and social cohesion. Social cohesion and religion-spirituality are common across Sufism, but the way the Mouride caliphate capitalizes on both political power and the centralization of economic resources has produced a distinctive sense of social belonging. The Wolofs have taken on Touba-based Mouridism to the extent that being Wolof is tantamount to being Mouride. From a young age, all Wolof children know that they are part of a community that provides for all the needs of its members and also know that they must work hard to produce as much wealth as possible for their *sheik* (master) and not to be a burden to the community themselves.

This combination has given the Mouriddiyyah brotherhood all-embracing power in Touba, the country's third largest urban agglomeration, and one of the *de facto* political and economic powers in the rest of the country. The power of the State is clearly in question in the face of Mouride power. Two examples illustrate Mouride power. Since independence, according to Rafael Crespo, the government has turned a blind eye to smuggling operated from Touba, and foreign remittances, controlled mostly by the Mouridiyyah, represented twenty-five percent of the state budget in 2003 according to official figures. The real amount, Crespo observes, is likely much higher.[9]

This power and these economic links are not confined to Senegal but have extended to other countries and capitals. Through local Mouride associations (*dahiras*), Touba presence is felt in seven of the world's top global cities: London, New York, Paris, Rome, Tokyo, Los Angeles, and Chicago.[10] These resources flowing from all over the world to Touba are helping to fulfill the vision of Amadou Bamba that Touba would be the "world capital."

The very strong social cohesion among the Mouride has meant that very few of them have become followers of Jesus. As mentioned above, Wolof Christians number less than fifty in the country as a whole. It seems that the efforts of the three churches studied in the capital, Keur Jamm, Keru Barkeel, and the Brethren assembly, have not been able to find in the gospel something that is good news for the Mouride community. On the other hand, the church that emerged from the steakhouse business and the Bethany Mission has obtained at least partial results with some *talibé* street boys (Mouride disciples). It is worth asking whether what these boys have found in the gospel is mostly a response to their homelessness or to their Mouride education. This would be a very important topic to study, given that several ministries work with street children, children who are a direct product of the Mouride philosophy of learning and the Mouride financial network.

In contrast with the pervasive presence of Mouride expressions of Islam among those of Wolof ethnicity, Islam as experienced in the villages of Fatick province is only superficially rooted within the community. It is mixed with many animist elements that constitute the true substratum of the Serere ethnic group.

The moderate level of religious freedom offered by Senegal gives prominence to the themes of integrality and proselytism. In contrast, the persecution and resulting secrecy prevailing in North Africa does not allow either integrality or proselytism to be openly manifested. Comparing the four churches, we find that Keur Jamm is integral but proselytizing. For this reason, despite their many positive social actions, the neighborhood looks at them with hostility. In fact, the enmity is mutual: for the Christians of Keur Jamm the Muslims are targets to be won or conquered for their ranks as they feel harassed, almost drowned in a "Muslim ocean" from which they have to defend themselves.

---

[9] Rafael Crespo, "Los 'Móodu-Móodu' y su Impacto en la Sociedad de Origen," in *Empresariado Étnico en España*, ed. Joaquín Beltrán, Natalia Ribas, and Laura Oso, vol. 12, Documentos Observatorio Permanente Inmigración (Madrid: Ministerio de Trabajo y Asuntos Sociales, Fundació CIDOB, 2006), 254, 257, http://www.cidob.org/es/content/download/4587/46036/file/12_crespo.pdf.

[10] Eric Ross, "Globalising Touba: Expatriate Disciples in the World City Network," *Urban Studies* 48, no. 14 (November 1, 2011): 2941, https://doi.org/10.1177/0042098010391300.

Keru Barkeel has been accused of proselytizing, but this seems more like an excuse, an indication that some authorities in the neighborhood are bothered by its presence. It has the appearance of integrality, because it tries to respond to various human needs, but both the Christian employees of the project and the church members have little friendship among themselves and have an inward-focused mentality. The Brethren assemblies in Dakar and in the villages exhibit integrality applied in a very different way: while in the villages the church is concerned with the welfare of the whole village, in Dakar they do not seem sensitive to the needs of their neighborhood and limit themselves to maintaining very good relations with the neighbors of their apartment block. The village church is very evangelistic but not proselytist.

5. Much Holism, Little Integrality

Our research and reflection has revealed underdeveloped, partial expressions and understandings of the broad idea of integral mission and the quality of integrality in most workers, projects, and churches. For many, integral mission means putting words and works together, or balancing projects and evangelism, or loving people. Of course, each of these phrases is completely true, but they reflect little depth of understanding of the concepts, just elementary stages in the theoretical-plus-practical formulation and implementation of the ideal of integral mission. The phrase that Leonardo Boff attributed to ecology can well be used to describe integrality:

> Ecology [integrality], as paradigm, entails taking a basic stance, always thinking holistically; that is, continually seeing the whole, which does not derive from the sum of the parts but from the organic interdependence of all the elements. This step moves beyond the thinking of modernity, which is purely analytical, split up, and disconnected.[11]

As some people we interviewed, colleagues from our missionary agency, PM International (PMI), commented: "Integral mission is something that is mentioned a lot in PMI, but nobody really knows what it is."

Our own experience of more than twenty-five years engaging with Latin American missionaries has made us aware of and to some extent understand the many pressures they face. These pressures are with themselves and in engaging with and living in Muslim cultures; but pressure is also faced when relating to their sending churches. These missionaries arrive bearing the practical and theological presuppositions of their sending churches, but they encounter a completely different reality, something that, more often than not, their senders

---

[11] Leonardo Boff, *Cry of the Earth, Cry of the Poor*, Ecology and Justice (Maryknoll: Orbis, 1997), 41.

do not understand. Even for themselves, it takes an average of three years of immersion in a Muslim-majority country to internalize the concept of integrality.

In general, we have observed a lot of holism, at least as used in its evangelical sense: the joining of two distinct things, word (or Word) and deed or evangelism and social work. However, we saw little that we would refer to as truly integral mission. We noted a great deal of interest in wanting to do good, but little focus on social transformation or, in other words, much relief (in projects) but little social and political action that addresses the causes (#5 of the Organizational Scale of Social Involvement, Chapter 5).

Another symptom of this limited understanding of integrality has been the lack of answers to the question, "What steps would be needed to advance integrality?" We expected to find holistic-type answers when visiting and interviewing workers from Keru Yakaar, the YWAM clinic in Dakar, precisely because of the general theological stance of their organization. In fact, the pastor of the church founded by YWAM workers nodded indirectly, but very politely, when we mentioned to him our perception of the holism of the clinic. Having been trained ministerially with World Vision International, he perceives the difference between holism and integrality. But we did not expect to find elementary (or reductionist) concepts and practices in our colleagues with PMI, which as an organization defines integral mission as one of its distinguishing characteristics. Does that mean that the organization has invested little effort in training its staff on that topic in recent years? That may well be the case.

6. Contextual Deficiency

Another set of findings is that the workers we interviewed displayed a seeming lack of understanding of how, in these settings, honor and shame and purity and defilement are applied to the gospel. They also showed an almost total lack of knowledge of Sufism.

While they seem to understand quite well the practical cultural characteristics regarding honor and shame, they do not seem to have taken the extra step of reading and understanding them in the Scripture, something that would enable them to apply those concepts to the gospel message; that is, finding a way to understand the gospel in terms of honor and shame.

Beyond the honor/shame pairing, the importance of the issue of purity and defilement seems to be hidden, even unknown, by these workers. This may be because the purity/defilement pairing is a concept deeply rooted in religion, and in that sense less visible to them than other elements of the culture. Understanding these concepts is very important, not just in cultural terms but including a grasp of the biblical implications of the concept and its relevance in books such as Numbers, Leviticus, Psalms, Hebrews, and much of the New Testament. This could help them reformulate their understanding of the gospel by including these mental categories, so important in African thought in general and Muslim thought in particular. Beyond its immediate relevance to the settings we studied, many practicing Jews, large social groups in India and Southern Africa, and a good part of Asian societies are culturally and religiously sensitive to the issue of defilement and purity.

Further, the workers we interviewed both in North Africa and in Senegal seem to be unaware of the essence and the extent of Sufism. They do not recognize that many of the practices they observe among their host communities are elements of the mystical current of Sufi Islam. When asked about the subject as applied to worship, liturgy, and church organization, they tended to emphasize a break from the practice of trances, which seems to be the only practice they could clearly identify as an aspect of Sufism. We find it inconceivable that so many of the workers simply do not know what Sufism is. How can this be, given that Sufi expressions of Islam play such a dominant, open, and even official role in North Africa and Senegal?

In contrast to this contextual deficit, the high level of local language performance of the Latin American workers is striking. It seems that the need to master the language, both administrative (French) and popular (Berber, Wolof, or one of the various Arabic dialects depending on setting), has permeated the priorities of the workers and mission agencies studied, and PMI in particular. On language skills tests we conducted, workers scored an average of sixty-six percent in comparison to the expected proficiency of an educated native speaker, a clearly commendable level.

7. Identity

Missionary Identity

Our research has shown the importance of a correct identity of the missionary. Initially we thought that the degree of integrality would be a decisive factor in the success of Latin missionary work. However, halfway through our research trip across North Africa, we realized that a correct identity is more important than integrality as a decisive factor. In Muslim contexts, the identity of the missionary as a "full-time Christian worker" is not appropriate. But this is precisely the identity with which they are perceived by their churches, by those who have sent them and support them financially, spiritually, and psychologically. In order to live and minister adequately for the long term in a markedly Muslim environment, workers need to reformulate their identity in ways that are acceptable and understandable to their Muslim neighbors.

In my 2008 Master's thesis, I, Christian, explored both the problems associated with an inadequate identity as well as the reasons behind a good identity and practical ways to consciously build it. The focus was an identity that Latin American workers and their families are comfortable with while also being both understandable to and acceptable within the Muslim environment in which they minister. Such a mono-vocational identity rejects the dual (bi-vocational) identity model. Instead, it is transparent, not camouflaged. Its genuineness and the associated sense of assurance are seen in the various social roles it lives out, one of which corresponds to the role of a pious Muslim.[12]

Our study has revealed the role that the project plays in the construction and appropriation of this new identity. The identity is derived from a direct relationship between the project and the worker: "I am a teacher at such-and-such a school," "I am a social worker at that center," or "I have a business in that neighborhood." In some cases, a worker may openly identify as a pastor. This direct, obvious relationship provides a lot of peace of mind both to the individual and to the family. It is quite the opposite of those who live a dual identity: a hidden one as "full-time Christian workers" combined with a public, artificial identity, which is little more than a cover to remain in the country and provide "contacts" (not people!) to whom to testify. The latter highlights the many cases of false or camouflaged identities. In fact, they are the majority among Latin American missionaries serving among Muslims.

On the contrary, a genuine and appropriate identity provides the worker with the necessary basis and peace of mind to establish other relationships, including those with the church linked in some way with the project, whether the relationships are direct, indirect, or mixed.

Identity of the Church

A clear and healthy church identity is another important topic for our consideration. A proper church identity contributes significantly to the sustainability and strength of a church. One of the churches studied, Grand Ville, has opted for a secret, clandestine, inward-looking identity. Another has chosen a semi-clandestine identity although it is known to the surrounding community. Made up mostly of men, it is a sort of community of mutual practical help, for example in the reconstruction of their homes. Note that this identity manifests a desire to serve the community, even if only in a limited way. The church in Gran Urbe constructed a rather similar identity, although in that church the component of service to society was smaller. It was a joyful, fraternal church that provided emotional and spiritual health to its members. Much the same could be said of the Brethren assembly in Dakar, except that it is not clandestine. Their church format is very welcoming; fellowship and times to gather together are important points in their understanding of the church. At the same time, they get along very well with their immediate neighborhood. In Dakar, Keur Jamm manifests an activist identity, clearly aligned with the "Christian culture." It scores quite high in integrality and tries by all means to relate to its neighborhood. However, its proselytizing attitude has raised a wall of hostility from its Muslim neighbors. It understands itself as the most Senegalese church in the capital, in contrast to the

[12] Christian Giordano, "Identity, Context and Message: Iberoamerican Mission in Muslim Lands" (M.Th., London, Brunel University, London School of Theology, 2008), 13-15, https://doi.org/10.13140/RG.2.1.2644.4241.

others whose membership is made up of foreign Africans. By contrast, Keru Barkeel has been searching for an identity without finding it.

In the two places studied, North Africa and Senegal, the local followers of the Messiah have chosen to identify themselves mostly as Christians. The insider movement model has not found acceptance among them.

8. Who Does the Project Serve?

Our reflections have convinced us that the project serves several interests in a positive way. First, it provides the missionary and their organization with a valid, transparent, and appreciated reason to remain in the country. The project constitutes a very important part of the missionary's identity. This is true not only in contexts restricted to the preaching of the gospel, but everywhere.

One of the relationships between the projects and the formation of a church is that, normally, the project allows the missionary to remain in the desired place long enough for the church to emerge. Also, the project provides identity and credibility to those who work in it. And finally, it provides opportunities, direct and indirect, to establish relationships with people both connected to the project and to the place in general. For all these reasons, a project plays a very important role in the establishment of a church in a pioneer area, in addition to its intrinsic value for the benefit of those for whom it is intended.

Likewise, the project serves the needs of the national population who, sensing the potential benefits, have requested such a project or action. In the best cases, they felt the need, negotiated on an equal footing with the worker and their organization, and together they designed the parameters of the project, each contributing a distinctive part. In this context, the missionary becomes an honorable guest, appreciated by the host society.

If a church already exists in the area, the project helps to demonstrate and reinforce the church identity in the community, whether positive or negative.

9. Gender

In our research and analysis, we have also highlighted the importance of issues related to gender with regard to church, gospel, and mission, especially in Muslim contexts.[13] The churches and projects we analyzed were, for the most part, lacking in a correct biblical understanding of such matters. Perhaps the only exception, and that only partial, has been the training projects in La Joya and the Spanish Center in Uzbekistan. However, both projects did not *consciously* address gender issues, nor did they advance discovering and experimenting ways of communicating the truths of the gospel regarding the position, dignity, and

---

[13] Our observations and comments are limited to issues such as how men and women relate to each other within the church, family, and society; for example, if they are together or separated during meetings, and roles that might be reserved for men.

role of women in Muslim contexts. They merely copied models that we take for granted in the West: women are worthy of education and respectful treatment. True, this is a first step, but much more could have been done.

Although women make up fifty-two percent of Iberoamerican evangelical missionaries, it seems that the gospel has not yet become good news for women, especially Muslim women. Let us note that the Latin *macho* background, both in society and in the church, has not helped in enabling helpful critical reflection on this subject. Although there are publications in English on this topic, there is an absence of published materials in Spanish or Portuguese on the topic of gender and Islam from a missionary perspective.

10. Projects: Help or Hindrance?

This question reflects the simplistic way in which churches and sending structures in Iberoamerica tend to consider this issue. It seems that utilitarianism has invaded all, or a large part, of recent Latin American evangelical missionary thinking. Too often, behind the search for "fruitful practices" hides an eagerness for "many visible results."

Some of our respondents have mentioned a negative relationship between project and evangelism. It seems that, in Turkey, the suspicion that all social aid is a gesture of proselytism has led to a reduction in the activity of both Christian and Muslim social work organizations and, on the contrary, to an increase in the social action of political parties whose campaigning is not frowned upon. As noted in Chapter 10, Christian emergency aid in the wake of the 1999 earthquake delayed the progress of the pioneer church in the area by ten years. It should be noted that this does not mean that social work cannot be carried out in Turkey, but rather that circumstances make it advisable to disassociate it from the church or evangelism. The social reality itself conditions the policy: the law does not allow the registration of foreign NGOs, although national organizations can operate normally.

Under different circumstances, it seems that for a few years some leaders of PMI, mainly in North Africa, discouraged open evangelism and discipleship by those missionaries who were involved in projects. Between the years 1997 to 2000, this generated tensions and the clear perception that the project did not contribute, and sometimes hindered, the formation of churches; this tendency has been corrected by the mission agency.

However, our research has shown that in most cases the projects contribute favorably to the establishment of new churches in pioneer Muslim contexts. We have already argued that a project facilitates the extended stay of missionary personnel, helps to define a new identity for them, is a training channel for national personnel and beneficiaries, and especially where there is a measure of tolerance or freedom, contributes to the public image of the church and how it fits in the community.

Even so, one of the cases studied, Keru Barkeel, seems to point to the fact that too much proximity is neither beneficial for the project nor for the church, at least in the Sahel.

Questions for Reflection and Discussion

1. Consider your own church in terms of its vitality, visibility, and age. What insights can you draw?
2. What is your own identity? What connection do the people around you see between your identity and your church or your faith in Jesus Christ?
3. What is the identity of the church you are part of? What strong or weak points can you identify related to this identity? How would you improve, or draw out the potential of your church and its identity?
4. If you are a missionary serving among Muslims, what caught your attention in this chapter? What ideas did you find to be accurate? Which raised questions in your mind? What would you suggest or add to the discussion?

For Further Reading

Bailey, Kenneth E. "Arabic-speaking Christianity: A Glorious Past and a Challenging Present" Lecture, first delivered at the Middle Eastern Presbyterian Caucus Banquet at the 216th General Assembly of the Presbyterian Church (USA), Richmond, Vir., June 29, 2004. http://www.pcusa.org/media/uploads/worldmission/pdfs/arabic_speaking_christianity_rev_dr_kenneth_e_bailey.pdf.

Ebin, Victoria. "International Networks of Trading Diaspora: The Mourides of Senegal Abroad." In *La Ville à Guichets Fermés*, ed. Philippe Antoine and Abdoulaye Bara Diop, 323-36. Dakar: and Future." In *Middle Eastern Presbyterian Caucus Banquet*, 1-11. Richmond, Vir.: 2004. IFAN/ORSTOM, 1995. http://horizon.documentation.ird.fr/exl-doc/pleins_textes/pleins_textes_7/carton01/010004580.pdf.

Internet Movie Database. "Kashf: The Lifting of the Veil." IMDb, 2008. http://www.imdb.com/title/tt1253580/.

Jenkins, Philip. *The Lost History of Christianity: The Thousand-Year Golden Age of the Church in the Middle East, Africa, and Asia – and How It Died.* New York: Harper One, 2008.

Stark, Rodney. *The Rise of Christianity: How the Obscure, Marginal Jesus Movement Became the Dominant Religious Force in the Western World in a Few Centuries*. San Francisco: HarperSanFrancisco, 1997.

Taylor, William D., Antonia Van der Meer, and Reg Reimer. *Sorrow and Blood: Christian Mission in Contexts of Suffering, Persecution, and Martyrdom*. Pasadena: William Carey Library, 2012.

Walls, Andrew F. "The Mission of the Church Today in the Light of Global History." *Word & World* XX, no. 1 (2000): 5. http://wordandworld.luthersem.edu/content/pdfs/20-1_20th_Century/20-1_Walls.pdf.

PART THREE

Conclusions and Missiological Implications

In the first part of this book, we dealt with the theoretical foundations of integral mission and development. In the second part, we described the details and contexts of the projects and churches and analyzed the relationships between them. In this third part, we take on a critical and constructive mode.

In this part, we will think critically about the Bible and development as we propose a theology and an alternative model of mission and development that we have called *Development-Salaam*.

12. The Biblical Perspective

At the dawn of humanity, relations between two brothers deteriorated to such an extent that one killed the other. Abel was a shepherd and Cain a farmer. What happened? Did things get out of hand for Cain during the quarrel? Could it be that he killed his brother by accident? Unfortunately, this was not the case. Both already knew what death was and how to produce it: quite a few lambs had already been slaughtered to make garments out of their skins. However, several events are striking in the biblical account. The first is God's conversation with Cain, a conversation that begins with a cautionary tone. Despite the fratricide, the dialogue between God and Cain is not broken off; they continue to talk – an incentive for us to not hastily break off communication with those who have offended or harmed us. Cain then goes away, but God preserves his life so that he can continue to live in society.

The Genesis account tells how Cain founded a family, had children, and built a city (Gen. 4:17). This fact has many implications for us. It is the second event that catches our attention: human beings are social; they like to live in community. A city or a village implies a certain number of families, who reside in the same place.

The biblical story provides us with only the minimum brushstrokes to lead us to its narrative objectives. From the account, we deduce that the list of names is partial, that between the lines it must have included quite a few women. We also note the passage of years, from one generation to the next.

Suddenly, the story takes an important qualitative leap: professions and arts appear. Jabal dedicated himself to making tents and raising cattle. He was a nomad who followed his flocks in search of pastures. By contrast, his brother Jubal was an artist. What? We would have assumed that life would revolve around production and survival, but the story takes us in a different direction. From an early age, there are people who appreciate music and art and dedicate themselves to it. Likewise, the story introduces us to the blacksmith Tubal Cain: a craftsman who combined artistic skills with smelting techniques. These three protagonists have names, they are specific people whose ancestry is provided. The third event is professional and artistic development. Humans, from very early on, manifested gifts for innovation and progress.

Linking these three events, we can draw initial theological reflections on development. God communicates with human beings; there is dialogue. Human beings like to form groups and build cities. Likewise, the emergence of professions and technical skills highlights the uniqueness of the individual and their gifts. Together, these factors speak of development. Therefore, God's creation is to be understood as a starting point. It can be enriched by the individual and collective gifts and abilities of persons made in the image of God, the creator. This is an important theological statement.

What should be the fundamental pillars of a theology of development? In this chapter, we will briefly consider some events and teachings from the Old and New Testament that will help us in our objective: to provide some initial ideas that contribute to a biblical theology of Development-Salaam.

Theology of Development

It would be very desirable to have a theology of development updated to the circumstances of the early twenty-first century. This should be a theology of development and well-being that would point to the new situations of globalization, multilateralism, post-colonialism, and the tendency towards a neo-liberal economy, among other factors. Unfortunately, since the 1980s, very little progress has been made on the issue of the theology of development. This is doubly true on the evangelical side of the Christian spectrum.

A theological analysis of the concept of development in the Bible must start from an exhaustive biblical study, focusing on the exegesis of all the texts related to development and social welfare. It must also enter into critical dialogue with the social, political, and economic disciplines that analyze current realities. Moreover, in the vision of the Global South, theology must dialogue not only with academia but also with praxis.

However, an exhaustive biblical study is far beyond the scope of this book, which represents a multidisciplinary and interdisciplinary approach, with a missiological focus. In the future, it will be the task of specialists in each of the disciplines involved: biblical scholars, economists, sociologists, historians, and theologians.

Initial Ideas

What we intend to do in this book is to advance some *initial ideas* regarding a theology of Development-Salaam. We define initial ideas as a first approximation of the foundational aspects of such a theology, still imprecise and needing development. These ideas are like the thick strokes of the painter's brush on a canvas that is just beginning to take shape. They are initial ideas because they intend to highlight an overall vision and the relationship between the various parts or themes. Expressed negatively, these initial ideas are the opposite of a *magnum opus* that would discuss all the themes and all the details in an exhaustive and masterly manner, in a discipline that is already mature. The Iberoamerican non-proselytizing development in Muslim lands that contributes to the establishment of Christian churches is far from being a mature discipline. In fact, it is just taking its first steps.

Hence, our purpose will be to attempt to give a bird's eye view of the social ideal that we perceive in the pages of the Bible. It will be a long road ahead to refine exegetically and hermeneutically that ideal, as well as to find practical ways to bring that ideal closer to the socio-ecclesial context of faith communities in Muslim contexts.

1. Old Testament

The Eyes of a Development Worker

Naturally, the eyes of development workers – those who have made development their profession or lifestyle, including social workers, some missionaries, and international aid workers – are particularly drawn to certain themes and stories from the Old Testament that evoke everyday situations for them. Reading the story of creation and the first advances of humanity through the eyes of a development worker raises important questions. Issues of culture, social relations, stratification of society, and environmental values, immediately come to mind. God is presented as a project manager. The creation story is structured in phases, just like a development project. And in each new creative act, God takes the time to stop, look at the completed, reason, evaluate and measure. "And God saw that it was good [...] that it was very good" (Gen. 1: 10, 12, 18, 21, 25 and 31).

Similarly, the creation account presents God as a creative artist and as a social regulator, among other roles. In these chapters, evil, sin, murder, and imperialism soon appear. Considering that Cain is presented as the first founder of a city and his descendants the fathers of extensive animal husbandry, metallurgy, and the musical and poetic arts also raises questions. One cannot but wonder: Is civilization, progress, and technological and cultural development the exclusive or characteristic heritage of the ungodly lineage? However, Cain is a model of a person reintegrated by God himself into society. That is to say, God did not try to prevent or limit the expansion of the descendants of Cain.

What stands out to us in this story, and in keeping with the example of the project-managing God, is that an aspect of the image of God in human beings is drawn out, their capacity for the development, fullness, or expansion of creation. We note that development for good implies the joining of forces and skills to build cities, forms of animal husbandry and metallurgy, and social rules of market and urban planning, as well as art. Paradoxically, the opposite is also true. Destruction, misuse of resources and intentional wickedness manifest themselves, not only on the personal level, but also on the collective, structural, and ecological levels.

Development workers also ask themselves: what is the concept of poverty and who is the poor person in the Old Testament? Alfonso Ropero notes that "The

Old Testament does not know the concept of 'poverty' as such, but only the poor, unfortunate, disinherited, weak, humble man, for whose description it uses seven Hebrew terms." Together with William Vine, he helps us see that the most important are three, whose respective meanings are as follows:

> **aní,** (H6041), "poor, weak, afflicted, depressed," whose root would have as its original meaning "to be stooped, humiliated, overwhelmed"; pl. *anawim*, occurs about one hundred and five times in the Old Testament.[1] This noun is frequently used in synonymous parallelism with *'ebyon* ("needy") and/or *dal* ("poor"). It differs from both in emphasizing some kind of disability or distress. A hired servant as one who is in a lower (oppressive) social and material condition is described both as an *'ebyon* and *'ani.*[2]
>
> **ebyôn**, (H34), "needy (person)." Biblical Hebrew attests it about 60 times, (33 times in the Psalms alone) and in all periods. This noun refers, first, to someone who is poor in a material sense. Such a one may have lost the land of his inheritance.[3]
>
> **dal**, (H1800), "one who is low, poor, reduced, helpless, weak." This noun also appears in Ugaritic. It occurs in biblical Hebrew about 47 times and in all periods. The *dallim* constituted the middle class of Israel – those who were physically deprived (in the ancient world the majority of people were poor). For example, the *dallim* may be viewed as the opposite of the rich (Ex. 30:15; cf. Ruth 3:10; Prov. 10:15). In addition, the word may connote social poverty or lowliness. As such, *dal* describes those who are the counterparts of the great: "Ye shall do no unrighteousness in judgment: thou shalt not respect the person of the poor, nor honor the person of the mighty: but in righteousness shalt thou judge thy neighbor" (Lev. 19:15; cf. Amos 2:7).[4]

It is important to note that, according to the image that the Old Testament gives us of the Israelites, during their period of slavery in Egypt they could in no way be considered rich or well-to-do. However, when they left Egypt, they experienced a completely different kind of poverty. They came out materially rich because their Egyptian neighbors gave them gold, silver, and clothing (Ex. 12:35-36; 2:21-22; cf. Gen. 15:14 and Ps. 105:37), but they became completely dependent for basic sustenance: food and drink, as well as protection from the scorching sun and the nightly cold of the desert. Although they possessed material wealth, they were utterly needy and vulnerable in essentials: that is, they were poor.

---

[1] Alfonso Ropero Berzosa, "Pobre-Pobreza," in *Gran Diccionario Enciclopédico de la Biblia* (Viladecavalls, Barcelona: CLIE, 2013). Trans. D. Greenlee.
[2] William E. Vine, Merrill F Unger, and William White, "Poor/Needy," in *Vine's Complete Expository Dictionary of Old and New Testament Words: With Topical Index* (Nashville: Nelson, 1996).
[3] Vine, Unger, and White, "ebyon."
[4] Vine, Unger, and White, "dal."

Following that same line of thought, the opposite of the poor and vulnerable is not necessarily the rich or affluent, at least not in the biblical social ideal. The ideal is to have enough and enjoy it with contentment. The ideal that the prophets dream of and preach is: "Everyone will sit under their own vine and under their own fig tree, and no one will make them afraid, for the LORD Almighty has spoken" (Mic. 4:4; cf. Zech. 3:10).[5] They are the "poor of the Lord," the "lowly of the earth" as defined in Zephaniah 2 and 3.

At the same time, some of the social and economic institutions of ancient Israel deeply appeal to development workers: the biblical concepts of land ownership, the equitable distribution of land in the division of tribes, the periodic remission of debts, the framework of protection for vulnerable people (widows, orphans, foreigners, day laborers), and so on. Even the resolute defense and positioning of God himself by and for the poor is a theme prompting deep reflection by those who have made social cooperation and development the object of their lives.

The most important institution for our study is the Jubilee and the remission of debts every seventh year.

> **Yobel**, (H3104) "blowing of the horn." The Septuagint usually translates this as "year of remission" or simply "remission" [...] The Jubilee year was announced with a trumpet blast, from which its name was derived. It is not mentioned in the book of Deuteronomy, and the only reference in the Pentateuch, apart from Lev. 25:1-55, is Num. 36:4.[6]

However, this is not a simple or completely clear subject. The Spanish-language *Nuevo Comentario Bíblico Siglo Veintiuno* [New Twenty-first Century Bible Commentary] comments on Leviticus 25 that,

> After chapter 19, chapter 25 has probably been the most influential chapter of Leviticus, [...] It is a complex chapter, in which three distinct economic practices have been brought together, along with parenthetical sections and exceptional clauses. These are: the sabbatical year (seventh); the Year of Jubilee (fiftieth); and redemptive procedures (at any time).[7]

Indeed, everyone was equally included in both practices of the Jubilee: rich and poor, men and women, urban and rural dwellers.

---

[5] The term, which is also used in 1 Kings 4:25 to describe the situation of the majority of the people in Solomon's time, may well be generic and written from the self-interested point of view of the established power. Even so, it reflects the Hebrew social ideal.

[6] Alfonso Ropero Berzosa, "Jubileo" in *Gran Diccionario Enciclopédico de la Biblia* (Viladecavalls, Barcelona: CLIE, 2013). Trans. D. Greenlee.

[7] James Bartley, José Luis Martínez, and Rubén O. Zorzoli, eds., *Nuevo Comentario Bíblico: Siglo Veintiuno*, 1st Spanish ed., eSword (El Paso: Casa Bautista de Publicaciones, 1999), s.v. Lev. 25.

The Socio-Religious Ideal

In the introduction to this section, we mentioned that our purpose was to discover the social ideal of the Old and New Testament communities of faith. Scientific studies of religion are always confronted with the problem of the representation of religion. An example of a current question might be: what is "true Islam" and where can it be seen to be fully practised?

In the case of early Israelite religion, the questions are complicated by the fact that the object of study is not observable today, it covers a very long time period, and because we lack sources of verifiable data. That is why we usually formulate the questions by dividing them according to more or less standardized epochs: the Patriarchs, the pre-monarchic era, the early and late monarchy of Israel, the Exile, and the Christian church of the first two centuries, to name a few.

The question we seek to answer in this chapter is what concept of development, of social and personal well-being, were held by the communities of faith reflected in the Old and New Testaments? Based on our answer, we intend to elaborate a theology of development.

From a purely empirical point of view, however, the answer is almost impossible to find. There is no sufficiently accurate and comprehensive answer covering such a variety of people, societies, and contexts to cover the entire time period described in the Old and New Testaments. Even if we were to formulate a partial answer, say at the time of the Exile for example, we would not be able to affirm that such a belief and conduct in development issues would have been believed and applied by all Israelites in that historical period. Surely, as in any society, there were variations, particular situations, dissident people, more progressive and more conservative sectors (to call them somehow) that did not subscribe to the formulated answer. A valid, verifiable, unique answer is impossible. That is why we have divergent approaches and theories about this concept of development.

For the purpose of this study, we have followed the path marked by the American anthropologist Clifford J. Geertz, former professor at Princeton, and representative of symbolic and interpretative anthropology. In his comparative study of Indonesian and Moroccan Islam, Geertz relies on the mythical character typical of each of these countries, to represent the whole of both religions.

Geertz draws on two historical figures, Sunan Kaliyaga of Indonesia, and Sidi Lahsen Lyusi of Morocco, who he uses as metaphors for the "true spirituality" of both peoples in the present time, an attempt to characterize the classical religious styles in Morocco and Indonesia.

> These men are metaphors. Whatever they originally were or did as actual persons has long since been dissolved into an image of what Indonesians or Moroccans regard to be true spirituality.[8]

To answer the question of what the typical spirituality of a country is – a question impossible to answer fully – Geertz turns to the symbol, to the character that embodies the religious ideal:

> What sacred symbols do for those to whom they are sacred is to formulate an image of the world's construction and a program for human conduct that are mere reflexes of one another.[9]

This is precisely the purpose of this chapter: to present an "image of the structure of the world" and a "program of conduct" that guided the faith and practice of the men and women reflected in the pages of the Old and New Testaments. Since we have not resorted to a historical personage turned legend, instead of resorting to symbol, we have preferred to call it the socio-religious ideal. This ideal is in no way intended to represent the actual behavior, as if it were a proven fact, of the inhabitants of ancient Israel and the Christians of the first centuries. What it does constitute is the ideal, or the program for human conduct as Geertz sometimes called it, that those ancient societies regarded as just and desirable.

Thus, the *Socio-Economic Characteristics* that we will outline below should be seen in that perspective: they represent the ideal that guided the social consciousness of the people in general. Of course, the daily reality must have varied considerably from this ideal, as we will see a little later.

Socio-Economic Characteristics

The socio-economic conditions of ancient Israel could be summarized as follows. At this point we will skip the nuances, the different historical epochs, as well as the struggles to establish or achieve these characteristics. We will deal with those issues later, but for now we are interested in the big picture. The mere fact that a people dream of these characteristics, and even more, that they put them in writing in their laws and in their sacred book, is in itself a fact to be highlighted.

- Israelite society was egalitarian, horizontal, with a low degree of hierarchy, in contrast to the surrounding societies that were feudal, monarchical, or imperial or with large landowners. The Israelites were organized by families, clans, and tribes.
- They did not own the land, they managed it. The land was God's property and its fertility, the rains, and good harvests were linked to obedience.

---

[8] Clifford Geertz, *Islam Observed: Religious Development in Morocco and Indonesia* (Chicago: University of Chicago, 2008), 25.

[9] Geertz, *Islam Observed*, 97.

- The economic and social system was aimed at the social health and viability of the smaller social units, the families and clans, rather than favoring the already wealthy. Family solidarity ties and the initial equitable distribution of land contributed to this objective.
- The economic system was one of *decreasing inflation*. The cycle of remission of debts every seventh year and the Jubilee every fifty years decreased – not increased – the value of the land. The large debts that a family could incur were not passed on to the next generation: every fifty years, the family could start over with sufficient capital (land and inheritance) for a decent life. Far from profiting from the misfortune of others, the needy were to be helped with gifts and interest-free loans.
- Justice was not the exclusive domain of the rulers, kings and the heads of clans and tribes, but of God through the priests. It was nearby, decentralized, and direct. A justice that was not "a question of the impartiality with which a formal standard of justice is applied, but of rightly satisfying those claims which are brought forward as a result of particular concrete relationships: justice is no abstract thing."[10]
- Responsibility for the weak was borne by all the people, each caring for those closest to them, in a system that (1) welcomed the stranger and the fugitive and (2) provided regularly for their needs through triennial tithes and the practice of leaving part of the crops and fruits in the field. The whole society was oriented to sharing, just as God shared his blessings, something seen in the laws on gleaning (Lev. 19:9-10).
- The land was not to be depleted; animals were not to be exploited. The land was to rest fully every seventh year. One day in seven was to be a day of joy and rest for all people, including foreigners, day laborers, and slaves. Animals were entitled to the same weekly rest as people.
- The king was not to accumulate power, wealth, horses, or wives. He was subject to rebuke by prophets and priests. One of his main functions was to be the guarantor of justice and equity for all.

Drawing these characteristics together helps us to perceive the ultimate purpose of these laws and practices and the economic concept that underlies the entire Bible. In the first place, it arose from the founding experience of the exodus from Egypt. In stark contrast to their slavery under the Egyptians, the Israelites are prompted by God to build a luxurious and artistic tabernacle; their response in voluntary contributions is an act of generosity and joy. Ropero emphasizes: "The voluntary nature of the work, the individual's role based on skill or talent, and the joy provided through collaboration: 'all generous of heart' (Ex. 35:5)."[11]

---

[10] Walther Eichrodt, *Theology of the Old Testament*, trans. John Baker, vol. 1 (London: SCM, 1983), 241.

[11] Alfonso Ropero Berzosa, "Economía," in *Gran Diccionario Enciclopédico de la Biblia* (Viladecavalls, Barcelona: CLIE, 2013). Trans. D. Greenlee.

Further, the sum of these characteristics clearly points to the eradication of systemic or radical poverty. "However, there need be no poor people among you, for in the land the Lord your God is giving you to possess as your inheritance, he will richly bless you" (Deut. 15:4). As Ropero observes, "The fundamental principle of these Israelite economic laws is found in a high moral concept: '[…] but love your neighbor as yourself' (Lev. 19:18)."[12]

Finally, the confession of faith, repeated again and again by Israel, indicates that God has led his people to a land and a style of society that the eyes of a development worker would describe as one of socio-economic well-being. In poetic language, the biblical text describes such a situation as "a land flowing with milk and honey" (Ex. 33:3; Lev. 20:24; Num. 13:27, etc.).

A Model Society

It is difficult to carry out a complex task or construct complex objects when you have never seen them, when you have never even dreamed of them, when they are governed by principles that do not come naturally to you. In those circumstances, a model helps a lot. When Moses had to build a tabernacle, the Bible tells us that God took him up the mountain, showed him a model, and told him to "make them according to the pattern (the design) shown you on the mountain" (Ex. 25:40, Heb. 8:5).

Similarly, Israel was to be a model, an example of society for the other nations. The divine choice of Israel was not motivated by favoritism or exclusivity, but to serve as a blessing and a beacon to all peoples:

> [The] nations […] will hear about all these decrees and say, "Surely this great nation is a wise and understanding people." What other nation is so great as to have their gods near them the way the Lord our God is near us whenever we pray to him? And what other nation is so great as to have such righteous decrees and laws as this body of laws I am setting before you today? (Deut. 4:6-8)

The whole life of Israel – themselves, their laws, the structure of their society, their faith, and their worship – was a model for the nations and a magnet drawing them toward God, who was the very center of Israel's life.

Walter Brueggemann, the North American Lutheran theologian, delves further into the concept of mediation. God is mediated in (becomes visible to others through) Israel. This concept, mediation, helps us to understand a relationship that is difficult to grasp, because it is "characterized at the same time by incommensurability and mutuality"[13] between God and Israel. In a way, God makes himself present (becomes visible) in Israel, and at the same time is very distant (different) from it. And this mediation, which takes place in a specific *time-space-history*, has clear social repercussions.

---

[12] Ropero Berzosa, "Economía,".

[13] Walter Brueggemann, *Theology of the Old Testament: Testimony, Dispute, Advocacy* (Minneapolis: Fortress Press, 2005), chap. 19.

The Reality: Epochs and Social Crises

Of course, Israel did not live consistently with its ideals. In fact, some of these were rarely fully applied. The age of the monarchy, marked by splendor and political development, represented a notorious departure from the ideal. The prophets raised their voices, acting as the collective conscience of the people and calling them back to the ideal, precisely because it was not being fulfilled. This discourse of return to the ideal and projection towards an envisioned ethical and solidary future, in accordance with the aforementioned ideal, is a fundamental part of the prophetic clamor.

Through the eyes of development workers, at least two great social crises can be discerned in the Old Testament. These are understood as moments of evident social fracture between the opulence of the few and the excessive poverty of the many. The splendor of the monarchy brought with it an inevitable fiscal burden (1Kings 4; 5:13ff; 12:4, 18) and a social class of officials. It was inevitable that time would consolidate an important social division: on one side the high officials and landowners, and on the other the immense majority of day laborers and poor rural inhabitants.

We glimpse this first social crisis in the denunciations of the early prophets. German Old Testament scholar Rainer Albertz thinks that in the monarchic era "social solidarity had been shattered" and that a wealthy urban class emerged, the landowners and moneylenders, who lived off the rents of their debtors who had become slaves. This social crisis was also clothed in religiosity, and that is why Amos, Micah, and Isaiah decisively reject the display of wealth in the liturgical celebrations of the ruling class, which they do not hesitate to describe as rebellion against Yahweh (Amos 4:4).[14]

Another social crisis can be seen in the fifth century BC, in the middle of the post-Exilic period, when the practice of social solidarity ceased to be a collective responsibility and became the decision of the individual. The episode recorded in Nehemiah 5 is clear proof of this, when the indebted Israelites cried out against the nobles and rulers. Already in the time of the Exile, an individual spirituality had begun to take shape, based on the Torah, which was to be consolidated in the two following centuries. The righteous, those who do practice their social commitment as a testimony of their adherence to the righteous God of the Covenant, are now the "true Israel."

Commenting on Isaiah 29:17-24, Albertz notes:

> They, the poor and oppressed, claimed for themselves that they were the real pious (*anawim*, v.19), the real Israel (v.22). We can see how here a special piety of the

[14] Rainer Albertz, *A History of Israelite Religion in the Old Testament Period*, vol. 2 (Louisville: John Knox Press, 1994), 1:322. See also Isaiah 5:8.

> poor developed from the social crisis; it was to be an important strand of Yahweh religion from early Judaism up to the New Testament.[15]

The Levites also played an important part in this lived-out collective memory of the socio-religious ideal, as we will explore shortly. The many crises and reforms in Israel's history, both political and religious, testify to how far from the ideal daily life could be. However, the simple fact of having a socio-religious ideal constituted a strong social impulse.

Disagreement and Divergent Visions

Through the eyes of development workers, we may also perceive in the Old Testament tensions and power struggles between groups competing to impose their vision of life and religion. Some consider the Levites as being a part of the poorer classes, and especially so following the centralization of worship in a single sanctuary and its subsequent destruction with the Babylonian invasion. Gerhard Von Rad, one of the fathers of Old Testament theology, always mentions them by adding the qualifier "landless" in parentheses, while Albertz identifies them unequivocally among the poor. The fact that they were poor and among the architects of the Deuteronomistic reform sheds light on the strong emphasis on the solidarity of that reform.

On the other hand, it is impossible to overlook the struggles between, on the one hand, the ruling class and the official religious structures and, on the other hand, the prophets. The religious reformers of the fifth and fourth centuries BCE are another of the pressure groups often noted in the text by development workers. Norman Gottwald, from his vision as a biblical scholar and Marxist activist, reads the entire Old Testament text in the light of these class struggles. For him, "biblical theology becomes 'historical-dialectical' biblical sociology."[16] Some of the "social conquests" may have been due to these struggles and pressures:

> [T]he priestly theologians, too, were concerned to abolish the social tensions and achieve more solidarity in society in order to benefit the impoverished small farmers. If they were the ones who attempted to develop the Deuteronomic reform model of a regular remission of debts (*shemitta*, Deut. 15:1-11) into a detailed social programme (Year of Jubilee, Lev. 25:8ff.), then it becomes clear how at this point there was more than a chance overlapping of interests. Rather, in social commitment to the protection of the weak groups in the population the concerns of the leading priests and laity came together in a common political aim.[17]

---

[15] Albertz, *History* 2:506.

[16] Norman K Gottwald, *The Tribes of Yahweh: A Sociology of Religion of Liberated Israel, 1250-1050 B.C.E.* (Maryknoll and London: Orbis and SCM, 1979), 47.

[17] Albertz, *History of Israelite Religion*, 1994, 2:481.

Hence Brueggemann, who focuses the understanding of Old Testament theology on what he terms the rhetorical enterprise of the text, clarifies that seeing these struggles:

> Our interpretive work is to attend to the way in which these several bids live in tension with each other and occasionally prevail over each other. Interpretation, in the end, cannot overcome the irascibly pluralistic character of the text.[18]

For development workers, weighing the various competing forces present in a development project is common practice. It is a routine part of stakeholder identification. Much of the success of a project depends on the wise management of these various divergent or even competing forces and interests.

In these paragraphs, we have described socio-economic characteristics that represented a civic-religious ideal, a desired style of spirituality. We have also seen that this ideal was shaped by time and power struggles. From these insights, two questions arise. First, it is worth asking whether these socio-economic characteristics were ever put into practice. This is a pertinent question and one that many have asked. Albertz answers by saying:

> The social legislation of Deuteronomy has constantly been branded as utopian and its practicability has been doubted. On this it should be commented that no reform movement, certainly not one with so strong a religious motivation as that of Deuteronomy, is conceivable without an utopia. Here indeed, no less was being undertaken than the attempt to break into and change an already relatively complicated social order in the light of the impulse towards liberation which was intrinsic to the religion of Yahweh in its beginnings. At no other time in Israelite history did the religion of Yahweh develop such social power as in this movement.[19]

Thus, it is reasonable to accept that the socio-economic characteristics described above were put into practice, albeit for relatively short or intermittent periods of time. Second, however, a reflection on the uniqueness of the Israelite social ideal can lead to discouragement or confusion. When we ask ourselves how we might put this into practice, or at least come close to that kind of society which would be a model for others, it seems that the gap is too great, that the gulf with today's society and circumstances is impossible to bridge.

Christopher Wright takes an important first step in the process of applying the Bible to the present. Considering Israel as a paradigm, his intent is to move beyond just looking for principles that can be applied in our present circumstances. Although his proposal falls short of the mark and does not dispel our discouragement over the absence of a robust, current theology of

---

[18] Brueggemann, *Theology of the Old Testament*, 126.

[19] Rainer Albertz, *A History of Israelite Religion in the Old Testament Period*, vol. 1 (Louisville: John Knox Press, 1994), 223.

development, we value his vital contribution and will build on it in applying these principles in the context of development projects.

Four Principles

In this chapter, we have been attempting to explore a theology of and alternative model of mission as seen through the eyes of development workers. The four principles Wright draws from the foundational chapters of Genesis can serve in the context of development projects as practical, easily communicable, and transferable. He finds in the creation story: resources for all, the right and duty to work, expectations of growth and trade, and equitable enjoyment of benefits.[20]

Shared access to natural resources: Land and natural resources are gifts that God has granted not only to a few, but to all human beings. In this divinely established order, there is room for private property, but the right of use granted to all is of higher standing than the right of possession of a few.

The right and responsibility of work: Work is also God's gift. God is productive; God works. In fact, work is an inherent part of productivity and human nature. It follows that work is a responsibility, as is allowing all human beings the possibility to work and thus fulfill their purpose.

The expectation of growth and trade: "Be fruitful and multiply" applies to all humans and all their means of production. God has provided sufficient resources for all humanity, as well as sufficient intelligence to distribute those resources equitably. Exchange and trade between peoples and areas of the planet with different resources are part of God's will. The divine purpose is not *accumulation* but *sufficiency* for all. This principle was later complemented with the regulation of the land (the land belongs to God, it returns to its owners every fifty years, and therefore speculation is eliminated).

Fair sharing of the product of economic activity: The responsibility to be productive goes hand in hand with the right to consume or equitably enjoy the fruits of our labor. This right is a fundamental part of *shalom*, the biblical concept of well-being. Denying the poor the possibility of enjoying their labor, or the employer keeping most of the profit by paying unfair wages to his workers, is characteristic of demonic systems. Justice, compassion, and generosity should guide distribution, attending to the welfare of all. And this is how God works, he who "causes his sun to rise on the evil and the good" (Matt. 5:45), who has established his covenant with the earth and its means of production (Gen. 8:22), and who distributes to all with liberality (Jas. 1:5, 17).

These same principles later govern the socio-economic life of the people in the Old Testament and in their eschatological hope. The biblical account is very practical and balanced. On the one hand, it establishes the ideal: "However, there need be no poor people among you, for in the land the Lord your God is giving

[20] Christopher J. H. Wright, *Old Testament Ethics for the People of God* (Downers Grove: InterVarsity, 2004), chap. 5; *God's People in God's Land: Family, Land, and Property in the Old Testament* (Grand Rapids: Eerdmans, 1990).

you to possess as your inheritance, he will richly bless you, if only you fully obey the Lord your God and are careful to follow all these commands I am giving you today." (Deut. 15:4-5). And yet, the same chapter acknowledges that poverty will not be completely eradicated: "There will always be poor people in the land. Therefore, I command you to be openhanded toward your fellow Israelites who are poor and needy in your land" (Deut. 15:11).

Hope is also clear. In the messianic kingdom, poverty will be unknown. In the last days, "They will beat their swords into iron plows and their spears into pruning tools. […] All will sit underneath their own grapevines, under their own fig trees. There will be no one to terrify them; for the mouth of the Lord of heavenly forces has spoken" (Mic. 4:3,4 CEB, see also Isa. 2:1-4); "I'm creating Jerusalem as a joy, and her people as a source of gladness. […] they will build houses and live in them, […] my chosen will make full use of their handiwork" (Isa. 65:21,22 CEB). This kind of hope, of course, does not point to idleness but to work and enjoyment; to a time of joy, harmony, and peace.

2. New Testament

Let us now turn to the New Testament, which presents a very different picture. The model is no longer a nation or society but a network of communities, a non-governmental solution to eradicate poverty and a new concept of global solidarity.

The New Testament World

Touching on them only briefly, let us consider some general characteristics of the societies of Palestine and the Mediterranean world. It was these characteristics that made up the environment in which the concepts and practice of development, welfare, and social solidarity of the first Christian communities developed.

Pax Romana: The two centuries between the first century BCE and the second century CE were turbulent times. Broadly speaking, Rome already ruled the entire Mediterranean and controlled all trade, but the numerous struggles and revolts on land and with pirates at sea complicated the political situation of the Republic, which was already in decline. General Pompey put down the revolt of Spartacus' slaves in 71 BCE and later put down the rebellion of Mithridates of Pontus in 65 BCE by incorporating Pontus and Bithynia as two Roman provinces. In the winter of 64-63 BCE, Syria and Palestine also became Roman provinces. Pompey returned to Rome laden with booty in the summer of 62 BCE.[21]

Meanwhile, Julius Caesar was consolidating his power and implementing far-reaching changes in the Republic. Octavius Augustus took advantage of these

---

[21] Johannes Leipoldt and Walter Grundmann, *El Mundo del Nuevo Testamento*, trans. Luis Gil, 2nd ed., vol. I (Madrid: Ediciones Cristiandad, 1977), 35.

changes and ruled as emperor from 27 BCE until his death in CE 14. At his death, he was deified by the Senate. Augustus was followed by Tiberius (14-37), under whom Jesus Christ grew up and lived, Caligula (37-41), Claudius (41-54) and Nero (54-58). After a year of instability, Vespasian and his sons Titus and Domitian ruled Rome with an iron fist during the years 69 to 96.

The *Pax Romana*, which began with Augustus, was based "on a system of slave exploitation, which not only and exclusively affected the slaves, but the entire population of the Empire that was not fortunate enough to belong to the elite, that is, the vast majority."[22] It was a peace imposed with blood and fire, using military violence as a tool, and whose main purpose was that taxes and goods could flow smoothly to Rome and its opulence.[23] In stark contrast to the *Pax Romana*, "the *pax evangelica* also includes reconciliation with others, [and] the mutual forgiveness of debts (Matt. 6:12)."[24]

Economy: The mainstays of the Palestinian economy were agriculture, handicrafts, and trade, according to Johannes Leipoldt and Walter Grundmann.[25] But the general situation of the country was precarious; Palestine had scant natural resources and could not supply its own needs. In the region of Galilee, large estates abounded, built on the backs of cheap and extremely vulnerable labor. However, there was not enough work for everyone and many emigrated. This was especially the fate of many sons who were not first-born, often faced with the challenge of mere subsistence. Many of these joined the ranks of the Jewish Diaspora, seeking better living conditions abroad.

Jerusalem, for its part, was in a separate situation, mainly due to the enormous economic movement centered on the Temple and pilgrimages. Beyond religion, Jerusalem was also the center of power and commerce. The city of that time is described by Bruce Malina, a former professor of New Testament at Creighton Catholic University as "the administrative, religious and market center for the towns or cities under its symbolic power."[26] Jerusalem, therefore, was home to priests, teachers, and merchants who worked in the temple, artisans and merchants of all kinds, and a small but powerful upper class composed of high temple dignitaries, politicians, and wealthy people. It was also home to many beggars, who lived on alms, this aspect of life highly regarded in the Jewish religion because of the merit it gave to the givers.

Limited goods and resources: To fully understand the economy of the New Testament world, we must keep in mind that the people of that time believed in what might fit into the concept of limited good; the concept of permanent growth of resources, so common in the West during the eighteenth to twentieth centuries,

---

[22] Ropero Berzosa, "Pobre-Pobreza GDEB." Trans. D. Greenlee.

[23] Leipoldt and Grundmann, *Mundo del Nuevo Testamento*, I:22.

[24] Ropero Berzosa, "Pobre-Pobreza GDEB."

[25] Leipoldt and Grundmann, *Mundo del Nuevo Testamento*, I:197.

[26] Bruce J. Malina, *The New Testament World: Insights from Cultural Anthropology*, 3rd ed. (Louisville: Westminster John Knox Press, 2001), 85.

was totally alien. Malina described in detail the characteristics of this way of thinking and its implications:

> The people presented in the pages of the New Testament would see their existence as determined and limited by the natural and social resources of their village, their preindustrial city, their immediate area and world both vertically and horizontally. [...] [E]xtensive areas of behavior are patterned in such a way as to suggest to one and all in that society as well as in nature – the total environment – all the desired things in life, such as land, wealth, prestige, blood, health, semen, friendship and love, manliness, honor, respect and status, power and influence, security and safety – literally all goods in life – exist in finite, limited quantity and are always in short supply.[27]

Therefore, if resources were limited and fixed, one could only increase one's possession or enjoyment by depleting the reserves of others. Thus, in the Mediterranean society of the first centuries of the Christian era, most people aspired to stability. The maintenance of the status quo was a very important social force. Since in peasant societies, all people are born with a measure of honor, regardless of their higher or lower social rank, the concern of honorable people was to preserve the honor portion of their own person (as individuals) and family. Maintained over time, this in itself constituted an increase in honor without causing harm to others.

Social relations were of two types: horizontal, governed by reciprocity, and vertical, of the patron-client type. Of course, there were always people who sought to accumulate goods, resources, or capital. However, this was frowned upon and was detrimental to the honor of those involved.

A correct understanding of the worldview of limited goods and resources becomes very important to clarify the relative concepts of poverty and wealth, as well as economic relations and the new socio-economic perspectives of the early Christian communities.

Social justice: Palestinian society was divided into three strata. On the one hand, the aristocrats, who belonged to or were related to the priestly nobility, and the high priest. They were a very small but influential and powerful group. Secondly, a wealthy class, made up of merchants and artisans, together with a part of the priests. Finally, the vast majority of the inhabitants, made up of day laborers, small farmers or herdsmen and slaves. Leipoldt and Grundmann, then Ropero, explain:

> Poverty increased in Palestine between the 1st century BC and the 1st century AD. The abusive exploitation of the country by kings and governors, as well as the wars and plundering that took place over and over again during the turbulent events of

[27] Malina, *New Testament World*, 89.

this period, contributed greatly to this fact. All this brought with it hunger and famine.[28]

> A truly high number of poor people was created by [Rome's] predatory imperial policy [...] The high standard of living and lavishness of the Roman elite [...] was fed by the hoarding of almost all surplus production, which meant that the share available to most of the population was barely enough to ensure their subsistence.[29]

Riches and Poverty in the New Testament

Various New Testament words describe the situation of poverty and need as well as the concepts of stewardship, management, and of being blessed. The Greek word *ptōchós* is the most common word used to describe severe or absolute poverty, as compared to *pénēs*, which is applied to people whose humble living conditions are dependent on their daily work:

> ***Ptochós***, [G3863] 1. Meaning.1. *ptōchós* as an adjective means "destitute," "mendicant." 2. *ptōcheúō* in the transitive means "to beg from someone," in the intransitive "to be destitute," "to lead the life of a beggar." 3. *ptōcheía* means "destitution," "begging." It is worthy of note that in distinction from *pénēs*, which refers to those who are poor and have to work for a living, the *ptōchós* group refers to the total poverty which reduces people to begging.[30]

The New Testament, however, completely redefines the concepts of poverty and wealth. Paul condenses into one sentence the entire gospel narrative regarding the example of Jesus Christ: "You know the grace of our Lord Jesus Christ. Although he was rich, he became poor (*eptócheusen*, third person singular, aorist) for your sakes, so that you could become rich through his poverty" (2 Cor. 8:9).

The collection that Paul organizes among the churches of Achaia and Macedonia is for the poor (*pénes*, economically fragile) of Jerusalem. We should not overlook this fact: Paul actively promotes this collection because he considers it particularly important:

> ***Pénēs***, [G3440] The LXX uses *pénēs* for Hebrew terms that denote the economically weak, e.g., day laborers with no patrimony of their own... In the NT, *pénēs* occurs only in 2 Cor. 9:9 (quoting Ps. 112:9). Giving to the needy is one of the good works for which God makes provision in believers.[31]

The gospel writers report how Jesus Christ constantly contrasted wealth and poverty, often using paradoxes, to completely redefine both concepts and the

---

[28] Leipoldt and Grundmann, *Mundo del Nuevo Testamento*, I:203-4.

[29] Ropero Berzosa, "Pobre-Pobreza GDEB."

[30] Ernst Bammel and Friedrich Hauck, "Ptochós," in *Theological Dictionary of the New Testament* (Grand Rapids: Eerdmans, 1964).

[31] Friedrich Hauck and Gerhard Kittel, "Pénes," in *Theological Dictionary of the New Testament*, trans. Geoffrey William Bromiley (Grand Rapids: Eerdmans, 1964).

way his disciples were to think. He says, "blessed are the poor," a shocking expression indeed:

> **Makharismós**, (N. 3108), "beatitude"; makharios (adj. 3107), "blessed, blessed", used 50 times. […] In the NT, it is Jesus Christ who pronounces the beatitudes, eight in Matthew's recension (Matt. 5:3-12) and four in Luke's (Luke 6:20-23). Matthew gives some of them a spiritual or interior meaning, while Luke gives them a more literal, material or external meaning. […] The antithesis of the beatitude is the admonition or threat, the famous "woes": "Woe to you who are now full! For you will be hungry" (Luke 6:25-26), which often, more than expressing a curse, constitute a prophetic announcement that not infrequently implies an exhortation to conversion in order to escape from evil.[32]

That is to say that these beatitudes and woes carry significant emotional force. Jesus is completely upending the concepts of happiness and security while giving them a renewed meaning as expressed to the kingdom of God. It is those who are rich in piety, purity and peace who are happy, secure for the future and authentically rich. A complete paradox!

In Luke 14, Jesus also contrasts Lazarus and the unnamed rich man; those invited to the banquet with the poor, the crippled, the lame and the blind. At the same time, He emphasizes that the poor do have something valuable to give, something of more value than the large offerings of the rich. The two *lepta* of the widow, poor by the standards of the time but rich according to Jesus' point of view (Mark 12:41), are a symbol of another way of looking at life, wealth, and poverty:

> In the parable of the great banquet, the poor are also the first to be invited to take the places of those who did not come (Luke 14:21). Lazarus, whose name literally means "God helps," is the prototype of the poor man welcomed by God (Luke 16:20, 22), while the rich man (whose name is not mentioned) who had no pity on him is the one condemned by God (cf. Luke 12:13-21).[33]

Indeed, in the New Testament there is evidence of a radical change in the way poverty and wealth are perceived. Bryant Myers rightly establishes three categories of people: the poor, the non-poor and the rich. But it is not only the concepts of poverty and wealth that are called into question by Jesus and his followers, but also the very essence of economics:

> **Oikonomia**, (Gr. 3622) from *oikos*, "household" and *nemein* "to administer," that is, "household administration." Although the etymological meaning of the term

---

[32] Antonio Cruz, "Bienaventuranza," in *Gran Diccionario Enciclopédico de la Biblia* (Viladecavalls, Barcelona: CLIE, 2013).

[33] Lothar Coenen and H.H. Esser, "Pobre," in *Diccionario Teológico del Nuevo Testamento* (Salamanca: Sígueme, 1985).

> economy means administration, especially domestic, in the NT it indicates the plan or ordering of salvation, its divine administration throughout history.[34]

But the New Testament expands the concept to refer to the task of the apostles and of every believer. That is why faithfulness is required of them, the highest standards of good praxis. Each and every one is an *oikonómos*, a steward:

> The apostle himself is an *oikonómos* in 1 Cor. 4:1: as a minister of Christ he is entrusted with the treasures of the gospel, and the first requirement is trustworthiness. Tit. 1:7 describes the bishop as God's steward, and 1 Pet. 4:10 calls on every Christian, as a recipient of a gift, to be a good steward of God's varied grace.[35]

Paul further broadens the concept by applying it to the upbuilding, the edification of the community of believers. Their task is to build, to contribute to good, to progress, to well-being. Every believer is also an *oikodoméō* (builder) in two senses:[36]

> a. An Apostolic Task. In Paul's letters *oikodomeín* is important. It denotes first an apostolic activity (2 Cor. 10:18; 12:19; 13:10). Paul may destroy when necessary, but his true work is to build up.
>
> b. A Community Task. Important also for Paul is the fact that the Spirit builds up the community. Edification for him has a charismatic and spiritual bearing. In 1 Thessalonians 5:11 we note a relation of individuals to the whole, a mutual interrelationship of individuals, and the charismatic nature of the process.[37]

This idea of building up is further seen in the word *synoikodoméō*:

> **Synoikodoméō.** [4254] This word means "to build together," passive "to be built together." In Ephesians 2:22 we do not have an imperative, nor is mutual fellowship the point. The reference is to the unity and totality of the structure in which Christ and the apostles are united with believers.[38]

Thus, administering the "ordering of salvation" is both an individual and community task focused on forming and structuring a totally different community. It is the community of the kingdom of God, a community of the end that now has come.

---

[34] Ropero Berzosa, "Economía GDEB."
[35] Otto Michel, "Oikonomía," in *Theological Dictionary of the New Testament* (Grand Rapids: Eerdmans, 1964).
[36] Otto Michel, "Oikodoméō," in *Theological Dictionary of the New Testament* (Grand Rapids: Eerdmans, 1964).
[37] Michel, "Oikonomía."
[38] Michel, "Oikonomía."

Jesus and Jubilee

It is important to note that on the occasion of his Manifesto, his programmatic statement in the synagogue of Nazareth, Jesus announces the fulfillment of the Jubilee in his ministry. It is the year of the Lord's deliverance (Luke 4:18, Is. 61:1).

We need to mention several aspects of this "Messianic Jubilee" that is fulfilled in Jesus Christ. In the first place, the radius of action of the Jubilee is widened. The beneficiaries are no longer only the Jews or those few foreigners who have taken up residence in Israelite territory. As Luke clearly recounts the story, Jesus explicitly teaches about the "year of liberation" with two shocking examples: Elijah was sent to a foreign widow, and Elisha healed a Syrian, both to the neglect of the many Israelite widows and lepers among the Jews. The aliens, the Gentiles, "the different" are now not only included among the beneficiaries of this re-defined Messianic Jubilee but are its first heirs! The shocking scope of this fact is often overlooked. Of course, Jesus' fellow citizens are outraged, but the scope goes far beyond that: it shatters all pretense of collectivism and corporatism.

This fact resonates strongly in a Muslim society, which typically is exclusive toward those who do not belong to its clan or extended family. We will touch on this later in our section on practical applications in *Islamia*. It also has much relevance for the church. A contemporary reading of the Jubilee should lead us not only to open our arms to those on the margins of society, but also to seek the welfare of people of other religions, even those with whom we have major disagreements or conflicts. The Jubilee of Jesus Christ is inclusive; it includes everyone.

Secondly, the blessings of the Old Testament Jubilee were linked to obedience. Leviticus 25, the quintessential text on the subject, makes this very clear: "Follow my decrees and be careful to obey my laws, and you will live safely in the land. Then the land will yield its fruit, and you will eat your fill and live there in safety" (Lev. 25:18,19). Likewise, detailing the blessings of obedience and the promises, the following chapter records that "'I will grant peace in the land, and you will lie down and no one will make you afraid. I will remove wild beasts from the land, and the sword will not pass through your country" (Lev. 26:6). The language of well-being, of *shalom* is evident: safe dwelling, fruitfulness of the land, abundance, and personal and social harmony. However, in announcing the new Messianic Jubilee, Jesus Christ takes upon himself the agency of blessing. He himself is their fulfillment. Obedience to the Law is no longer required to enjoy inclusion, liberation, reconciliation and rest, the characteristic fruits of the Jubilee. Calvin Tiessen writes:

> As he opens his public ministry with a proclamation of 'the year of the Lord's favour' (Lk. 4:19), Jesus profoundly reiterates and then 're-orients' the agentive principles of the jubilee narrative. The delineation between responsive blessings and cooperative blessings, which was stressed in the Levitical jubilee, is now

> removed as Jesus takes on primary agency for the attainment of both. He declares, 'The Spirit of the Lord is *on me*, for he has anointed *me* [...] He has sent *me* [...]' (Lk. 4:18 (ESV)). The covenantal contingency of obedience that was required of God's people in order for them to continue to live under the blessings of his covenant with them was declared 'fulfilled in your hearing' (Lk. 4:21).[39]

Finally, we can discern a clear link between the Jubilee and Pentecost, one of the foundational markers of the church. The outpouring of the Spirit is a sign of the fulfillment of the Jubilee, of the Kingdom of God. John Stam notes:

> Again, the Spirit is poured out, now on the body of Christ, on the day of the birth of the Church, and again the Jubilee is practised. It is very possible that the very name "Pentecost," as the fiftieth day after the Passover of Israel, was related to the Jubilee, as the fiftieth year within the century. Some have even claimed that Pentecost occurred in a Jubilee Year, but either way, Pentecost fulfilled the double promise of Isaiah 61: the Spirit was poured out on the church, and the faithful distributed their goods.[40]

The Unstoppable Kingdom

The social ideal announced through the Old Testament legislation becomes reality. The end has come. "The kingdom of God is at hand," Jesus repeats again and again. The eschatological jubilee is here. It is no longer a moral aspiration or a social ideal. It is "the foolishness of God" (1 Cor. 1:25) come true.

The first disciples undoubtedly understood it this way, and that is why Luke can affirm that there was no needy person in the community (Acts 4:34). They faced the difficulties and assumed the paradoxes-utopias of the Kingdom-Jubilee. It is in that context – the arrival, in Jesus, of the eschatological Jubilee – that the socio-economic dynamics set in motion by the first Christian communities must be understood. The description of the first Christian community cannot be read only from a social perspective, but also from an economic perspective. And the new Jubilee in Jesus Christ is the key to understand it properly. Ropero clarifies:

> This is how, following the death of Jesus, his disciples and the first Christian communities understood. [...] These disciples behave in a radically new way; what

---

[39] Calvin Tiessen, "Jubilee, Discipleship and Social Rest," *Transformation* 36, no. 2 (May 16, 2019): 113-26, https://doi.org/10.1177/0265378819837763. Emphasis in original.

[40] Juan B. Stam, "El Año de Jubileo," *Blog de Juan Stam* (blog), December 18, 2007, https://juanstam.com/posts/el-ano-de-jubileo-tres-partes. See also Harold Segura Carmona, "A Clean Slate!," *Transformation* 36, no. 2 (May 16, 2019): 135-40, https://doi.org/10.1177/0265378819839605.

> is new is the understanding of the community as God's new society and a sign of new social possibilities brought about by God.[41]

According to American sociologist of religion Rodney Stark, the combination of the solidarity demonstrated by believers in Jesus in the first four centuries and their socio-economic practice were key elements in the impact they had on the entire empire. In addition, Stark mentions the Christian birth rate, the status of women, the supportive Christian response to epidemics, and the dismal urban, social, and sanitary conditions of Greco-Roman cities. Speaking of Antioch, the fourth largest city in the empire, Stark states:

> Any accurate portrait of Antioch in New Testament times must depict a city filled with misery, danger, fear, despair, and hatred. A city where the average family lived a squalid life in filthy and cramped quarters, where at least half of the children died at birth or during infancy, and where most of the children who lived lost at least one parent before reaching maturity. A city filled with hatred and fear rooted in intense ethnic antagonisms and exacerbated by a constant stream of strangers. A city so lacking in stable networks of attachments that petty incidents could prompt mob violence. [...] Since Antioch suffered acutely from all of these urban problems, it was in acute need of solutions. No wonder the early Christians missionaries were so warmly received in this city. For what they brought was not simply an urban movement, but a *new culture* capable of making life in Greco-Roman cities more tolerable.[42]

The experience of a city or of a situation as miserable as that of Antioch (and of present-day societies) should lead Christians to an "ethical indignation," to use an expression of the Brazilian-Korean theologian Jung Mo Sung, which moves them firstly to reject the possibility of not being indignant, of being indifferent and, secondly, which leads them to dream that another city, another society is possible, at this time, in the present context.[43]

This is precisely what the followers of Jesus Christ did during the first three centuries of the Christian era, setting in motion an alternative approach to relationships, community, and economics.

Model Communities

Just as the Old Testament presented us with a society and nation, and with it a series of laws, the New Testament approaches socio-economic issues from

---

[41] Ropero Berzosa, "Economía GDEB."

[42] Rodney Stark, *The Rise of Christianity: How the Obscure, Marginal Jesus Movement Became the Dominant Religious Force in the Western World in a Few Centuries*, 1st pbk. (San Francisco: HarperSanFrancisco, 1997), 160-62.

[43] Jung Mo Sung, "The Human Being as Subject: Defending the Victims," in *Latin American liberation theology: the next generation*, ed. Ivan Petrella (Maryknoll: Orbis, 2005), 1-19, https://www.academia.edu/5259533/The_Human_Being_as_Subject_Defending_the_Victims_-_Liberation_Theology_Next_Generation.

another, quite different angle. There are no longer laws, the nation of Israel no longer has a preeminent or privileged place, membership is no longer based on blood or lineage, but is voluntary and goodwill has replaced coercion.

The nation has taken a back seat and now the community of believers is the center of attention. Membership is open to all; it is multi-ethnic, cutting across social classes and affluence. The community brings together slaves and masters alike, women and men, children and the elderly. Some communities are majority Jewish, others are mixed Jewish and Gentile, and others are openly Gentile. Each community is distinct, organized according to its needs, and moves in different cultural molds. Religious pluralism, rather than monotheism, is the environment in which New Testament faith communities move. In general, these faith communities are surrounded by a hostile environment. They may be held with suspicion or distrust, and often persecution. At the same time, society, which looks at the community from afar and does not dare to join it, admires the conduct and example of the believers. They enjoyed the general esteem of the people (Acts 2:47), unbelievers who observed their good works and would eventually glorify God (1 Pet. 2:12).

Down with Poverty

The large group of believers in Jerusalem naturally and spontaneously found a way to end poverty within the community of believers: they shared as the need arose. The system was simple, voluntary, supportive. They had made their own the teaching of the Torah: "There need be no poor people among you" (Deut. 15:4). They had found a practical way to put into operation their version of the eschatological Jubilee, which had been made present in the person of Jesus Christ. And yet, this version of the Jubilee has provoked, on the one hand, a great deal of rejection and, on the other hand, indifference. Let us explain.

Together with some colleagues involved in development projects, I attended one of the multiplex sessions of Cape Town 2010, the Third Lausanne Congress on World Evangelization. The three speakers presented their topic to the best of their ability given the limited time and translation constraints. At the end, chatting with these colleagues, I brought up the subject of the "Jerusalem solution," to which they objected with a virulence that surprised me. According to them, this short-term solution led to their need for outside help within a few years.

The view of my colleagues is shared by many. Some hold that view in a sweeping way: holding resources in common is not a preferred or appropriate way to meet needs, nor is this early church example normative. Further, they hold that it caused the later poverty of the Jerusalem church. Others hold these positions, although in a more measured expression. Some commentators choose to tiptoe around the issue; they may simply fail to comment on the issue in their text or give it merely marginal attention. Finally, a few authors are moderately favorable to this idea, while fewer are openly in favor of practice today of the kind of sharing of goods carried out by the early church.

We also find it symptomatic that in books on development theology the tendency is to comment on the needs of the poor and to praise Paul's and James' instructions on sharing and generosity. The Jerusalem church's example in the face of poverty, however, is largely ignored.

Should we set aside the "Jerusalem solution", the sharing of goods by the early church, on the assumption that it is neither applicable nor useful today? We certainly would not presume to recommend its application on a general or global level, but in the small project setting, we are inclined to think that it could be very useful.

The case studies in this book have also highlighted several full or partial examples of sharing of resources. The steakhouse in Dakar began with the assets of the missionary couple put at the disposal of the business and the training of street children. Likewise, the Fatick village in the interior of Senegal shares its work force to attend to the needs of widows or sick people, for example by helping harvest their fields, its public prayers for all its neighbors, and its services such as the community water well. The practical example of the missionary, sharing their money, their work, and even their own life and family in the reconstruction of North African houses destroyed by the earthquake is another example. Some other examples have been given within the community of believers: the church in the North African city of Gran Urbe, the solidarity among the missionaries themselves when someone has been in need (notably due to the freezing of bank assets by their home countries, Argentina and Venezuela).

Global Solidarity

In this new model for the world, embodied by the New Testament communities, another important characteristic stood out: a sense of global solidarity. The communities of one country and continent supported those of another with personnel and offerings according to the needs and possibilities of each.

Solidarity with the needy at home was extended to include the needs of other congregations or of traveling apostles and preachers (Phil. 4:16). They organized collections, designated messengers-custodians of the funds, and took care of the international logistics to get these funds to the communities (2 Cor. 8-9, 1 Cor. 16:3). That is to say, they felt part of a global church, worldwide, spread throughout all countries, a growing church interconnected by bonds of love and solidarity.

This global solidarity constitutes a step beyond the understanding of solidarity in the Old Testament. J.M. Sung, looking for realistic ways to express this global solidarity, warns against the danger of thinking that there is no alternative, that it is not possible in the present circumstances to introduce socio-economic and spiritual changes. According to him, we must not fall into the trap (old trap of the left) that no progress is possible from within capitalism. That is what some would have us believe: that there is no alternative. But yes, there is much room for improvement, "even if one does not have the strength to replace it." To be radical is to stand alongside the poor, to learn from history and to propose viable changes, recognizing the limits that the historical moment itself imposes. "No form of social organization is definitive... all human societies are historical and can be criticized, modified or overcome."[44]

3. The First Three Centuries

This section is only a brief note in which we offer an example of how the Christians of the first centuries dealt with economics, social issues, and development. We include it because it establishes the nexus, the continuity between the narratives of the New Testament and the practice of the early church. We note that praxis is one of the components of Latin American theology. Of course, a detailed study of the first three centuries of Christianity will reveal the complexity of the historical, theological, and phenomenological study and conceptualization of the development of Christianity. Here we have limited ourselves to a generalization regarding the praxis of Christian *diakonia.*

One of the responsibilities that the Jerusalem believers assumed was to care for the widows. They established a list, a system of daily distribution, and a fund that was given to the apostles for their administration (Acts 4:35). Paul and his teams took these same instructions to the churches they were founding in Asia Minor and Europe. The instructions remained in force not just until the later years of the first century (1 Tim. 5:9) but continued for at least the next three centuries. This was not just private practice but institutional, according to celebrated German theologian and historian Adolf von Harnack.[45]

But this concern was not limited just to the widows. Orphans, the ill, prisoners, the enslaved, and all of the disenfranchised by society were included in this truly revolutionary service.

Fernando Bullón comments:

> This widespread practice [...] of ministry among the poor [was] established by the church. [...] The sick were healed, comforted, visited, and supported; innocent prisoners, those persecuted, or imprisoned for debt were also visited, consoled, and assisted; where possible, ransom was paid, even at risk. Those sentenced to the mines were searched, visited, and sometimes ransomed. [...] The redemption of slaves became a solemn act, supervised by the clergy, with a document of emancipation being read at the altar, so that the assembly could ratify the freedom of the slave. Estimates of the number of slaves set free by large Christian

---

[44] Jung Mo Sung, *Se Deus Existe, Por Qué há Pobreza? A Fe Cristã e os Excluídos*, 3rd ed. (Sao Paulo: Paulinas, 2000), 64-65.

[45] Adolf von Harnack, *The Mission and Expansion of Christianity in the First Three Centuries*, trans. James Moffatt, The Cloister Library TB92 (New York: Harper Torchbooks, 1962), 147.

> households range from 1250 to 8000, showing the commitment against slavery on the part of solvent families when they embraced the Christian faith.[46]

As for the sharing of goods mentioned above, there is also evidence of its continuity in the first centuries. Paul maintains that teaching: "the one who receives instruction in the word should share (*koinoneito*) all good things with their instructor" (Gal. 6:6). Giuseppe Ricciotti notes that the community of goods was widely taught and practised until well into the second century.[47]

The same idea is taken up by Pope Francis, citing the conclusive words from the fourth century of St. John Chrysostom: "Not to share one's wealth with the poor is to steal from them and to take away their livelihood. It is not our own goods which we hold, but theirs."[48]

Valdir Steuernagel, likewise, in analyzing the form that the Christian mission took under the rule of Julian the Apostate, notes the enormous specific weight that Christian social work represented in the society of the time (362-363 AD).[49] Further, Fernando Bullón draws our attention to the fact that "within the teachings of the church fathers as a whole, communication in economic and social life is undoubtedly the most common and characteristic doctrine, since it is *on it that the patristic authors in general constantly and unanimously agree*."[50]

4. Practical Suggestions for *Islamia*

And now we suggest a few ideas for putting some of the biblical recommendations into practice in Muslim environments.

From below. Just as the Messianic Jubilee was initiated from the margins of power and society, so too can some of the dynamics that we have analyzed be understood with regard to the projects under consideration. Business as mission, the empowerment-liberation of the *talibé* boys from the steakhouse in Dakar is not spectacular. But it is undoubtedly a clear example of Jubilee expressed among the destitute of society. The same can be said of the welding school, the literacy and computer project in North Africa (La Joya), as well as the Spanish Center in Uzbekistan, to name but a few. They were (some of them still are) a witness from the margins of inclusion, reconciliation, and Jubilee rest. Almost

---

[46] H. Fernando Bullón, *Historia de la Iglesia y Responsabilidad Social*, vol. 2, Misión Cristiana y Responsabilidad Social Series (Buenos Aires: Kairos Ediciones, 2009), 43-44, 54. Trans. D. Greenlee.

[47] Giuseppe Ricciotti, *The Acts of the Apostles: Text and Commentary*, trans. Laurence E Byrne (Milwaukee: The Bruce Publishing Company, 1958), 97.

[48] Francis, *The Joy of the Gospel: Evangelii Gaudium* (Frederick, Md.: The Word Among Us Press, 2014), para. 57, https://www.vatican.va/content/francesco/en/apost_exhortations/documents/papa-francesco_esortazione-ap_20131124_evangelii-gaudium.html.

[49] Steuernagel, *Obediencia Misionera*, chap. 2.

[50] Bullón, *Historia*, 2:60. Emphasis added.

always, Iberoamerican non-proselytizing missionary work in Islamic lands is done from below, with few resources whether economic, human, or of influence. They are often small initiatives, but they can be understood as a current parallel to the liberating dynamics, the Jubilee dynamics, that we find in the New Testament.

Economic freedom. If the Exodus is to be taken as a model – and certainly in Scripture it is – then God intends economic freedom for his children and subjects as an essential part of salvation. This has political, social, economic, and spiritual implications. Employment training and communal resource-generating initiatives should be much more prominent in missionary projects. The CEDIES project in Uzbekistan is a notable example in this regard. It contributed directly to both training and employment for a good number of students. Another example is the welding project in the city of Villa Hermosa which was recognized as the best quality training in the country.

Community economic initiatives. In strongly monotheistic religious societies, such as Muslim societies, it is possible to transmit theocentric and neighbor-centric economic concepts. Since the extended family units of Muslim countries and the rural patterns of society are very similar to those of ancient Israel as described in the Bible, concrete initiatives such as the Jubilee, the gleaning at the margins of harvests, positive discrimination towards the weak in society, and offerings or collections for the needy, would be easily understood and adapted. The two projects benefiting the handicapped (which we have mentioned only briefly) are examples of care for the needy. Another project (outside the scope of this research) runs a Spanish and English language school for profit and gives all the profits to an association for the care of children with cerebral palsy; the teachers are missionaries who donate their work. However, many more initiatives could be implemented based on biblical models mentioned above, such as a communal policy of solidarity and collaborative economy.

Interest-free loans. The subject is already well known in Muslim societies. There are many writings on the subject and banks that work as closely as possible to this principle. The Archbishop of Canterbury mentioned the Christian and Muslim overlap on this point saying, "The Christian tradition has always been cautious about interest and for many centuries it was very much of one mind with the Islamic tradition, but after the 16th century that changed."[51] Making possible interest-free, or extremely low interest, loans for vital and productive needs would represent a significant advance for Iberoamerican missionary agencies in the lands of Islam. As yet, we are not aware of any such projects carried out by Iberoamerican entities.

Sabbath rest. In many places of strong Islamic influence, Friday is already partially established as a day of rest. The concept underlying Sabbath and Friday prayers is not the same, but the similarity is certainly evident. Would it be

---

[51] Ekklesia, "Archbishop Urges Christians and Muslims to Create Fairer Lending," Ecumenical News International, October 21, 2008, https://old.ekklesia.co.uk/node/7816.

possible for Christian communities and development projects in rural areas of Islamic lands to redefine the content and practice of Sabbath rest? In fact, some churches in the Muslim areas we have termed "exclusivist" gather on Fridays, since the other days are working days. How to apply Sabbath rest to projects, giving it biblical meaning, is a topic that has not yet been explored.

Interreligious dialogue. The projects we have studied are involved in forms of dialogue with people and institutions of other faiths: they can be considered interreligious dialogue initiatives. The mere fact that those perceived to be *kafir* or infidels, non-Muslim people and their organizations, are working for the development, the integral well-being, of the followers of Islam is in itself very striking. We have indicated above how Jesus extended the radius of benefit of the Jubilee to those outside the borders of Israel. This countercultural fact has its parallel in the projects studied. In each of them, expatriate Iberoamerican followers of the Messiah sacrificially demonstrate concern for the *shalom* of those who are not of their religion. In addition, as a sign of interreligious goodwill, they are supported by Iberoamerican Christians who sacrificially give to benefit Muslim groups.

The same cultural conception once held by the Jews, seeking the good only of relatives and co-religionists, is an intrinsic part of today's Muslim societies. In the analysis of the rural integral project in the Gran Urbe area, we have seen the astonishment of many who asked: "Why are you doing this for us? I would never do something like this for an infidel." For many, the blessing of peace expressed in the greeting, *As salaamu aleikum*, is reserved only for believers. Likewise, after a period of hospitality, the infidel is invited to convert to Islam or, at best, to become a second-class citizen, a *dhimmi*, who is prevented by systemic constraints from prospering. But in such a society, it would be inconceivable to actively and intentionally seek the good of the other, the infidel, the different. The essence of Islam is submission, conformity. However, the inclusion advocated by the projects we have studied constitutes an important contribution to society: inclusion for the weak and excluded from society, for those who do not belong to the extended family, for non-Muslims, in short for those who are different. This kind of inclusion could certainly be further enhanced and disseminated.

Collective rules and procedures. Another practical action to consider has to do with the *results of development*. Indeed, once the benefits of improved health, economy, and social welfare begin to manifest themselves, it is easy for unsupportive and hoarding attitudes to sprout (or sprout again). This is especially true in groups in which the principles of the Jubilee have not taken root, when the rest of society (those who are not linked to the project in question) live by other standards. For solidarity and mutuality to endure over time, they must be embedded in collective rules and procedures. Personal convictions are not enough to maintain solidarity and the spirit of mutual aid over time; it must materialize in, first, a change of worldview, based on the intrinsic value of each person and the sacred (divine) value of creation. This derives from the concept of the image of God. Likewise, second, it must be translated into rules, procedures, and even laws that consolidate a way of doing and relating to others. It is therefore a matter of finding local equivalents of the Jubilee rules, as well as equivalents of theological, ontological, and social justifications for them.

Social agents of *shalom*. Directly related to the above, for community *shalom* to endure, take root, and grow, it will be indispensable to invest in the development of social agents of *shalom*: people dedicated to promoting the values and practice of the Messianic Jubilee, that is, promoting peace, reconciliation, inclusion, rest, and social welfare. The theoretical tools are familiar to the missionary-development workers we studied: discipleship expressed in the dynamics of transferring values, character, and practice into apprentices. However, there are no precedents and materials for such discipleship of social agents. It is a pending task.

Finally, we mention four concrete actions that have already appeared, in one way or another throughout the analysis of the cases studied, but which we summarize here.

1) *Public prayer* must be a constant and characteristic part of the Development-Salaam projects. It is the ultimate expression of the desire for the well-being of others and of the community. Muslim spirituality includes prayer, usually public, although there are important differences, to which due attention should be paid.

This is not the place to deal with this subject in depth. Suffice it to mention that Muslim prayer is ritualistic and repetitive (the same words are always repeated); it is gender-segregated; it is concerned with the welfare and advancement of the *ummah*, the Muslim faith community, not the whole of humanity or society, nor does it include creation as the object of divine activity. It also constitutes a "wall of defense," protecting women and children from the malicious attacks (proselytizing and chicanery) of the infidels, which is why in the mosque the men form a line, side by side, each man's foot touching his prayer neighbor, forming a wall.

2) Promote *interreligious dialogue*. We are convinced that, in addition to carrying out projects, witnessing to the faith of the Messiah and founding churches, it is necessary to invest in dialogue. Dialogue is not evangelism; it does not seek to convince the other or to win arguments. The purpose of dialogue is knowledge and mutual respect. The British missiologist Andrew Kirk explains that interreligious dialogue is based on five principles:

- Respect for the dignity and integrity of all human beings.
- The need to represent other people's views fairly.
- The need to hear and consider what others say about our beliefs and practices.
- The call to work together in common projects that seek justice and reconciliation in society.
- Mutual witness.

To which Kirk clarifies:

> There is a sense in which all religions are 'evangelistic' in intent, in that they see themselves as the guardians of crucial insights into the nature and meaning of life itself and how it should be conducted, which they have an obligation to share.[52]

3) *Working together*. This could seem obvious. In fact, all the projects we have analyzed have intentionally sought cooperation, from the grassroots level, with people and national institutions. But this bears repeating. It includes working together for the good of the community as one of the key practical actions. Note that this is not always the case in projects carried out by foreigners (both missionaries and secular), who only employ nationals, but who are far from working together.

4) Exercise *joint solidarity in the face of needs, calamities, and emergencies.* Few things unite a community as much as facing adversity together. We have seen the example of the rural church in the Fatick villages in the interior of Senegal. They attend to the needs of widows and the sick, and mediated a neighborhood dispute. However, on the ground, other situations may arise as a pressing need arises.

We conclude this chapter with a clear statement of the Bible's commitment to development in both the Old and New Testaments – that is, the development of a more just, caring, and ecological society – by means of a concrete and visible model, whether it be the Israelite socio-economic ideal or that of the Christian communities. This model is summarized and condensed in the Old Testament word *shalom*, the word which will be the subject of the following chapter.

Questions for Reflection and Discussion

1. What three lessons have you learned, or have been reaffirmed, through reading this chapter?
2. What aspects of the biblical ideal of social well-being are you putting into practice? What others could you implement?
3. Who provides "the bread" (the basic necessities) for your family and you? How does sharing your resources with others seem? Please give reasons for your responses.

[52] J. Andrew Kirk, *Mission under Scrutiny: Confronting Current Challenges* (London: Darton, Longman & Todd, 2006), 28-29.

For Further Reading

Blomberg, Craig L. *Neither Poverty nor Riches: A Biblical Theology of Material Possessions*. New Studies in Biblical Theology 7. Leicester and Downers Grove: Apollos and InterVarsity, 1999.

Malina, Bruce J. *The New Testament World: Insights from Cultural Anthropology*, 3rd ed. Louisville: Westminster John Knox Press, 2001.

Murton, Zoe, and Tearfund. "Land Rights." *Paso a Paso*, 2018. https://learn.tearfund.org/en/resources/footsteps/footsteps-101-110/footsteps-105.

World Council of Churches. "São Paulo Statement: International Financial Transformation for the Economy of Life," October 5, 2012. https://www.oikoumene.org/resources/documents/sao-paulo-statement-international-financial-transformation-for-the-economy-of-life.

13. *Shalom* and *Salaam*

> I have seen their ways, but I will heal them.
> I will guide them,
> and reward them with comfort.
> And for those who mourn,
> I will create reason for praise:
> utter prosperity to those far and near,
> and I will heal them, says the Lord.
> But the wicked are like the churning sea that can't keep still.
> They churn up from their waters muck and mud.
> There is no peace (*shalom*), says my God, for the wicked.
>
> (Isaiah 57:18-21 CEB)

1. *Shalom*: the Biblical Ideal

Introduction

The Bible sets forth a broad ideal of society for believers and, in terms of eschatology, for the cosmos as a whole. No single word in modern English or Spanish captures its full meaning. *Shalom* refers to the global and total well-being of the individual, the community, and the entire cosmos, in all their facets and relationships. God's desire for his people and for all of his creation is condensed into this single Hebrew word, which we have brought untranslated into our own languages.

In this chapter, we will focus our efforts on a synthesis of the *characteristics* of *shalom* as recorded in the Old Testament and on *eirene* in the New Testament.

Shalom in the Old Testament

The word *shalom* is difficult to analyze and describe. It has become a commonly used word but at the same time it carries a dense religious meaning. G. Lloyd Carr notes that:

> *šālôm* and its related words *šālēm*, *šelem* and their derivatives, are among the most important theological words in the O.T. *šālôm* occurs over 250 times in 213 separate verses.[1]

Peace and well-being: The Spanish Jesuit Luis Alonso Schökel, a scholar on biblical Hebrew, notes that the term *shalom* points to "peace, tranquility, serenity, calmness, calm, concord; prosperity, well-being, bliss, [and] bounty" while clarifying that "Peace and prosperity merge into an inclusive concept; sometimes one of the two aspects comes to the fore."[2]

A primary meaning of *shalom* refers to well-being, with strong emphasis on the material (e.g., Jdg. 19:20, 1 Sam. 16:6, 2 Sam. 18:28, and Ez. 5:7). Alonso clarifies that it sometimes reflects a state (1 Sam. 25:6, 2 Sam. 17:3, 20:9, 2 Kings 4:26, 5:21, Jer. 6:14, 8:11, Job 5:24, 21:9, Prov. 3:17), at other times it refers to an attitude (1 Sam. 17:4, 1 Kings 2:13), while 2 Kings 9:11, 17-19, 22, and 31 play with ambiguity between the two meanings. It may refer to the state and attitude of the individual, but more often than not it has direct or implied connotations to relationships of all kinds. In the following quotations, we realize that *shalom* is much more than peace; it is well-being, salvation, harmony, absence of fear, full realization, fulfillment or being complete.

> The word is used when one asks or prays for the welfare of another (Gen. 43:27; Ex. 4:18; Jdg. 19:20), when one is in harmony or agreement with another (Josh. 9:15; 1 Kings 5:12), when one seeks the good of a city or country (Ps. 122:6; Jer. 29:7). It can mean material prosperity (Ps. 73:3), or physical security (Ps. 4:8). But it can also mean spiritual well-being. It is peace that relates to righteousness and truth but not to wickedness (Ps. 85:10; Is. 48:18, 22; 57:19-21).[3]

> As a verb, in the simplest form (qal) shalam, it means, to be at peace, to be complete, to be finished, to be safe and sound, to be happy, to be at the top, to pay, etc. The meaning of this root is similar in all the Semitic languages in which it is documented.[4]

***Shalom* is integral**. *Shalom*, as an integral and integrating concept, includes many connections to other positive aspects of life such as joy, tranquility, love, life, and a promising future. Gottfried Vanoni writes that:

---

[1] G. Lloyd Carr, "Shalom," in *Theological Wordbook of the Old Testament*, ed. Gleason L. Archer, Bruce K. Waltke, and R. Laird Harris (Chicago: Moody, 1999).

[2] Luis Alonso Schökel, "Shalom," in *Diccionario Bíblico Hebreo-Español* (Madrid: Editorial Trotta, 1994). Trans. D. Greenlee.

[3] F. Foulkes, "Paz," in *Nuevo Diccionario Bíblico*, ed. James D. Douglas (Barcelona: Certeza Unida, 1991).

[4] María José Cano Pérez, "Paz en el Antiguo Testamento," in *Cosmovisiones de Paz en el Mediterráneo Antiguo y Medieval*, ed. Francisco A. Muñoz and Beatriz Molina Rueda (Granada: Universidad de Granada, 1998), 29-61, index of the book: http://wdb.ugr.es/~rimon/paginas/publi/capitulos/index.php.

> [*Shalom*] evokes other associations. The opposite of *shalom* is not properly war but evil or misfortune. There are interesting positive expressions that we find in the setting of *shalom*: love and compassion (Jer. 16:5), life (Mic. 2:5; Prov. 3:2), future (Ps. 37:37), salvation (Is. 57:19; Jer. 14:19; 33:6), health (Ps. 38:4), blessing (Ps. 29:11), good (fortune) (Ps. 34:15; Jer. 14:19), joy (Is. 55:12), and quietness and security (Is 32:17; 57:2).[5]

As an integral concept, it cannot be only partially had; it either is or it is not; it is either had or not had. When it is had, it is enjoyed integrally. At the same time, it is always subject to improvement and growth, it is never total or complete.

***Shalom* is relational**: True *shalom* has important individual dimensions, of course, but above all it is relational. It arises from a relational God and is replicated in the multitude of relationships of human beings, society, and the whole of creation. *Shalom* is *shared* integral well-being yet we offer it to others as a blessing, as a greeting, in fact the greeting par excellence in Hebrew and Jewish society.

***Shalom* is a divine gift**: As many authors point out, the biblical concept of *shalom* is centered on God himself, his nature, and his gifts. God is the primary source of integral well-being; humans receive *shalom* as part of a covenant with him. But what is more, *shalom* is the very characteristic of God. "Yahweh is *shalom*" exclaims Gideon (Jdg. 6:24). This is even more evident in the prophesied Messiah, the King of peace (Heb. 7:2), the Prince of Peace (Is. 9:6), who himself will "be our peace" (Mic. 5:5) and who will speak peace to the nations (Zech. 9:10). The priestly blessing (Num. 6:24-26) is a clear example of how he who is graced by God with *shalom* also receives blessing, protection, and grace. This integral well-being is therefore a blessing, a grace, a treasure to be preserved.

In the message of the prophets, the use and implications of *shalom* arouse strong controversy. Here, the meaning of the term is broadened to denote the whole spectrum of salvation. *Shalom* is contrasted in these prophetic texts with righteousness. Micah accuses the false prophets of being driven by gain (Mic. 3:5). Jeremiah confronts those who proclaim "peace, peace" when just the opposite is true (Jer. 28). Ezekiel condemns false prophets in the same terms (Ez. 13:16). As Gerhard von Rad has noted:

> As may be seen from Is. 48:18 and 54:13, more than political peace is now at issue, for peace is associated with righteousness. The term still embraces welfare and

---

[5] Gottfried Vanoni, "Schalom als zentrale biblische Botschaft," *Theologisch-praktische Quartalschrift* 141, no. 1 (1993): 5. Trans. D. Greenlee.

> peace, but it has the more comprehensive implication of salvation in its total range and scope.[6]

***Shalom* is eschatological**: Our description of the range of meaning of biblical *shalom* would not be complete without referring to its eschatological aspect: *shalom* begins now but will be completed in the divine future. We have mentioned that biblical *shalom* finds its expression in the Messiah. We must add that this is its ultimate expression, linked to the kingdom, and that it constitutes the hope that inspires all biblical authors, as well as believers of all times. Drawing further from von Rad:

> The promise of *shālôm* in the fuller sense brings the term into the orbit of eschatological expectation. The term may not always occur, but when restoration of paradise is prophesied, international peace promised (Is. 2:2ff.), or a humble king of peace awaited (Zech. 9:9-10), we have a proclamation of peace of the widest possible import.[7]

***Shalom* is contextual and ecological**: We mentioned earlier that *shalom* is a relational concept. Two of these relationships cannot be overlooked: social peace and ecological peace. *Shalom* does not exist in a vacuum; there is no *shalom* without context. These relationships exist between humans and society and nature. Above all, relationships of *shalom* are found between humans and the Creator, the social God who wants cosmic *shalom*. Because God cares about social justice, and because he will bring about the redemption of creation, humans – we who bear the image of God – must seek and cultivate those same relationships of integral well-being. Vanoni notes that:

> The bond between justice and peace […] is perfectly integrated into the biblical concept of *shalom* and extends like a crimson thread into the New Testament. For Paul, too, it is certain: "For the kingdom of God is not a matter of eating and drinking, but of righteousness, peace and joy in the Holy Spirit" (Rom. 14:17). […] No, *shalom* in "peace and security" cannot be had without justice: "The fruit of that righteousness will be peace; its effect will be quietness and confidence forever. My people will live in peaceful dwelling places, in secure homes, in undisturbed places of rest" (Is. 32:17-18).
>
> A further perspective is drawn from the linkage between [these] texts. […] "[T]ill the Spirit is poured on us from on high, and the desert becomes a fertile field, and the fertile field seems like a forest. The LORD's justice will dwell in the desert, his righteousness live in the fertile field. The fruit of that righteousness will be peace; its effect will be quietness and confidence forever. My people will live in peaceful

---

[6] Gerhard von Rad, "Peace-Shalom (OT)," in *Theological Dictionary of the New Testament*, ed. Gerhard Kittel and Geoffrey William Bromiley (Grand Rapids: Eerdmans, 1995).

[7] von Rad, "Peace-Shalom."

> dwelling places [...] how blessed you will be, sowing your seed by every stream, and letting your cattle and donkeys range free" (Is. 32:15-20): Here we no longer speak only of the intertwining of "justice" and "peace." This theme is central, but it would be meaningless outside the context of creation transformed and made safe. The desert turned into a garden is the field in which "justice" can bring forth shalom.[8]

This ecological dimension of *shalom* is intimately related with development, as we shall observe later.

***Shalom* is resisted**: But the biblical description is far from idyllic. Walter Brueggemann notes that integral well-being, *shalom*, implies a tension between order and justice, between the real and the prophetic. This tension leads to transformative action, social action, "active intervention to transform society."[9] True *shalom* is hated and resisted by the world, which continues to seek peace according to its own rules, with imposition and force. But we are assured, this world is falling and the new one is rising! "The prince of this world [...] has no hold over me" (John 14:30); he has no power. It is a struggle, and it is a sadness that gives birth to joy.[10]

As we shall see, this broad biblical concept, *shalom* or integral well-being, connects culturally and religiously with the Muslim concept of *salaam*.

Eirene *in the New Testament*

The Septuagint and the Gospels: It is logical to ask ourselves if there is continuity between the Old Testament concept of integral well-being and the New Testament understanding of peace. Moreover, do Jesus and his disciples extend the concept or do they simply reformulate it? The Septuagint offers a perfect bridge to answer part of these two questions. Indeed, the Septuagint translated the Hebrew *shalom* primarily with the Greek word *eirene*.

The New Testament develops the concept of peace consistently with the meaning attributed to *shalom* in the Old Testament. Judging by its use, the word peace, *eirene*, has great importance in the thought of Jesus and Paul. In fact, it "occurs in each of the books of the NT, save in 1 John."[11] All the uses of the word *shalom* are found, to a greater or lesser extent, repeated in the New Testament, although the emphasis will be quite different.

Of course, in the New Testament, the word peace is still a greeting, but on the lips of Jesus it acquires a new force. "Go in peace" Jesus says both to the sick

---

[8] Vanoni, "Schalom," 5-7. Trans. D. Greenlee; Scripture passages NIV.

[9] Walter Brueggemann, *Peace* (Atlanta: Chalice Press, 2001), 112.

[10] Brueggemann, chap. 10; Margot Kässmann, "Creative Thinking for Peace or Blessed Are the Peacemakers," *The Ecumenical Review* 63, no. 1 (2011): 5-15, https://doi.org/10.1111/j.1758-6623.2010.00088.x.

[11] William E. Vine, Merrill F Unger, and William White, "Peace/Eirene," in *Vine's Complete Expository Dictionary of Old and New Testament Words: With Topical Index* (Nashville: Nelson, 1996).

woman (Mark 5:24) and to the woman who had lived a sinful life (Luke 7:50). Or again, "Peace be with you" as he stands among the disciples in the upper room after the resurrection (Luke 24:36; John 20:19, 21, 26). The angels' "peace on earth" greeting to the shepherds was connected with a message of salvation "good news [...] a Savior" (Luke 8:10-14). Following this line, the disciples, when they are sent out, will be told that upon entering a house or city they must offer this peace that goes beyond a mere greeting: it is the very announcement of the promise of salvation (Matt. 10:12, Luke 10:5 and parallels).

However, the peace that Jesus announces is cryptic, it seems to be contradictory. "Do not suppose that I have come to bring peace to the earth. I did not come to bring peace, but a sword" (Matt. 10:34). It is a different order of peace, peace of another kind. Likewise, especially in Luke's writing, the peace of Jesus contrasts with the concept of *Pax Romana* (Acts 24:2). Paulus Widjaja, a Mennonite who grew up in the Muslim setting of Indonesia, observes that:

> The Greeks understood peace as a state of mind, an inner harmony that results in emotional stability, a personal inner tranquility. The Romans understood peace as a state of law and order where there is a balance of competing self-interest between power groups maintained by military force. The NT is distinctive, retaining the range of OT understanding, while introducing the new dimension of fulfilment by Jesus of the OT messianic peace, and in the way peace takes shape in the church as a messianic community.[12]

We have already mentioned the connection that the synoptic Gospels make between peace and salvation. In fact, this is one of the characteristics of the concept of peace throughout the New Testament. On the other hand, the gospel of John associates peace with the sacrifice of Jesus (16:33).

Paul's Letters

Paul widely mentions the concept of peace in all his writings. He establishes three characteristic connections: the direct relationship between peace and reconciliation, justification, and life. In fact, in numerous Pauline passages, *eirene* (peace) could be replaced by *zoe* (life) without changing the meaning of the passage. The best example is probably "The mind governed by the flesh is death, but the mind governed by the Spirit is life and peace" (Rom. 8:6). On the other hand, for Paul peace is a tangible concept, to be embodied in the new messianic community. Peace must be pursued (Rom. 14:19), maintained in daily relationships (1 Th. 5:13; 2 Cor. 13:11; Rom. 12:18), and it must permeate every thought (Phil. 5:7). Likewise, Paul adapts the rabbinic greeting "mercy and peace" with the expression "grace and peace." These words of greeting are present in most of his letters, usually complemented in the letter's farewell by invoking the "God of peace."

---

[12] Paulus S. Widjaja, "Peace," in *Dictionary of Mission Theology: Evangelical Foundations*, ed. John Corrie (Downers Grove: InterVarsity, 2007), 280.

Werner Foerster, who groups his analysis of peace in the New Testament into three major categories of thought, emphasizes the meaning of peace: "the eschatological salvation of the whole person":

> Thus in Luke 1:79 *eirḗnē* is the awaited eschatological salvation. In Luke 2:14 again peace is the salvation that has now come to the earth. […] Paul calls God the God of peace who will crush Satan (Rom. 16:20) and secure our total salvation (1 Th. 5:23; cf. Heb. 13:20-21). Peace, then, embraces the salvation of the whole person, and in Christ this is *already present* as the power of God.[13]

We must emphasize that the peace of the New Testament does not reach only to the reconciliation of individuals with God, but transcends all nations, all conflicts. It is a peace that breaks down the barriers erected by centuries of prejudice between Jews and Gentiles, that overcomes the differences between women and men, and between warring nations. That peace has been made possible not by the enlightenment of Greek thought, nor by Roman military might, nor by the application of Jewish ritual purity laws, but by the victory of the cross of Jesus Christ. Quite a paradox! This aspect has important implications for us, as we will develop later.

***Eirene* and mission to Islam**: In the concept of peace, we find a powerful answer to the question, "Is it ethically appropriate to establish Christian communities in Muslim-majority lands?" The gospel of peace in Jesus Christ offers a distinct element of reconciliation in today's difficult relations between Muslims and Christians, and between the West and Islam.

Let us note in the text of the sending of the seventy-two (Luke 10:1-9), how the mission of the ambassadors of Jesus Christ is, first, justified: the workers are few… ask the Lord… to send out workers. The workers sent to the family of Islam are still few, very few, and Jesus himself thought it lawful to send forerunners "to every town and place where he was about to go" (Luke 10:1).

But the mission is, second, characterized by vulnerability: "like lambs among wolves," along with the precariousness of means "do not take a purse or bag or sandals" (Luke 10:3-4). It is a mission from below, without power and without being imposed.

The eligibility of the missionary visit, third, is emphasized twice more: "When you enter a house […] if not, it will return to you […] When you enter a town and are welcomed […]" (Luke 10:5-6, 8).

There is no hint of the messengers imposing their message, not a trace of domination. The choice rests on the host, on the one receiving the visit. That is, the messengers or missionaries cannot impose either their presence or their message. This is the complete opposite of a religious war or a clash of civilizations. The announcement of the presence, of the approach, of the

[13] Werner Foerster, "Eirene," in *Theological Dictionary of the New Testament*, ed. Gerhard Kittel and Geoffrey William Bromiley (Grand Rapids: Eerdmans, 1964). Emphasis added.

kingdom of God is marked by two signs: the priestly impartation of communal peace for the home, and the miraculous healing of the sick, in the name of the King. It is mission conceived as word, deed, incarnation, and the power of the Holy Spirit.

Synthesis of Biblical Concepts

We have briefly considered the chief characteristics associated with the idea of peace in both the Old and New Testaments. Peace is the biblical ideal of personal and communal well-being that arises from God himself. It affects all relationships: with oneself, with one's close neighbor, with the distant "other," and with nature, and is based on a unique relationship with Jesus Christ himself, the Lord of peace. It is an integral, believing, relational, contextual, and eschatological concept.

We now propose the concept of *shalom-salaam* as a cultural, religious, and hermeneutical bridge of interpretation of everyday life that will help us carry out development as a form or reconciliation in Muslim lands. Let us now explore Islamic practice and the teachings of the Qur'an to see what concept of peace we find.

2. The Muslim Concept of *Salaam*

The words *shalom* and *salaam* share a common Semitic source; the Muslim concept of peace, *salaam*, is also very broad. It shares many common roots with the Jewish and biblical concept of peace and is a basic concept in the Qur'an and Islamic theology. The meaning of the words *shalom* and *salaam* goes beyond the Western concept of peace to include the notion of salvation, well-being, fulfillment, solace, and prosperity. These are broad and inclusive concepts.[14]

The Muslim concept of peace in the Qur'an is derived from the roots *slm* and *slh*, from which come the terms *salam* and *sulh*: "peace."[15] "In total there are one hundred thirty-eight references to terms derived from the root *slm* and one hundred seventy-nine derived from *slh*."[16] The analysis of these multiple quotations from the Qur'an reveals two large blocks of related yet very different meaning.

Inner peace. The first set of meanings has to do with the individual, inner peace that believers experience from Allah as they submit to the divine precepts. It is a divine gift, related to blessing, which is understood as a reciprocal

[14] Royce Anderson, "A Definition of Peace," *Journal of Peace and Psychology*, 2004, 102.

[15] C. Gómez Camarero et al., "Una Lectura del Corán desde la Paz," *Miscelánea de Estudios Árabes y Hebraicos* 46 (1997): 116; Earle H. Waugh, "Peace," in *Encyclopaedia of the Qur'an*, ed. Jane Dammen McAuliffe (Washington, DC: Georgetown University, 2013).

[16] Gómez Camarero et al., "Lectura," 117.

covenant between humans and God. Without any doubt, peace emanates from Allah himself. It is therefore a concept of deep belief linked to spiritual life. Peace is even a name of God, although in a lesser sense than in the Bible. A single verse in the Qur'an mentions this fact: 59:23 "Allah is He, than Whom there is no other god – the Sovereign, the Holy One, the Source of Peace (and Perfection), the Guardian of Faith, the Preserver of Safety [...]."[17]

A prominent meaning in the Qur'an, linked to this same general concept of inner peace, is the use of *salaam* as a greeting. It is the greeting received by the prophets, exchanged by Abraham with the angels (11:69), prescribed for Muhammad after the ritual prayer, and characterizes the community of believers. It becomes the Muslim greeting *par excellence*. It is often used in the plural to include the two angels or spirits that accompany each person. It should be noted that non-believers do not enjoy this greeting, except perhaps in response (in its abbreviated form). However, the Sufi tradition elaborated a contrary view in great detail, recommending greetings, hospitality, and blessings to all, including to strangers according to Muhammad al-Bukhari (810-870).[18] Its fulfillment is the supreme happiness experienced in paradise, the house of peace, *dar al-salām*, characterized as a garden. The faithful believer will no longer experience fear, terror, and suffering (21:97-103), but joy and peace (36:55-8). This Muslim concept of peace, then, includes a strong eschatological component.

Functional peace. The second major meaning has to do with functional peace, or peace in action. This is the aspect of peace expressed in the social life of the community and its relations both internally and in the context of the struggle with non-believers. It is a social and political peace aimed at the consolidation of the *ummah*:

> This root [*slh*] has a range of meanings including "to act uprightly, to be upright" to "to impose peace," "to rectify, to set things right, to put things in order," "to come to an agreement," "to reconcile or be reconciled," "to establish concord."[19]

It is a peace to be won, requiring struggle, negotiations, and covenants. Several commentators note that the verses referring to the latter meaning are predominantly Medinan or from the second Meccan period, when Muhammad was confronted with the need to act as a political leader.[20] The practical and

---

[17] English language quotations from the Holy Qur'an are taken from International Institute of Islamic Thought, ed., *The Meaning of the Holy Qur'ān: Complete Translation with Selected Notes*, trans. Abdullah Yusuf Ali (Washington, DC: Amana Corporation, 1989).

[18] Valerie J. Hoffman, "Hospitality and Courtesy," in *Encyclopaedia of the Qur'an* (Washington, DC: Georgetown University, 2013), http://www.brillonline.nl/entries/encyclopaedia-of-the-quran/hospitality-and-courtesy-COM_00086.

[19] Gómez Camarero et al., "Lectura," 121.

[20] C. van Arendonk and D. Gimaret, "Salām," in *Encyclopaedia of Islam* (Leiden: Brill Online, 2013).

active application of peace was contextually applied by Muhammad during that period.

Many other meanings are closely related to both sets of concepts: friendship, solidarity, help, refuge, repentance, forgiveness, and purification. These occur mostly among the *ummah*, but sometimes also in relationship with non-believers.[21] But we must not limit ourselves to merely a textual or exegetical study of the Qur'an. The tendency on the part of Christian thinkers is to study Muslim concepts with a reductionist approach: to limit ourselves to the text of the Qur'an. To do so is a grave error. As Francisco Franco Sánchez, of the University of Alicante, illustrates, the analysis of the context, the history, and the facts about Muhammad must complement the study of the text of the Qur'an. It is necessary to understand the circumstances that motivated the formation of the Islamic religion and society in order to get a real idea of the concept of peace from the Muslim point of view.[22] Indeed, the very existence of the Hadith is rooted in that hermeneutical reality: the narrative, anecdotal details, and non-quranic sayings of the Prophet and his Companions are almost as important to the Muslim ethos as the Qur'an itself.[23]

In this context, there is an important variation in the concept of peace between the early Meccan period – when the Muslim community was a minority in society – and the Medinan and later periods, when Muslim society is properly transformed into a confessional state:

> Out of one hundred five references to peace in the Qur'an, there are sixty-one Meccan verses and forty-one Medinan verses that are related (even if tangentially) in Arabic to the semantic concept of peace. In contrast to war, *salaam* is mostly mentioned in the Meccan period, which we interpret as being due to the fact that the term should be understood more in the meaning of "submission" and the related idea behind "Islam." Here, it is also used as a salutation, rather than pointing to the idea of peace itself. In comparison, the verses that speak of *aslaha* as "to impose peace, to keep the peace" are mostly related to the Medinan period, during which the new Islamic state was established.[24]

---

[21] Gómez, Molina, Pérez, and Vidal, from the University of Granada, detail in their article, whose title in English is "A reading of the Qur'an from the perspective of peace," each of these meanings connected to peace. Gómez Camarero et al., "Lectura."

[22] Francisco Franco Sánchez, "La Noción de Paz en el Pensamiento Religioso Islámico y su Plasmación en al-Andalus," in *Idees de Pau a l'Edat Mitjana: Reunió Científica. XIII Curs d'Estiu Comtat d'Urgell Celebrat a Balaguer els Dies 2, 3 i 4 de Juliol de 2008; Sota la Direcció de Flocel Sabaté i Maite Pedrol.*, ed. Flocel Sabaté, Collecció Aurembiaix d'Urgell 13 (Lleida: Pagès, 2010), 161-84, http://hdl.handle.net/10045/16616.

[23] For a feminine view of the context of the quranic verses, see Geneviève Chauvel, *Aïcha: La Bien-aimée du Prophète*, 7th ed. (Paris: Librairie Générale Française, 2009).

[24] Franco Sánchez, "Noción de Paz," 170.

In addition to the socio-political context, in Muslim cosmology, one cannot separate the understanding of peace from its opposite, war. In fact, the latter is mentioned many more times than the former. "In Islam, peace, as a religious fact, is not approached in a systematic way," affirms Franco Sánchez. "The concept of peace is related to, and is deduced to a great extent from, what Islam affirms about war, about which there is an abundant literature."[25] As we have already indicated, this concept of functional or active peace has to be earned. Strategies for achieving social and political peace range from military intimidation to open warfare to asymmetrical treaties or pacts in which recognition of the sovereignty of the *khalīfa* (emperor, Muhammad's successor) and his taxes are predominant. Submission is the all-governing principle. In Islam, peace and submission go hand in hand since they are derived from the same linguistic-semantic root.

A clear example of these four interrelated aspects (war, peace, context, and the variety of meanings of the concept and its practice) is found in two verses of the sura of the Retraction, *at-Tawba*:

> 3. […] And proclaim a grievous penalty to those who reject Faith.
> 4. (But the treaters are) not dissolved with those Pagans with whom ye have entered into alliance and who have not subsequently failed you in aught, nor aided anyone against you. So fulfil your engagements with them to the end of the term: for Allah loveth the righteous.
> 5. But when the forbidden months are past, then fight and slay the Pagans wherever ye find them, and seize them, beleaguer them, and lie in wait for them in ever stratagem (of war): but if they repent, and establish regular prayers, and practise regular charity, then open the way for them: for Allah is Oft-Forgiving, Most Merciful.[26]
> 6. If one amongst the Pagans ask thee for asylum, grant it to him, so that he may hear the Word of Allah; and then escort him to where he can be secure. That is because they are men without knowledge. (Qur'an 9:3c-6)

Verse six comes from the early period of Islam, and details the practice of *amān* that:

> Consisted of a security guarantee according to which the *harbī* (the polytheist, the Christian or the Jew) could avail himself of the protection of a Muslim, as long as he remained in the territory of Islam, for a period of less than one year; after that time, two possibilities were offered to him: to become a *dhimmi* and pay the [associated] tax or to adopt Islam; otherwise, the *musta'min* was taken, guaranteeing his safety, to his place of origin.[27]

---

[25] Franco Sánchez, "Noción de Paz," 173.
[26] This verse is noted under the name *ayatus-saif*, the verse of the sword, which abrogates the earlier pronouncements on relations with non-Muslims.
[27] Gómez Camarero et al., "Lectura," 136.

But, as we see in the prevailing Sunni interpretation (expressed in the commentaries of the convert Melara Navio, published by the King Fahd Complex), this verse is abrogated, while the previous verse (that of the sword) is the ruling one.

Our brief study has revealed two major meanings of peace according to the Muslim understanding: an internal meaning and a sociopolitical meaning. The first developed and prevailed in the early period in Mecca while the second is related to Medina. As we move ahead, we anticipate many points of contact between the biblical and Muslim understandings of peace, although we will observe a different ultimate goal and a different path towards achieving peace.

3. Development-Salaam: Cultural Connections

In the previous two sections, devoted to the biblical ideal and the Muslim concept of peace, we have presented a summary of their conceptions of peace. We can easily perceive certain similarities as well as differences. The impression of similarity is considerably reinforced by the experience of living in a majority Muslim country. Here we will attempt to highlight the aspects that present the greatest potential for those engaged in integral development in a Muslim context, what we have called Development-Salaam. Our intent is to highlight the positives in that which we have observed. We want to place value on what the Muslim community is proud of and desires that we emphasize.

- *Salaam* is theocentric, religious. In the mind of every Muslim, *salaam* comes from Allah. Moreover, there is no salaam without fear of God. One of the names of Allah is precisely *As-Salaam*: the giver of peace. (cf. Jdg. 6:24; Is. 9:6)
- It is concerned with the communal and social. *Salaam* is inherently collective; it is welfare for the individual in the community. (cf. Num. 6:24-27)
- It is integral. True and complete salaam is all-encompassing, harmonious. Partial salaam (which concerns only one area of life) is only a foretaste of the comprehensive and total salaam that fulfills the deepest aspirations.
- Is relational. He is interested in promoting healthy relationships. *Salaam*, well-being, and harmonious relationships with oneself, one's family, one's community, and God are one and the same.
- It transcends class and rank divisions. Both the poor and the rich, the powerful and the weak need and aspire to experience true *salaam*.
- It is generous. *Salaam* is the sincere wish for the other, expressed in every greeting: "*As salaamu aleikum*" (Allah's peace be upon you/with you). The pursuit of salaam is focused on the neighbor, the other both near and far.

These points of overlap should not, however, lead us to overlook the differences, aspects requiring the most attention when embarking on a Development-Salaam initiative. There are significant differences.

One of the aspects that we will have to cultivate, both theologically and practically, is that of contentment. We need to show that *salaam* and envy are incompatible. God has commanded "You shall not covet" (Ex. 20:17) and "be content with what you have" (Heb. 13:5). We must teach, encourage, and cultivate this truth in the face of the consumerist spirit that the West globally propagates. Contentment is not a common or desired concept in Islam (unlike resignation, which is).

A second difference is the very weak relationship that the Muslim concept of *salaam* has with creation. The relationships emphasized by *salaam* are human ones, almost ignoring the harmony with nature created by God. The whole concept of stewardship of creation, sustainable management of resources, cleanliness and hygiene of public spaces, and pollution are topics little known to our Muslim friends (in relation to *salaam*) but are included in the idea of biblical *shalom*.

Third, differences in the concept of justice, and in how peace is achieved, are also important. Timothy Woods notes that:

> At the heart of Islam is the imperative to create a godly community, a people at peace with God and one another. This demands action, and lays upon believers the call to *jihad*, the duty to struggle to apply God's will and purpose. [...] In Islam, peace will be attained through struggle against injustice, and by commanding the right.[28]

It is the duty of every Muslim to promote the justice on which peace is based, as well as to fight against the injustice that hinders it. Every believer has a certain executive power with respect to the law of God (the *shari'a*). The concept of peace and justice in Islam is linked to geography. There is no compassion or tolerance when Muslims lose or are expelled from their homes and territories (e.g., Palestine). Currently, there is a unanimous feeling (among Muslims) that the *ummah* is suffering violence and oppression, both politically and from global capitalism.

David Shenk's reflection, comparing the paths to peace of Jesus, Constantine, and Muhammad, is very pertinent. Jesus deliberately chose suffering as a way to defeat, in his own body and with his "peaceful resistance," the various forms of violence that Jews, religious leaders and political leaders exercised against him. By contrast, Constantine and Muhammad chose violence and military might or piracy and ambushes to impose their rule.[29] Shenk notes:

---

[28] Timothy J. Woods, "Islam, Peace and the Quest for Justice," *Theology* 109, no. 852 (November 1, 2006): 412-20, https://doi.org/10.1177/0040571X0610900603.

[29] David W. Shenk, "Three Journeys for Peace: Jesus, Constantine and Muhammad," in *Anabaptists meeting Muslims*, ed. J. R Krabill, D. W Shenk, and L. Stutzman (Scottdale, Penn.: Herald Press, 2005), 25-39, http://www.mwc-cmm.org/sites/default/files/website_files/mis_com_fd_shenk_d._three_journeys2.pdf.

> The Muslim Hijrah takes us in the opposite direction to the way chosen by Jesus. Messiah-centered peace is the way of the cross. The peace of the Messiah is in receiving and offering forgiveness.[30]

The very radical distinction between *dar el-Salaam* and *dar el-Harb* (house of peace and house of war) again points us to the radical difference in the methods of achieving peace. Development-Salaam should pay close attention to these distinctions.

Fourth, the growing polarization and mutual enmity between a large part of Muslims and the West cannot be ignored. Both sides have fomented confrontation, the "clash of civilizations." The question of peace cannot be approached simplistically and naively. There are many, on both sides, who foment violence and rejoice in it. The events of 2015 and 2016 with the rise of Daesh/ISIS, the wars in Syria and Yemen, and the growing wave of attacks in Mali, Paris, Turkey, Belgium, and elsewhere charge the atmosphere of confrontation between "Islam" and "the West."

Therefore, despite the many cultural, semantic, and outward similarities between the concepts of *shalom* and *salaam*, the serious differences in substance make it necessary to work toward the redevelopment of values, if the Development-salaam proposal is to have any chance of success.

4. Development-Salaam: Connections with Development

As we have already seen, development is not a uniform concept, equally understood by all. It is expressed through a variety of approaches and is directed toward different ultimate purposes. The results of a comparison between development and *shalom-salaam* have greater points of contact with models of the Other Development or Human Scale Development type discussed earlier, and less continuity with neoliberal/neoconservative and structural positions.

The table overleaf is not based on assumptions of equal, comparable categories. Rather, we intend it to help visualize differences and similarities between the broad concept of "development" and the broad concept of "*salaam/shalom*." It visually draws our attention to the many points of contact between the two concepts, as well as the fundamental differences.

As we have seen earlier, the ultimate purposes of development, especially state-sponsored development, include important doses of profit, westernization, and power struggles as well as the promotion of a humanist worldview. We must then ask ourselves what are, or should be, the goals of development-*salaam*:

---

[30] David Shenk and Ahmed Haile, "Peacemaking and Church Formation," in *From Seed to Fruit: Global Trends, Fruitful Practices, and Emerging Issues among Muslims*, ed. J. Dudley Woodberry (Pasadena: William Carey Library, 2008), 326.

Development	*Salaam/Shalom*
Is empirical; searched for facts; develops plans and projects	Is relational and intuitive, it is perceived
Is an inherent part of the Western mindset	Is primarily understood and appreciated among Semitic peoples
Assesses and works towards objectives	Is a state, a condition
Is achieved	Is lived
Focuses on needs	Focuses on the positive and on an ideal
Dreams of a better future (principally material)	Dreams of a better future (principally relational)
Is human, material, and of this earth	Is all-encompassing (Col. 1:16-20)

Figure 7. Comparison Development-Salaam

> I know the plans I have in mind for you, declares the Lord; they are plans for peace (*shalom*), not disaster, to give you a future filled with hope. (Jer. 29:11 CEB)

God's goal is well-being, future, and hope, for all, especially the weakest in society: orphans, widows, foreigners, the poor. That is the measure and goal of *shalom*. It is the restoration or righting of all relationships, in an atmosphere of justice and joy (Rom. 14:17).

Peace and mission: In relation to Christian mission, peace is both the way and the means to a life in fullness. It has both individual and socio-political implications. Development-Salaam, which we have just begun to outline, could be a way to promote human, socio-political, and ecological development, carried out jointly by Christian activists (followers of the Messiah) and Muslims. It would thus contribute not only to the harmonious progress of local communities, but also demonstrate that a non-confrontational relationship between Christians and Muslims is possible.

5. Conclusion

These theoretical reflections, motivated by our research among several development projects, will help us build the proposal that we will present in the final chapters. Together with considerations of integrality, the various concepts of development and the understanding of *shalom-salaam*, they contribute to a proposal for a new approach aimed at:

- a reformulation of the identity of Iberoamerican workers in order to become intrinsically religious, integral, relationship-oriented salaam agents oriented to the global welfare of the community, and
- a first outline of a theology of Development-Salaam.

Questions for Reflection and Discussion

1. Have you worked or lived with Muslims? What was your experience? To what extent does such a pleasant or unpleasant experience condition you?
2. Have you ever visited a mosque? Have you ever asked a Muslim to help you understand their faith and practices? What did you learn?
3. If you are a missionary or a Christian development worker serving among Muslims, what ideas initially came to mind as you considered the bridge between Development and *Salaam*?

For Further Reading

Dennett, Bill, and John R. Reid. *Sharing the Good News with Muslims*. Homebush West, NSW, Australia: Anzea, 1992.

Fileta, Jason, Tearfund, and Micah Challenge. *Live Justly: Global Edition*. Portland, Ore.: Micah Challenge and Tearfund, 2017. https://learn.tearfund.org/en/resources/tools-and-guides/live-justly-global-edition.

Kateregga, Badru, and David W. Shenk. *A Muslim and a Christian in Dialogue*. 2nd ed. Harrisonburg: Herald Press, 2011.

Schirrmacher, Christine. *The Islamic View of Major Christian Teachings: The Role of Jesus Christ, Sin, Faith, and Forgiveness; Essays*. Ed. by Ruth Baldwin. The WEA Global Issues Series, Vol. 2. Bonn: Verlag für Kultur und Wissenschaft, 2008. https://iirf.eu/site/assets/files/91402/wea_gis_2_-_christine_schirrmacher_-_the_islamic_view_of_major_christian_teachings.pdf.

14. Outline of a Theology of Development-Salaam

1. Introduction

In this section, we intend to outline the main ideas of a theology of Development-Salaam, consistent with the reflections and considerations we have made so far. It is intended as a reflection on the reality of development initiatives carried out by Iberoamerican development workers serving in Muslim contexts. This reflection draws on four sources: biblical reflection, the Christian church's understanding of development or progress over the centuries, an in-depth analysis of the hybrid Latin-Muslim context, and finally a personal component arising from our own experience as a married couple, establishing churches and directing development projects for some forty years.

In synthesis, *this reflection is developed within the lines of integral mission, from a contextual hermeneutic, but applying an epistemological and dialogical contextualization.* Our approach is evangelical, that is, it gives first place to the Bible, but it broadens the two sources of traditional theology (Bible and tradition) to include first, the current context in which theological action takes place and second, the experience of our personal life. In this way, the participants dialogue and interact with their context, with their current understanding of the Bible, as well as with ancient interpretations of the biblical text, in order to respond to the new questions that reality poses to them. Finally, we seek a contextualization that goes beyond external forms and incarnation or translatability. In this proposal, we try to go a step further, towards a reading of the Scriptures from local knowledge, questioning Western epistemology and establishing a constant tripartite dialogue between the reality of the Muslim context, the reflections of the Church in other latitudes and the Bible. The ultimate purpose is to contribute to doing theology from the Latin-Muslim hybridization.

2. Large Themes

It is not easy to deal with such a broad subject, one which carries so many ramifications. That is why we have thought of structuring it around eleven core themes in order to coherently organize the concepts and achieve an integral and solid final result. Development-Salaam moves within the framework of the *kingdom of God*, expresses itself through *music, proverbs, and stories*, moves away from the *Western* development model, to articulate its own contextual religious identity, expressed in new *gender and caste* relations. Development-Salaam formulates the gospel from its own categories of *honor and purity*, in continuity and discontinuity with *Israel*, has articulated a new understanding of *conversion and ecclesiology*, is essentially *missionary*, and has an alternative understanding of *economics, property, and resource management*, all wrapped in *salaam*. In listing these eleven axes or themes, we realize at once that they are of varying importance and breadth, but we do not want to establish an order of priorities or a ranking of importance. They are all necessary and in fact form part of a whole.

To help understand the relationship of these eleven axes to each other, we will compare them to the various elements of a house: the environment and context in which the house sits, the ground, four columns that support the four corners of the house, the roof, the windows that bring light, the exterior walls, and a truss that, at the height of the roof joins together the whole building giving it additional strength.

Figure 8. Courtyard of an Andalusian House

The Kingdom of God: the Environment or Context

The kingdom of God was the central theme of Jesus's message. It was the central theme of the preaching of the apostles: "Jesus Christ is Lord" (or king). No missiology can ignore considering the kingdom without running the risk of losing its way. Frequently, the Iberoamerican missionary enterprise has identified the purpose of its mission with the establishment (planting) of churches. This error is common among servants and agencies working in the

Muslim world. Let us understand each other well. We do not want to undervalue church planting. On the contrary, we have dedicated more than forty years of our lives to this noble work. But church planting is the penultimate goal of mission.[1]

In the Latin-Muslim hybridization, this is an easily understandable issue. On the one hand, the kingdom of God has been the central theme of Latin American integral mission and, on the other hand, Muslim societies are theocratic in their own ethos, in their essence. Theocracy is the government of God, whether direct or mediated through his ministers. Muslims understand that God is the supreme king and ruler. They believe that God's rule permeates (or should permeate) all aspects of society. This is why we have proposed that missionary workers in Islamic contexts use *explicit religious language*. We define explicit religious language as "that which adopts Islamic cultural expressions to refer to God, his kingdom and sovereignty, but goes beyond that, eliciting reactions of awe or surprise." Muslim societies use a multitude of idioms naming God, which everyone repeats almost without thinking. For example, when getting into the car and starting a journey, "Allah go with us" is often said. Explicit religious language will change this formula a little to raise questions and admiration: "May the Most High be with us."

Considering development in the light of the kingdom helps us to keep perspective, because the kingdom adds Christological, ethical, ecological, and eschatological dimensions to the mere soteriological content. Kingdom and development go hand in hand. The latter points to and finds its purpose in the former. At the same time, the kingdom is broader than development and the church; it has much broader and deeper dimensions without which both the church and development miss something vital.

But it is not an easy or simple subject. Suffice it to recall the many and constant misinterpretations of the kingdom. In New Testament times, we may think of the Jews in general, the disciples of John, those who, like Simeon and Anna, expected "the consolation of Israel", the apocalyptics such as the Essenes. In our times, among our missionary partners there will be those who understand the kingdom as something within the heart of the believer, or those who identify it with the Church, those who cast it into the future, into the Millennium, and even those who equate the kingdom with the betterment of society. On the Muslim side, it will be necessary to fight any temptation to identify the kingdom of God with *dar al-Islam* (the house of Islam), that is, a geographical and political concept imposed from above and from the logic of power. It will be necessary to return again and again to the Bible, to the history of the Church and to the Islamic/Muslim context in order to understand the kingdom of God from the perspective of the Development-Salaam.

---

[1] Orlando E Costas, *Liberating News: A Theology of Contextual Evangelization* (Eugene: Wipf & Stock, 2002), 56-57; Bryant L. Myers, *Walking with the Poor: Principles and Practices of Transformational Development*, Rev. ed. (Maryknoll: Orbis, 2011), 79.

But, returning to our illustration, the environment – the context of the kingdom on which the house is built – is saturated with hope and a vision of the future. It is not possible to think of the kingdom of God only in past or present. The eschaton is always present. In our own story, our experience as children and young people was just the opposite. Faced with the questions of the present, our church asked: What did the apostles teach? That is a very laudable question in itself, but it was rarely balanced with the future ideal. As a result, we lived looking to the past, taking for granted that the early church was the best of all time.

This future-oriented approach provides an important balance to Islam's tendency to focus on the past, to idealize it. In the specific case of the projects, we believe that it is appropriate to develop a hermeneutic (an orientation of the whole project) of the future, with an eye to the consummation of the kingdom as the ideal model for the present. In a certain sense, it is an eschatological orientation because it takes the New Jerusalem as the model of development.

This orientation to the future contrasts with the vision that takes Eden as a model, that is to say that it understands the goal of development as a return to a restored Garden.[2] "Your kingdom come, your will be done on earth as it is in heaven" is the prayer balanced between the eschatological, complete kingdom and its daily and progressive advance, mediated by the prayer of its subjects, here on earth.

Economy, Land, Property, and Resources: the Ground

The ground on which our theological "house" is built is a biblical and alternative understanding of economics, property, and resources. It is derived from the Bible, and in many respects is alternative to both Western practices and the teachings of Islam.

To turn them into practical reality, the four principles enunciated by Christopher Wright will have to be studied, put into verse or proverb form, drawn out, and widely disseminated: resources for all, the right and duty to work, expectations of growth and trade, and equitable enjoyment of benefits. Development-Salaam economics recognizes that everything we have is a gift from God and has translated that truth into everyday reality. At the same time, all activities, projects, and ethics are imbued with a simple but revolutionary motivation: "watch out for what is better for others" (Phil. 2:4 CEB; Eph. 4:28). It is a theocentric and neighbor-centric economy.

Development-Salaam economics makes it clear that the consumerist system fostered by disembodied capitalism and the globalization of markets has become a problem. From the believer's perspective, it is clearly sinful. Plain and simple.

---

[2] Among others, see Leonardo Boff, *Cry of the Earth, Cry of the Poor, Ecology and Justice* (Maryknoll: Orbis, 1997). Note how the Muslim concept of Paradise is also associated with a garden.

"You shall not covet" is the divine commandment. Let us remember that, in a Muslim society, a divine commandment has extraordinary force.

We have mentioned some practical applications that could be implemented in urban areas: job training, economic empowerment, self-sufficiency, microcredit, rest and enjoying the Sabbath, public prayer for the common welfare, and training of welfare agents. In rural areas, this could include gleaning of harvest fields, periodic tithes given to the poor, rest and joyful weekly celebrations – all of these familiar customs that might even look like some form of Jubilee. This is not simply a matter of uncritically applying practices of Bible times to our own time but of looking for an equivalent, considering Israel as a paradigm.

A Non-Western Model: the First Column

Two reasons lie behind the negative term in this section heading. On the one hand, the purpose of an important part of state-sponsored Western development has been to conquer the rest of the world with its consumerist and humanist model of society (as seen, for example, in Truman's "let them be like us" expression). Likewise, whether rightly or wrongly attributed to the West, we are concerned with the profit motive at the expense of the weakest, and in particular directed toward the Global South (as expressed, for example, in the theory of dependency, discussed in Chapter 3). In recent years, this disembodied profit-driven goal has been increasingly fueled by China and India, each with its own peculiarities. On the other hand, the widespread suspicion in the Muslim world is that any development initiative is a covert aggression against its very Islamic nature. Hence our proposal that development projects carried out by Iberoamerican workers and mission agencies should dissociate themselves from the Western model. The proposal of Development-Salaam includes the idea that the Iberoamerican development agencies should reformulate their identity, both negatively (which we do in this section) and positively (which we will do in the following section).

A non-Western model also includes an express break with all traces of imperialism, whether Western, Christian, or Islamic. Development-Salaam serves another King and lives under another banner. This must be made very clear not only to the development workers themselves, but also outwardly to the world for which the projects and churches want to be a model and example. From the beginning and throughout the Bible, God claims first place and therefore rejects all forms of imperialism. Babel (Gen. 11) is the first clear message in this sense. From then on, God always works on the margins of, and in contrast to, the great empires; with a small nation, or with a numerous but scattered and not very powerful church. In contrast, the history of empires has been a constant useless, overwhelming, and dehumanizing expense. Development-Salaam is called to follow, imitate, and exemplify the eternal kingdom, humanizing, just, inclusive, presided over by the Lamb who was slain. In front of the human emperor stands the righteous Servant.

Coupled with this, we have already mentioned the deliberate rejection of warmongering language. This is a theme mentioned repeatedly in some missiological works relating to Islam. Finally, another rejection is to favor primarily the rich and powerful. That is the essence of the current neo-neo model; it is also the trend in Muslim societies, but it is not the way of Development-Salaam. All biblical teaching focuses on caring for and helping the weak and building a caring and egalitarian community and society.

Religious Identity: the Second Column

In this section, we deal with the identity of the development workers and the agency they work for, as well as the identity of the development project. If in the previous section we talked about rejecting a certain model, now we are building an identity of our own. The two most common options are to adopt either a secular or a Christian identity. We have already discarded the former, because of its association with the West and its values. We propose to reject also the second, the option of presenting ourselves as Christian workers or agencies. Rather than being a help, the label "Christian" is a great hindrance, an almost insurmountable difficulty, when serving in Muslim societies.

This label carries with it a number of negative connotations that are very difficult to avoid. A religious identity, although not "Christian" (Western), coupled with the *explicit religious language* mentioned above, and accompanied by an active and open but non-threatening evangelism, is a radical departure from what our Muslim friends would expect from a "Christian."

It is often taken for granted that, in contexts hostile to the gospel such as in Muslim-majority countries, evangelists should be discreet, sharing their message very slowly, without arousing suspicion, trying not to make a fuss. The idea is to avoid confrontation and gain trust through so-called friendship evangelism.

We hold just the opposite view. Evangelism, by its very nature, cannot be discreet, go unnoticed, be done half-heartedly or in secret. The essence of evangelism is to call people to a radical change to follow Jesus Christ. This cannot be done discreetly. The purpose of the messenger of the King of kings is not to go unnoticed; on the contrary, their whole life must bear witness to the lordship of Jesus. What the integral evangelist wants is to be noticed. They avoid unnecessary cultural offense. There is one offense that cannot be avoided, the scandal of the cross (Gal. 5:11), but all other stumbling blocks, all those due to language and cultural barriers, must be set aside by the evangelist operating in another culture.

Our proposal is to adopt, in a transparent manner, the identity of honorable guests, followers of the Messiah, messengers of the King, and God-fearers. "We are agents of Salaam, promoters of harmonious welfare derived from the King" would be the motto of the proposed new identity.

In this style of open evangelism associated with this religious identity, the messengers of the King:

- Communicate their faith with minimal cultural offense, that is, using appropriate cultural forms,
- Do not hide their faith in Jesus Christ,
- Openly confess their love for the nation and their intention to bless it in the name of the Messiah,
- Do not hide their intentions; they openly express their role as ambassadors of the King and their desire that their hearers should decide to follow the Messiah,
- Constantly name God using his names,
- Are perceived as God-fearing (honest, righteous, true, etc.),
- Provoke admiration,
- Provide opportunities in which people can ask them about their life and their faith,
- Take the initiative to offer prayer, to pronounce a blessing, or to minister spiritual liberation, health, and peace,
- Use proverbs that name God and spiritual themes,
- Are known in their setting as people who fear God, people who are righteous, followers of the Messiah, and similar descriptions.

In addition to adopting a religious identity that applies to the development workers-missionaries and the agency, what about the project itself? For the project to be enduring, it must have a history of its own and make sense, fitting into the overall story of the community. At the same time, it must fit into God's story for the world. It is a matter of identity. In the convulsive world in which we live, many peoples are redefining their identity. In the case of Muslim peoples, the list is very long: Kurds, various Afghan ethnic groups, the countries South of the Sahara, and Berbers, to name just a few.

Beyond the identity of the project, to whom does the project belong? Whatever the theory, in most cases the project belongs to the workers, the agency, and those who finance it. We propose that in this intentional change of identity we should also approach things so that in daily, practical reality it is clear to everyone that the project belongs, in this order, (1) to God, the giver and sustainer of all things; (2) to the local beneficiaries, and (3) to the workers and facilitators as well as to the supporting agency.

Gender, Caste, and Slavery: the Third Column

Every generation and every culture poses its own questions concerning *Isa al-Masih* (Jesus the Messiah). Questions related to gender are numerous and very present in the Muslim world. Women want to know what advantage Christianity offers to them. They are impacted by the example of Christian marriages as well as the way the Messiah treats women in the "Jesus" film. At the same time, doubts arise, as Chantal Logan notes. "The teachings of Jesus: Good news for whom?" as well as "Is the Church radical enough when it meets the *Ummah*?"[3]

The answers are not as positive as we might like. Current models of conversion and of churches are not reaching women in equal numbers. We have to ask why, among Muslim men who have become followers of Jesus, so few wives have also come to faith through the example and instruction of their husbands.[4] The Latin-Muslim mix further complicates the situation. Latin American workers come from a social and church background dominated by *machismo*. How should we face this unanswered theme?

First, we observe that in Latin American societies (and the West in general), men and women live in the *same world* and compete to gain influence in that same world. By comparison, in Muslim societies, men and women live in *separate worlds* that virtually do not touch and with minimal interaction. Women have full rights in their world and virtually none in the world of men, while men have the rights in their own world but virtually none in the world of women. The theme is complex, but to accept principles of gender that arise from the evaluations, subsidies, and criteria imposed by Western donors on development projects is not enough. It is urgent that Latin American workers-missionaries develop a theology of gender in accordance with Scripture, in particular modeled in the story of creation and of the new Jerusalem (once again the hermeneutic of the future) in clear contrast with a "theology of masculine domination," that is a direct consequence of the Fall (Gen. 3:16b) perpetuating its noxious effects. That is to say we need to understand gender complicated passages (that some could understand in a misogynistic form) in the light of the full development of the Bible.

In this sense, *all* projects, not just those directed toward women, should include biblical values of gender. This needs to be done with sensitivity as is appropriate for "guests in a foreign land" understanding and teaching the theological and practical reach of existing as *bi-unity*, man and woman.[5]

We dream of a new movement of local churches in Muslim contexts that, instead of reinforcing the male domination of the culture, challenges it in radical and, at the same time, gentle and non-threatening ways.

---

[3] Chantal Logan, "Is the Gospel Good News for Muslim Women?," in *Anabaptists Meeting Muslims: A Calling for Presence in the Way of Christ*, ed. James R. Krabill, David W. Shenk, and Linford Stutzman (Scottdale, Penn.: Herald Press, 2005), 141-53.

[4] Note that just the opposite was the characteristic of the gospel in the first four centuries. The gospel was attractive to women, so that they constituted the majority of the membership, and a large number of women won their husbands to their new faith. See among others, Rodney Stark, *The Rise of Christianity: How the Obscure, Marginal Jesus Movement Became the Dominant Religious Force in the Western World in a Few Centuries*, 1st pbk. (San Francisco: HarperSanFrancisco, 1997).

[5] Paul King Jewett, *Man as Male and Female: A Study in Sexual Relationships from a Theological Point of View* (Grand Rapids: Eerdmans, 1990).

Another very important theme, one of the main columns of our house, is the issue of caste. When speaking about caste, we consider not only India but also several Muslim countries, like Bangladesh or Pakistan, that hold to a form of that social system. William Carey and his colleagues were known and honored throughout India for their struggle against the burning of widows. As we saw earlier, the Christians of the first centuries were known for rescuing thousands of slaves. Unfortunately, however, today only a few Christian minority groups are known in India for their struggle against the unjust and inhuman caste system. Let us clarify that Hinduism is not intrinsically opposed to conversion to Christianity or any other religion. Its belief in thousands of gods allows it to admit one more, as long as the new believers remain in their caste and follow the social dictates of their social group. But opposition is fierce as soon as the caste system and the impossibility of inter-caste mobility is questioned.

The caste system determines that some castes are up and others down on the social, economic, educational, and political ladder. Mobility from one caste to another is not allowed. This fact is totally contrary to the spirit of the Bible which stipulates (1) the radical equality of all human beings before God, (2) the commandment of progress and the legitimate possibility for all to enjoy equally the resources given by God to all, and (3) the possibility of change, and in particular of turning from other gods to Jesus Christ (and vice versa). The Bible makes it very clear that Jesus Christ came to break down the barriers that sin has erected between human beings with one another and with God (Eph. 2:14; Col. 3:11; 1 Cor. 12:13; Gal. 3:28).

The caste system has also condemned some two hundred fifty million people to virtual slavery. Dalits or untouchables are not even included in the caste system. They are under all castes and are virtual slaves to do all the menial jobs that the other castes do not want to do. Slavery and human trafficking continue to be common practice throughout the world, a large part of them in India, in Muslim countries, and unfortunately, also in our country, Spain. Slavery and human trafficking constitute the second most lucrative business on the planet.[6]

---

[6] This is a complex and broad subject. In 2017, the ILO estimated the number of victims of forced labor at 21 million people. As an introduction, see David A. Feingold, "Trafficking in Numbers: The Social Construction of Human Trafficking Data," in *Sex, Drugs, and Body Counts: The Politics of Numbers in Global Crime and Conflict* (Ithaca: Cornell University Press, 2011), 46-74, https://www.degruyter.com/document/doi/10.7591/9780801458309-005/html; Louise Shelley, *Human Trafficking: A Global Perspective* (Cambridge: Cambridge University Press, 2010); Katharine Bryant and Todd Landman, "Combatting Human Trafficking since Palermo: What Do We Know about What Works?," *Journal of Human Trafficking* 6, no. 2 (March 14, 2020): 119-40, https://doi.org/10.1080/23322705.2020.1690097; Patrick Belser, "The Economics of Slavery, Forced Labor and Human Trafficking," in *The Encyclopedia of Law and Economics* (Rochester, N.Y.: Elgar Publishing, May 11, 2008), https://papers.ssrn.com/abstract=1838369. For Spain, see: Europa Press, "La Trata de

A Development-Salaam missiology cannot ignore this fact, nor can it fail to take a clear public stand against this scourge. How will the slaves believe in Jesus if the followers of the Messiah they know, the development workers and national believers, maintain their rejection of slavery in silence? The New Testament gives us examples of firmness on this point, albeit in non-threatening ways.

Conversion and Church: the Fourth Column

Development-Salaam theology understands conversion more as a process than as an instantaneous act or crisis. Many who have worked for years in Muslim contexts agree on this point: they see conversion as a succession of small steps toward Jesus Christ and the kingdom of God, a progression. David Greenlee and Rick Love, both with many years of experience in Muslim contexts, mention seven lenses and the many facets of conversion.[7] Donna Entz relates several examples of these micro-conversions in Burkina Faso.[8]

The goal is not to incorporate isolated individuals but family groups into the church. The preference for group or collective evangelism minimizes the impact of Western individualistic style on decision-making. Instead of gaining individuals for the Christian faith in this model the goal is to win a complete natural group, usually an extended family, taking much care to respect the leader or head of the group. In societies having honor as a key marker of relationships, it is not only inadequate to push someone as an individual to make an important decision, as it becomes an affront to the honor of the entire group. This does not mean that we should entirely avoid individual conversations and Bible study nor abandon the idea of individual conversions. We are speaking of how people make decisions. The maxim "if something is good for me it must be good for my family" governs close societies and those with a strong group cohesion. In this way, the individual who has recently become convinced of the validity of the Christian faith will share their discovery with the extended family and, eventually, all may come to a decision to follow Jesus Christ. As this moment approaches, the individual will live their new faith within the limits of the extended family in ways that stimulate the entire group but without bringing

---

Personas En El Mundo, En Datos y Gráficos," Datos, October 2020, https://www.epdata.es/datos/trata-personas-mundo-datos-graficos/427; Europa Press, "El Tráfico de Personas en el Mundo en Diez Datos" (May 6, 2016), https://www.europapress.es/internacional/noticia-trafico-personas-mundo-diez-datos-20170506174236.html.

[7] David Greenlee and Rick Love, "Conversion through the Looking Glass: Muslims and the Multiple Facets of Conversion," in *From the Straight Path to the Narrow Way: Journeys of Faith*, ed. David Greenlee (Waynesboro, Ga.: Authentic Media, 2006), 4.

[8] Donna Entz, "Burkina Faso," in Krabill et al., *Anabaptists Meeting Muslims*, 201.

shame upon them. John Kim offers an interesting case study along these lines based on a cluster of Muslim family groups in Southeast Asia.[9]

Anthropologist Paul Hiebert's set theory could be helpfully applied here. First, he describes sets or groups defined in terms of a center or a boundary (extrinsic or intrinsic sets). He then explores two other categories: well-formed sets, which have a sharp boundary, and fuzzy sets, which do not.[10] Churches made up of those with a Muslim background can easily be understood as centered groups, focused on a relationship with Jesus, having a clear difference between membership and non-membership but where conversion is understood as a progression toward the center, and where faithfulness and commitment to Christ is the primary variable.

This understanding of conversion certainly has many practical repercussions for the church. On the one hand, it changes the church's perception of itself, it changes the makeup of its membership: principally family groups along with some unmarried singles, as compared to a group of extracted converts[11] made up mainly of unmarried singles.

In the same way, it changes its relationship with its surrounding environment: isolated or integrated. It also changes its sense of being a closed group, hermetically cut off, or a group that is open and welcoming. This final point is very sensitive in settings in which the church is surrounded by persecution. It is not easy to maintain an open, welcoming spirit among those who are seeking the Lord or have recently come to faith in Jesus when there is a strong possibility of betrayal and of traitors within the group. Finally, this progressive perception of conversion minimizes the separation between evangelism and discipleship, something that fits well integral cultures like that of many Muslims.

Evangelism based on this group approach leads naturally to group decisions that, without doubt, will affect our ecclesiology, for example in deciding the time and place of baptism, accepting new members, and how to apply discipline.

Above all, Development-Salaam theology seeks to keep the objective clear: that the community of believers should be an alternative model that the

---

[9] Kim briefly recounts the process of introducing the gospel into a rural Southeast Asian cluster, following the church planting movements model (CPM) outlined by David Garrison. John Kim, "Muslim Villagers Coming to Faith in Christ: A Case Study and Model of Group Dynamics," in *From the Straight Path to the Narrow Way: Journeys of Faith*, ed. David Greenlee (Waynesboro, Ga.: Authentic, 2006), 239-54; John Kim, "The Anotoc Story Continued: Group Dynamics within an Insider Movement," in *Longing for Community: Church,* Ummah, *or Somewhere in Between?*, ed. David Greenlee (Pasadena: William Carey Library, 2013), 169-80; V. David Garrison, *Church Planting Movements: How God Is Redeeming a Lost World* (Midlothian, Vir.: WIGTake, 2004).

[10] Paul G. Hiebert, *Anthropological Reflections on Missiological Issues* (Grand Rapids: Baker, 1994), chap. 6.

[11] Extraction evangelism pushes new believers to make individual decisions, often accompanied by alien values and lifestyles, which leads to rejection and isolation by the subject's original community.

surrounding community and society can admire and imitate. It aspires to form churches, communities, or development projects that are open, attractive, and ready to share the blessing of God, knowing that each should "watch out for what is better for others" (Phil. 2:4 CEB.)

Missionary in Essence: the Roof

The theology of Development-Salaam is missionary in its very nature; it lives by and for the mission of God, the *missio Dei*, because its identity is rooted there: "My Father is always at his work to this very day, and I, too, am working" (John 5:17). This concept is closely related with all the rest: personal identity, the kingdom, economy, and so on. Mission is not just one more activity added onto many other important things but is the organizing theme of all of life. The entire Bible, from the first page to the last, is missionary in essence: it is the revelation of the purpose of God and His missionary action in human history. Consequently, Development-Salaam follows the same steps. Mission goes far beyond evangelism; it includes a dynamic relationship with society and the world with a view to their transformation according to the model of the kingdom of God. Development – the transformation of individuals and of the institutions of society – and mission go hand-in-hand. Therefore, from here on we will refer not to the theology but to the missiology of Development-Salaam.

This missiology has to formulate its own theology, from the critical reflection on its praxis, in the hybrid Latin-Muslim framework. While neither subordinated to Western theology nor anti-Western, it should be in close contact with other theologies or missiologies of the Global South.

Honor and Purity: a Window

Two windows allow light to stream into and add color to the house of our illustration. The first we mention is an understanding of the gospel seen through the categories of honor and purity.

Fortunately, the last few years have seen the emergence of a great deal of reflection and publication on the subject of honor and shame, offering us a deepened biblical understanding in general and application to evangelism in particular.[12] Roland Muller has probed these insights and adapted them to

---

[12] Consider in particular the authors linked to the Context Group and their exegetical commentaries drawing on the social sciences. Bruce J. Malina and Richard L. Rohrbaugh, *Social-Science Commentary on the Gospel of John* (Minneapolis: Fortress, 1998); Bruce J. Malina and John J. Pilch, *Social-Science Commentary on the Book of Revelation* (Minneapolis: Fortress, 2000); Bruce J. Malina, *The New Testament World: Insights from Cultural Anthropology*, 3rd ed. (Louisville: Westminster John Knox Press, 2001); Bruce J. Malina and Richard L. Rohrbaugh, *Social-Science Commentary on the Synoptic Gospels*, 2nd ed. (Minneapolis: Fortress, 2003); Bruce J. Malina and John J. Pilch, *Social-Science Commentary on the Letters of Paul* (Minneapolis: Fortress, 2006); Bruce J. Malina and John J. Pilch, *Social-Science Commentary on the Book of Acts*

Muslim settings.[13] However, the missiology of Development-Salaam must undoubtedly reformulate its understanding of the gospel from these two mental categories so typical of the Muslim world: the pairs of honor and shame, and purity and impurity. On the other hand, evangelism based on the mental categories of law and guilt (following Anglo-Saxon-German cultural models) makes little sense to the Muslim listener. Therefore, it is not only a matter of understanding the culture, but of re-reading the Bible from the honor-shame and purity-impurity pairings. It is about how we do theology: understanding the cultural reality in the light of the Bible, as well as knowing how to transmit the biblical truths from the concepts of honor, shame, purity, and impurity.

However, if at least something has been published about honor and shame, the pairing of purity and impurity has yet to be explored. There are practically no exegetical and anthropological works on this subject, a theme that is very foreign to the Western mentality. Nevertheless, data from the field shows the affinity of Muslim believers with the books of Leviticus and Hebrews in which purity and impurity are linked to holiness and obedience and their opposites. Even if some thought and writing has been done on these issues (in English; much is still needed in Spanish and other languages) touching on evangelism, there is still a long way to go in applying these mental categories to the field of development and to community life and dynamics.

Israel: another Window

We have previously seen that Israel should be a model and a channel of blessing for all nations. There seems to be a pendulum effect among evangelicals: from a marked "spiritual Zionism" to forgetting Israel altogether. The importance and place of Israel in God's plan is a concept that cannot be overlooked, especially when working in Muslim countries. However, the opposite tends to be the norm in Iberoamerican missionary work and in the literature focused on mission in Muslim contexts. All mention of Israel is avoided, except to warn, defensively, that the current State of Israel should not be confused with its biblical namesake.

Focusing on the practical implications in the field of development, Israel can and should serve as an analogy for each project, so that the beneficiaries learn: "You are blessed to be a blessing to others. Learn from the example, good and bad, of Israel. God blessed them to be a channel of His blessings to the whole world. See what happens when a people hoard for themselves the benefits of God, or think themselves God's favorites, or conquer by force what God has

---

(Minneapolis: Fortress Press, 2008); John Van Seters, *The Pentateuch: A Social-Science Commentary*, 2nd ed. (London and New York: Bloomsbury T&T Clark, 2015); David Arthur DeSilva, *Honor, Patronage, Kinship & Purity: Unlocking New Testament Culture* (Downers Grove: InterVarsity, 2000).

[13] Roland Muller, *Honor and Shame: Unlocking the Door*, (Philadelphia: Xlibris Corporation, 2001); Roland Muller, *The Messenger, the Message, the Community: Three Critical Issues for the Cross-Cultural Church-Planter* (Osler, Sask., Canada: CanBooks, 2006), www.canbooks.com.

promised to give them." It doesn't take many arguments to convince a Muslim community to see evil amongst the Jews! But this can help them to understand why they have come to that situation, and how they themselves can very easily be in the same condition. Of course, one should not minimize the profound differences in perception of history and its consequences that both cognitive universes (Christians and Jews vs. Muslims and Palestinians) maintain.

There is a long way to go, much to be explained, from the side of the biblically-minded development workers. The idea we are advocating, still in incipient form, is to reverse the situation mentioned above: to change the silence on Israel by an abundant mention and explanation of Israel's biblical role in God's plan and its practical consequences regarding Development-Salaam. The latter is a very powerful argument: the very idea of becoming (as they see it) as evil as a Jew is a repulsive thought for any Muslim.

Instead, as project managers, we can tell them, "You are a small example of what God is doing globally; you are a community with a mission. Moreover, Allah (God) is great! There are no impossibilities for Him! Will there be any greater miracle than to see Jews, Egyptians, and Syrian Iraqis walking together in harmony? God has promised it (Is. 19:19-25) and His Word – equivalent in the Muslim worldview to God Himself – is always fulfilled."

A Development-Salaam missiology works toward both a spiritual and historic continuity with Israel. At the same time, both as lived reality in the life of the people and of the development project, there is both an ethnic discontinuity and a methodological discontinuity: God's choice and the way he works with Israel is unique. In pursuing this, the emphasis is on the future, on what God is going to do with us, Latin-Muslim hybrids, with our Muslim friends, and with Israel, all together. We are moved by a hermeneutic focused on the future: we live sustained by the hope of the kingdom of God.

Cultural Expressions: the Walls

Development-Salaam missiology is expressed in concrete Muslim cultural patterns, through music, proverbs, stories, and rituals. In this case, we have been considering a hybrid house, fruit of the Latin-Muslim cross-breeding that characterizes the development projects carried out by Iberoamericans in the lands of Islam.

But let us note again that there is no such thing as "the Muslim world." There are many different cultures that share Islam as their unifying element. In other words, the missiological "house" built in Algeria need not look like the one built in Turkey or Indonesia or Mali, to name just a few of the forty plus countries where Muslims make up more than seventy per cent of the population. In each of them, various ethnic groups and cultures coexist. In other words, the cultural, ethnic, and linguistic variety of Islam is enormous.

Secondly, culture is dynamic and internal to or inseparable from life itself (a postmodern concept of culture). That is, we are not talking about folklore or external elements such as dress, customs, or language. We are trying to say that the house itself, all of it, will have to be thought through and structured from the cultural approaches of each people. Therefore, the results may be quite different from case to case. Yes, there will be similarities across settings. And yet, the development project should be different and unique in each case – dare we say completely and radically different? – if we really allow it to be thought and structured from the cultural reality and concerns of the community. This is not an easy ideal to achieve. As we mentioned before, at the end of the colonial period, churches and denominations were able to pass the baton to their sisters in the Global South, while Western Christian development agencies still held all the key resources and decision-making power. There is still a long way to go.

But development projects and initiatives in Muslim contexts will have some distinctive characteristics, in particular, a special use of music, proverbs, stories, the place of elders, and relationships.

Don McCurry asserts that in the heart of every Muslim there is a longing for spiritual music. According to him, music is an essential part of God and so are human beings who have been made in His image.[14] In centuries past, Sufi musicians found very successful ways to use music to express their spirituality and thus spread the Islamic faith throughout much of Africa, Asia, and Europe. Development-Salaam missiology will have to find musical ways of expressing itself, different from the use of music in the Latin churches.

An important part of the task of Development-Salaam missiology will be the teaching of values. Here, again, stories, parables, and proverbs will be of paramount importance. As a general rule, when Westerners want to be well understood, they try to express their theme or subject as simply as possible. They choose simple words, which any listener can understand, avoid unnecessary details, and focus on the main point or fact. In contrast, a Muslim will make use of a proverb, a metaphor, or an image. The more sophisticated, the better. Sophistication lies in the need for interpretation, even if the proverb is very simple. Important ideas must be "well-dressed." The way the message is expressed is as important as the message itself. The underlying idea is that wisdom should not be wasted on foolish or uninterested people. That was the advice of the Lord Jesus: "Do not give dogs what is sacred; do not throw your pearls to pigs." (Matt. 7:6).

The Upper Beam

Finally, an upper beam or truss joins the whole house at roof height, to give it stability. A truss is made from a strong material, a kind of clamp that serves to strengthen things that must stand up to great pressures. Our "truss" is the concept of *shalom-salaam* that we described in the previous chapter. It is a generous, believing vision of life and reality that seeks the integral well-being of all, in a harmonious way. It is "the peace of God that exceeds all understanding" (Phil. 4:7 CEB); it is a miraculous, supernatural element that brings a distinctive characteristic to our "missiological house." It is a rare commodity in all societies, Muslim or not, and

---

[14] Don McCurry, *Healing the Broken Family of Abraham: New Life for Muslims*, 2nd ed. (Colorado Springs: Ministries to Muslims, 2011).

therefore an important element of witness and mission. It is also an attractive feature of the house. The integral well-being that comes from God unites and consolidates the other elements we have discussed: the kingdom, the economy, identity, gender and social relations, church, mission, and honor and cleanliness as well as the grafting of "Gentile branches" into the original olive tree, Israel (Rom. 11:17); these all help to reorient the culture. It is the sense of satisfaction and belonging that is achieved when a community has developed a solid and coherent theology of its own. "Peace [...] to the Israel of God" (Gal. 6:16).

3. Conclusion

It is still too early to expect a well-developed contextual theology to have been expressed in each of the Muslim contexts we have studied. However, we have noted hints of what we are seeing, as well as some aspects of what might emerge in the near future. As is normal, the first generation of national believers and churches will be heavily influenced by the culture of their spiritual parents, in this case Iberoamerican cultural expressions. We hope and expect that the second and third generations will develop completely local models, even if they incorporate elements of the global evangelical culture.

Questions for Reflection and Discussion

1. Make a list of the features that make your church "of the land" (or not). That is, what is typically English, Welsh, Korean, Singaporean, American, etc. about your region and ethnic group as expressed in the church?
2. How would you apply the concept of group conversion and decision-making to the essentially family-based Latin American societies? How would this group concept affect your own church's practice in matters such as liturgy, finances, evangelism, etc.?
3. How would you apply to your church community the concepts of economics, land, property, and resource management mentioned in this chapter and in Chapter 12?
4. If you are a missionary serving among Muslims, what ideas have come to mind as you considered the concepts of open evangelism and religious identity?

For Further Reading

Evans, Alex, Richard Gower, and Tearfund. "The Restorative Economy: Completing Our Unfinished Millennium Jubilee." Tearfund, 2015. https://learn.tearfund.org/~/media/files/tilz/research/tearfund_therestorativeeconomy_summary.pdf.

Holwerda, David E. *Jesus and Israel: One Covenant or Two?* Grand Rapids and Leicester: Eerdmans and Apollos, 1995.

Muller, Roland. *The Messenger, The Message, The Community: Three Critical Issues for the Cross-Cultural Church-Planter*. Osler, Sask., Canada: CanBooks, 2006.

Van Engen, Charles E. *Transforming Mission Theology*. Book and ePub. Pasadena: William Carey Library, 2017.

Wilber, Charles K, and Amitava Krishna Dutt, eds. *New Directions in Development Ethics: Essays in Honor of Denis Goulet*. Notre Dame: University of Notre Dame Press, 2010.

15. Development-Salaam

As you read this chapter, you will note that the lessons and reflections we present can be applied to any context and not just to Muslim societies. Ultimately, reflecting on mission, on personal identity as well as ecclesial identity, and on involvement in society, are the tasks of every follower of the Master, of every church, of every mission agency, in whatever part of the globe they are working. For this reason, we encourage you, as you read, to compare your own situation to the content of this chapter. The questions at the end of the chapter, as well as the suggested readings, are focused precisely on making that bridge between the lessons that we draw from the Muslim mission fields and those that the reader finds in their own context.

1. Summary: Looking Back, Moving Ahead

What have we learned so far, and what conclusions can we draw? We have come a long way, both theoretically and practically, by examining the history of some individuals, projects, and churches. Let us take a short pause, catch our breath in a sense, and briefly review the key milestones of the road we have traveled. This will help us focus our energy as we move towards the goal: our own reflection.

The heart of this book grew out of academic research in which Christian had developed a theoretical framework for the analysis and interpretation of a group of individuals, development projects, and churches. This is what allows us to reach the conclusions that we now offer, organized around four themes.

Redefined Concepts of Development

The development approach that we, Charo and Christian, propose in this book is based on the concepts of Bryant Myers and Manfred Max-Neef, adding a spiritual and religious vision from the hybrid Latin-Muslim space. Indeed, Myers' understanding is framed in non-official development, in the action of development-focused NGOs, but from a Christian perspective. His perspective was broadened by a student of his, Jayakumar Christian,[1] who brought his Indian understanding of the spiritual dimension (non-visible spiritual realities),

[1] Jayakumar Christian, *God of the Empty-Handed: Poverty, Power and the Kingdom of God*, 2nd ed. (Brunswick East, Vic., Australia: Acorn Press, 2011).

developed the systemic dimension, and added the cosmic dimension, thus situating development in an all-encompassing Hindu worldview. For his part, Max-Neef adds a more general understanding that includes the official sector in the overall picture of development that nevertheless remains "on a human scale," fleeing the myth that economy of scale is always better. For Max-Neef, Schumacher's slogan, "small is beautiful," translates into a critique of "gigantism."

Building on the ideas of Myers, J. Christian, and Max-Neef, we have begun to construct our own concept, more appropriate to the needs and circumstances of development projects carried out by non-proselytizing evangelical Protestant missionaries in Islamic contexts. We have argued for the need to renounce the camouflage, to define a form of development that respects the authorities and the national society. This form of development bears a markedly religious character, wrapped, in fact, in explicit religious language. It distances itself from Western models of development and therefore describes itself as Development-Salaam.

Expanded Understanding of Integral Mission

Considering the importance of incarnation in missionary work, integral mission in Islamic contexts is comprised of the harmonious combination of word, deed, incarnation, and the power of the Holy Spirit, in that order. For those of us who live and minister in Muslim contexts, this concrete incarnation will be lived out against the backdrop of an Islamic worldview. Most often, this incarnation will consider the role of popular Islam and Sufism among the community, while finding creative ways to incorporate important ceremonies of the local culture and religiosity into our personal practice as well as into the church in formation.

It is from this expanded concept of integral mission that we have clarified the concept of integrality. In a way, integrality can be understood as a measure of the quality and depth with which integral mission is being reflected in a concrete situation. For this reason, integrality is always a path, an aspiration, which is normally perceived in its absence.

New Missionary Identity

Closely linked to the above, an integral understanding of mission goes hand in hand with an integral, mono-vocational, transparent missionary identity that fits the social role carried out by the missionary. The Iberoamerican missionary in the lands of Islam has four problems: the identity of the missionaries, their clash with a very different cultural context, and the content of their message. From the Western and compartmentalized point of view of the Latin American missionary, these seem like three problems, but the Muslim hosts are shocked, not by the different things that their Latin friends do (after all, everyone knows that foreigners do and say strange things!), but precisely by their lack of coherence or integrality. What they are (or say that they are), what they do, and what they talk about do not match: the fourth problem. In Muslim cultures, which are characterized by integrality and give more importance to the whole than to the parts, this lack of integrality becomes the main obstacle to the credibility of the missionary.

To address this problem, the missionary needs not only to confront the three initial problems, but also to integrate them into a single, coherent whole.

Reflection over Praxis

Finally, critical reflection on *praxis* constitutes the fourth axis of the theoretical scaffolding we have used. We have examined the practice of both individuals and organizations, that is, mission agencies, projects, and churches. This daily experience questions, transforms, and drives a new way of seeing and doing things, a new theory of concrete missionary practice.

While practice is the repetition of an activity to improve skill, *praxis* is the intentional analysis and reflection on the action to help form and refine theory.

In the words of Charles Van Engen:

> The concept of praxis helps us understand that not only the reflection, but profoundly the action as well, is part of a theology-on-the-way that seeks to discover how the church may participate in God's mission in God's world. The action is itself theological, and serves to inform the reflection, which in turn interprets, evaluates, critiques, and projects new understanding in transformed action. Thus the interweaving of reflection and action in a constantly spiraling pilgrimage offers a transformation of all aspects of our missiological engagement with our various contexts.[2]

Reflection on praxis is not a common element in classical European and North American theology, which more highly values pure theory. However, it constitutes a vital part of Latin American theological work. Also, reflection on praxis is crucial in some methodologies used in the social sciences, for example in Participatory Action Research.

2. Missiological Paradigm

Polarization: Instrumental and Integral

We have analyzed two missiological positions that describe the mission approaches of Iberoamerican workers in the lands of Islam. We will call them instrumental and integral.

We have summarized in a table four levels of involvement between evangelism and social work or development: as pre-evangelism, as a hook or bridge, as an accompaniment and inseparable. (Illustration 1, Chap. 5). The first three levels are framed in the "theology of the primacy" of evangelism over social work, reflected in Section 6 of the Lausanne Covenant. However,

---

[2] Charles E. Van Engen, *Mission on the Way: Issues in Mission Theology* (Grand Rapids: Baker, 2000), 26.

interviews with field workers have suggested that their personal positions align mainly with two of these levels: the second and the fourth; that is, for some, the project they (or others) are involved in is a hook or a bridge to evangelism. One of my informants serving in North Africa explained, "The project is a springboard to stay in the country and have contacts." Others, conversely, understand that project and evangelism are inseparable.

We have labeled the two types of responses, the two levels expressed in the field, as *instrumental* and *integral*. As we pointed out when discussing integrality, for some, in fact, the majority of those we interviewed, evangelism is a bridge to their fundamental goal: to see souls saved and churches formed. It might even be thought of as a "hook." Note the proselytizing conditioning factors in the term. That is to say that the project is an instrument to reach the goal of their mission. For others, project and evangelism are completely inseparable; they are part of the goal of bringing the kingdom of God to people, societies, and relationships. In other words, project and evangelism are integrally linked. Note that both positions are contradictory, they are not degrees of the same general category. They are incompatible.

Many times, a development project is used as a pretext for obtaining a residence visa, but with the intention of dedicating oneself, as much as possible, to evangelism. Such a deceitful manner is often accompanied by "entry strategies" designed at the organizational level by the sending church and/or the missionary agency. Thus, on an ethical level, we can consider the elaboration of these entry strategies as intentionally and collectively fabricated lies.

The opposite position, which we have advocated in this book, is transparency coupled with cooperation with national organizations, associations, or churches. The two positions are contradictory and incompatible.

The Concept of Integral Mission: Not Yet Fully Established

As we read some authors, we are given the idea that forty years of discussion has led to integral mission becoming well-established in the contemporary Latin American evangelical panorama. On the contrary, our field research has demonstrated the scarce penetration of the concept within Latin American mission agencies and their personnel, especially as far as mission to Islam is concerned. Moreover, Latin American workers who have opted for integral mission often feel misunderstood by the churches that have sent them and faithfully support them, precisely because the integrality of their churches is questionable. That is, their integrality is partial, it has not gone beyond uniting word and deed. For this reason, they expect the missionaries they have sent to use the projects in which they are involved to produce new believers and new churches.

In our opinion, integrality still divides evangelicals, now nearly fifty years since the landmark Lausanne 1974 conference. It is a question that we have not yet resolved. It is a question that came up again – with a force that surprised Christian – at the 2010 Lausanne III conference in Cape Town. On the one hand,

Ruth Padilla deBorst advocated on Tuesday for integrality, then on Wednesday John Piper defended the importance of "preventing eternal suffering in hell." These two plenary speakers were only the tip of the iceberg, but we present them as illustrations.

To qualify the expression that integral mission is established, perhaps it would be better to say that while it is no longer just a topic of academic discussion, or even that it remains the position of a small minority, it seems naïve to suggest that it is a majority view. We think that many missionaries, theologians, and others do hold to this position. But, we ask, has it truly been comprehended and adopted by most of those in places of influence, the leadership of the global evangelical institutions such as the Lausanne Committee for World Evangelism and the World Evangelical Alliance along with those who finance them?

3. Theologically Responsible Mission

We have focused our writing on the ideological and theological presuppositions that drive the development project or the organization behind it, and on the ultimate objectives of development. Ethical components that have emerged in the analysis of each group of projects come into consideration here. We need to ask ourselves if our model of mission is theologically responsible. Is it sound and healthy?

Theology

From the beginning of creation, the *human-in-bi-unity* has been commissioned by the *God-in-tri-unity* to expand his project both qualitatively and quantitatively.[3] The image of God in the man-woman includes the capacity for development, fullness, and expansion of God's good work. The people of Israel were constituted as a social model for the other nations (Deut. 4:6-8). The characteristics of that model, related to development, were: an egalitarian and horizontal society, organized by families and clans; dignified work and administration of God's land, whose fertility was linked to obedience; a socio-economic system focused on the welfare of the smaller units (family and clan) instead of focusing on the strengthening of the rich; an economic system of decreasing inflation through the remission of debts every seven and fifty years; justice was close, decentralized and direct; the responsibility for the care of the poor and vulnerable (widows, orphans, and foreigners) fell on all the people directly; the land was not to be depleted; Sabbath breaks included the land, the animals and all the workers; and finally, the entire people were a channel of God's blessing to all the nations. *Shalom-for-all,* both present and eschatological, was the goal, and solidarity, justice and the fear of God were the way to achieve it.

---

[3] Moisés Chávez, *La Ishah: un Estudio Etnohistoriográfico. La Mujer en la Biblia y en el Pensamiento Hebreo.* (Miami: Caribe, 1976), 35.

In the New Testament, the situation is more like a *non-governmental* model. Goodwill replaces compulsion, and the community of believers takes center stage. The Jubilee is reinterpreted in the person of Jesus Christ, extends its benefits to all humanity, and goes from being cyclical (every seven and fifty years), to becoming permanent at Pentecost, the feast of the Messianic Jubilee that pours the Holy Spirit on representatives of all nations. The membership of this community is open and multiethnic; it overcomes social class, gender, and age. Caring for the needy is considered a priority, the responsibility for which lies with both the community (collective) and its members (individual). Solidarity extends globally, crossing borders, and with principles of good management and transparency. The communion of goods quickly and spontaneously solved the problem of poverty in the large church in Jerusalem.

In the first three centuries, social concern was a distinguishing characteristic of Christians, which eventually shook the moral conscience of the Roman Empire. Widows, the sick, prisoners, slaves, orphans, and others in need were regularly cared for by Christian communities. This was the common practice in all Christian communities until the fourth century.

Missionary Inclusivity in Islamia

The descriptions of the people, projects, and churches that we have presented point to *life-in-movement*. This missionary paradigm will not be complete, it will not achieve "theological responsibility" without operating inclusively. Hence the importance of the five statements that follow.

Mission is Life

First of all, integral mission is life. It does not fit into definitions, although they may be helpful. It does not resolve priorities; it does not separate or dissect. A dissection would provide us with many details, but it would be a fixed photo without context. Instead, integral mission represents an attempt, always partial and unsuccessful, to see the whole in movement and is dependent on the context. That is why integral mission should always be redefining itself, adapting to the rapid changes that the globalized world of the twenty-first century imposes on us. What we must do is constantly evaluate the *quality of life*. That is, to ask ourselves how close the expression of integral mission we practise is to the ideal that we are discovering every day in the contextual reading of the Bible, the guidance of the Spirit, and the missionary community of faith.

Orlando Costas asked more than forty years ago if mission is from the road or from the balcony. René Padilla remarked "the gospel is a call to follow Christ on the way, not to contemplate him from the safe distance of the balcony."[4] Probably neither the way nor the balcony of the twenty-first century are the same as they were when those questions were raised.

---

[4] C. René Padilla, ed., *Bases Bíblicas de la Misión: Perspectivas Latinoamericanas* (Buenos Aires and Grand Rapids: Nueva Creación and Eerdmans, 1998), 322.

It seems that Latin American mission has polarized both perspectives too much and needs a new interactive perspective. Latin American activism has pushed some tens of thousands of missionaries onto the path of cross-cultural mission. Some have reflected with much success and have produced a good amount of quality literature, but they have not reached the masses of our churches. Will we find concrete mechanisms that will enable us in an interactive way to distance ourselves a few steps so that we can both observe from the *perspective of the balcony* without losing contact with the *movement of the road*?

Various Visions of Integral Mission

Secondly, we perceive different, nuanced visions of integral mission that proceed from different starting points and are rooted in distinct emphases. This is the case between the Latin American vision and the hybrid Latin-Muslim version that we have tried to describe. In the past, the Latin American Theological Fraternity focused almost exclusively on giving birth to a missiology of and for Latin America. Is this still the way forward in the globalized world of the twenty-first century? In our opinion, it seems to us that Latin Americans should look at the whole world with Latin eyes in order to make theology applicable to today's globalized Latin America, and that Africans should do the same with African eyes, and Europeans, and Asians, and so on.

Note that what we suggest is far from the *McDonaldization* of theology. For too long Europe and North America have looked at the world with Eurocentric eyes, have told all nations which theology they should believe, and furthermore have packaged it in books, CDs, and videos, posted it on the Internet, and sold it to the whole world. For our part, we are just presenting an opinion to be scrutinized in the ongoing discussion. It is the opinion of some simple missionaries with modest resources, born Mediterranean, of parents or grandparents married in Africa, and who collaborate with Latin Americans in Muslim contexts in Africa, Asia, and Europe.

Truly Biblical Development

Third, we believe it is vital to promote true biblical development. The development discourse of this world, which has become popular since the end of World War II, only serves the interests of the empire of power and the global market. It is that drastic. The Sustainable Development Goals are simply a mirage to hide the personal and structural sin of our world. As Jean Ziegler, member of the UN Human Rights Council and rapporteur on the Right to Food, has put it, "it is not about giving more, but about stealing less."[5] Some might

---

[5] David Rojo, "Jean Ziegler: 'La Solución al Hambre no es Dar más, Sino Robar Menos,'" [The solution to hunger is not to give more but to steal less] Attac Acordem, September 27, 2011, http://www.acordem.org/2010/09/27/jean-ziegler-la-solucion-al-hambre-no-es-dar-mas-sino-robar-menos/. See also, Jean Ziegler, *Betting on Famine:*

think that we support the withdrawal, the non-involvement, of God's children and the church in the transformation of people and of our societies. Quite the contrary! God has been building his kingdom since the beginning of the world, and he has invited us to participate in that mission. But it is a different kingdom (John 18:36), a different love (John 13:34-35), a different peace (John 14:27). It is the story of two cities, Babel and the heavenly Jerusalem, the imposter city and the city of God. "God's mission is about creating the second city (or community or world, if you like) while the Empire is trying to create the first" as Simon Penney points out.[6]

Unfortunately, many Christian development organizations seem to want Babel to look as much like Jerusalem as possible, not realizing that the difference between the two is profound, radical, and unbridgeable. Many Christian organizations carry out development with a humanistic foundation varnished with Christianity. That is why, we insist, it seems vital to us to promote, and to show – with examples – a humanizing development, one that is not based on accumulating more goods and comforts, but on the contrary, one that connects people with God, with their neighbor, with the other, and with God's creation. This is a development that walks, not towards "progress" but towards true *shalom-salaam*.

There is No Mission Without the Church

Fourth, there is no integral mission and no true development without an integral church. They go hand in hand, inseparably united. But founding or establishing just any kind of church does not work. The reductionist, cut-down, comfortable versions of the church do more harm than good. A little bit of truth (and church) in small doses immunizes people against the whole truth and against the committed and vibrant church. Could it be that the Latin evangelical missionary movement is vaccinating people against the gospel by creating *church lite*? It is a strong statement, but one that directly concerns us as Iberoamerican evangelicals when considering the fruit of our work. Countries like Guatemala, Honduras, and El Salvador are saturated with evangelical churches seemingly on every corner yet have some of the highest violent death rates in the world.

The integral church is a community of disciples, missionary, just, generous, and supportive; it looks to the future (to the kingdom) to live in the present. It is a *community*, not a schedule of worship. It is a family of people with fraternal bonds, who live, decide, and do things together, who support each other. It is made up of *disciples*, not members; that is, people who follow Jesus Christ on a daily basis; who are learning and putting into practice what they learn as a way of life. The integral church is *missionary* by nature. It lives for the world, not to

---

Why the World Still Goes Hungry, trans. Christopher Caines (Chicoutimi, Quebec: Bibliothèque Paul-Émile Boulet, Université du Québec, 2018).

[6] Simon Penney, "Does Development Work? Asking the Question Again in the Shadow of the Empire," *Encounters Mission Ezine*, no. 14 (2006): 24–26..

satisfy itself, not even for its own survival. The healthy (integral) church is always on the verge of extinction, giving and giving, beyond what it has. Poor, yet making many rich, as Paul described himself and his teammates (2 Cor. 6:10).

The integral church oozes hope from every pore of its skin, so much so that it cannot help but look to the future, to the kingdom of God. This forward-looking orientation fills it with enthusiasm to live in the present. It rejects both the *super-realized* eschatology, that which believes it can bring a quasi-paradise to earth by its own efforts and revolution, and the *other-worldly* eschatology, which isolates itself from the world to live an absent spiritualism, waiting for the Millennium.

Starting such churches, with this sort of DNA embedded from the beginning, is no small challenge, as we have seen in the stories of the people, projects, and churches described in this book. But, following Romans 1:16, it is there that we see that the gospel is God's own power for salvation to all who have faith in God, to the Jew first and also to *the Muslims*, if you will grant us this freedom of terms.

The Complete Picture

Myers warns development workers of the importance of seeing the whole story and of thinking holistically.[7] For those involved in development projects or church planting it is crucial to remember again and again that neither church planting nor community development is the ultimate goal of mission, at least not from an Integral Mission perspective:

> "What do you do, good man?" asked the King of France to a stonemason who was fashioning masonry stones in the bustling construction site of the cathedral of Notre Dame. "I hew stone, Majesty," replied the workman reverently.
> "What do you do, my good man?" again asked the king to the fellow who was working beside the first.
> The stonemason sprang to his feet, and with a lighted gaze exclaimed:
> "I am helping to build the great cathedral of France, your majesty!"

Both stonemasons did exactly the same job but had a very different perspective of the big picture. May we have the same breadth of vision. Each of us should heed Paul's instruction: "Don't think of yourself more highly than you ought to think. Instead, be reasonable since God has measured out a portion of faith to each one of you. We have many parts in one body, but the parts don't all have the same function. [...] We have different gifts that are consistent with God's grace that has been given to us" (Rom 12:3-6 CEB).

Integral gospel, integral church and discipleship, Development-Salaam, kingdom-minded society, they all form a whole, a harmony toward which we are on our way: "A new heaven and a new earth, where righteousness dwells" (2 Pet.

---

[7] Bryant L. Myers, *Walking with the Poor: Principles and Practices of Transformational Development*, Rev. (Maryknoll: Orbis, 2011), chaps. 3, 6.

3:13 CEB). The center of all this harmony is God himself and his glory. "Holy, holy, holy, is the LORD Almighty; the whole earth is full of his glory" (Is. 6:3 CEB). In very general lines, Protestant theology has placed the human being and our salvation as the central message of the Bible, while the Catholic Church has done the same with the church. It seems to us that, on this point, Orthodox theology has better grasped the focal point of this immense and at the same time harmonious picture: only God and his glory are at the very center of the universe, of History with a capital letter, and of course of the Bible. To think otherwise is dangerously close to idolatry.

The specific task of each disciple, each local church, and each organization is likely to be different. For some of us, it may be to act as agents of *salaam* and form *tariqah* (brotherhoods) of *Isa al-Masih* in Muslim lands. May God grant us the grace to do so with the big picture in mind.

4. Development-Salaam

Development-Salaam is part of our proposal to reformulate the idea of development from a biblical, faith-based perspective, easily understandable in Muslim contexts. It is a way of disassociating ourselves from the Western interpretative framework of development, to "invent it differently," to borrow the expression of the Colombian anthropologist Arturo Escobar.

Our proposal is that missionary organizations and their workers adopt this whole broad concept, Development-Salaam, as an identity framework. Linked to theologically responsible missiology this framework sets the parameters for describing both their work and their Christian identity in the lands of Islam.

Bridge of Knowledge

We have taken the Muslim concept *salaam* as a religious, knowledge, and cultural bridge for the practice of a development reformulated according to the biblical model in the Latin-Muslim hybridization. For this purpose, we have compared the scope of the words *shalom* and *salaam*, their differences and similarities, as well as a theological framework: a theology of Development-Salaam.

Comparison of Shalom and Salaam

The biblical word shalom encapsulates in a single word God's desire for his people: the overall *and* complete well-being of the individual, the people, and the entire cosmos. We have used five qualifiers to describe *shalom*: as an integral, believing, relational, contextual, and eschatological concept. As such an integral concept, it cannot be half-hearted. You either have it or you do not, and therefore you enjoy it integrally. But it is always improvable, until it culminates in the fullness of the expected kingdom.

Our analysis has shown many important similarities between the Jewish and biblical concept of *shalom* and its Arabic and Muslim equivalent *salaam*. On the one hand, they share a Semitic linguistic root. On the other hand, the fact that both *salaam* and the word "Islam" come from the same semantic expression gives us an idea of the central importance that the *salaam* concept has in the Muslim religion in general and in the Qur'an in particular. The more than three hundred quranic quotations relating to *salaam* have led us to two major categories of meaning: first, the inner, individual peace that the believer experiences, conveys through greetings, and will enjoy in fullness in paradise. Second, functional peace, which has to do with society – the community of believers – and its internal and external relationships, and which is directly linked to the consolidation of the *ummah*, the worldwide Muslim community. This second Islamic concept of peace cannot be understood in isolation from its opposite, war. Peace is manifested when submission (Islam) is added to victory.

However, our study has also brought to light the points of divergence between the two concepts. The many similarities should not lead to the naïve assumption that *shalom* is equivalent to *salaam*. Both the ultimate goal and the means to achieve peace-well-being differ considerably, as David Shenk has noted in comparing the paths to peace of Jesus, Constantine, and Muhammad, as we explored in chapter thirteen. Consequently, we have proposed the concept of *salaam* as a bridge to true Development-Salaam as well as the need to constantly renew our focus on the means to achieve *salaam*. This becomes concretely applied when we give serious thought to the ultimate objectives as we consider or propose a development project. This bridge of knowledge constitutes a paradox: *shalom* and *salaam* are quite different; the proposal of this book is to stress the connotations of biblical *shalom* in the cultural garb of Muslim *salaam*.

Theological Proposal

We have proposed a theological and ideological framework that, on the one hand, builds on the modern Western concept of development and at the same time distances itself from it. It describes the main lines along which biblically-inspired, integral development work should be carried out by Iberoamerican agents in Muslim contexts. We present this proposal of Development–Salaam missiology for consideration by our colleagues, non-proselytizing Iberoamerican missionaries serving among Muslims who have adopted integral mission as a frame of reference.

We have structured our proposal into eleven components that have been compared to the structure of a house. Applying this Development-Salaam missiology, we propose to go one step further, changing the terminology of humanitarian, cultural and development projects to "Development-Salaam project." It is not enough to change ideas. This change of ideas must be accompanied by a change of vocabulary if the substance of the issue is to be properly understood and perceived by the recipients. The purpose is to disassociate the project from Western humanistic ideology and the idea of progress and in its place to a focus that includes belief and is God-fearing, a relational focus that is directed toward integral well-being (*salaam*).

A Proposal of Identity

The identity of the worker or development partner as a full-time missionary has no place in most Muslim settings. Christian missionaries are not allowed, either by the authorities or by society. Moreover, the very word missionary carries very negative connotations. But it is precisely this missionary identity that underlies why their church (in their home country) has sent them and continues to offer them financial support.

Many add another identity, frequently as a façade or cover-up, to become, for example, a businessperson, a language teacher, a worker in a development project, or similar. In other words, the worker has two identities, one in their country of origin and the other in their country of service, one public and the other secret or hidden. This is what we have called the dual identity model. Since the people among whom the missionary lives easily see through this artificial identity, credibility is lost or never achieved. The dual identity model becomes, in practice, a sort of *missionary suicide* for those who practice it, disqualifying them from their intended purpose: to do mission in a given Muslim context.

The model we propose advocates a real identity, one that is adopted; it is not layered on top as a disguise. The integrated identity seeks to be as transparent and true as possible. In most Muslim cultures, the concept of privacy is quite different from what is usually practiced in Western societies more inclined to individualism. The front door of the house is open all day long; people often look in through the window to see what is going on in the house, and there are very few secrets between neighbors. In such circumstances, the failure of the dual-identity model is not surprising, and the virtues of a transparent identity are appreciated.

Likewise, messengers who have opted for an integrated identity take on a real job or occupation, one that they are qualified to do and enjoy doing. With enthusiasm, they dedicate time and energy to it as a way of blessing the society in which they are guests with their skills. In the exercise of their professions, the workers establish natural relationships with people, sharing their Christian faith in genuine, non-artificial ways. Spiritual conversations will arise without fail and, eventually, will lead to discipleship or "apprenticeship" situations.

Social Role

If identity defines who you are, the social role is the set of behaviors appropriate to that identity. For each identity, society establishes a pattern of expected behavior and defines social roles. Each culture may assign different behaviors for the social role expected for a given identity. For example, Spanish teachers tend to be friendly with their students and facilitate interaction with their class. That is the expected behavior for their social role. In contrast, Moroccan teachers are expected to be distant, use a directive style, and always be correct. Moroccan students would feel disoriented if their teachers behaved as Spaniards do and vice versa. The social role is defined by a whole series of behaviors, standard of living, style, vocabulary, schedules, and so on. The followers of the Messiah must act in ways that are in accordance with what society expects of the social role and identity they have chosen. It is therefore essential to integrate the social role with the identity.

Some workers might opt for a religious social role, one of the many offered by Muslim societies. It could be a religious teacher, a wandering religious storyteller, a religious troubadour or musician, or even a holy man, called a *marabout* (Arabic), *pir* (Persian, both men and women), *muchtahid* (Persian), *salid* or *al-salih* (Arabic), *sidi* (Arabic), or *dede* (Kurdish). Some of these social roles will be reserved for veteran workers, fluent in the language and culture. Depending on the region of the world, some roles may only be filled by men, although there is always ample room for women in every culture.

Another option is to look carefully at the way in which some pious individuals exercise spiritual functions to teach, guide and bless others, and learn from them. Let us keep in mind that in many ascribed status societies[8] (including most societies in Africa and Asia) technicians and Western-educated people (such as engineers, doctors, and teachers) are often considered lacking in spiritual wisdom.[9] Their Western education has focused them only on the material. Occasionally, some of these technicians manifest spiritual abilities, and exercise an additional social role in the community as a peacemaker, a giver of blessings, or a teacher of spirituality. These rare individuals know how to change from one role to another. The King's messengers should study that skill and incorporate it into their own lives. Since many of the King's Iberoamerican ambassadors work on technical projects, they should pay special attention not to become trapped in roles that exclude spiritual activity.

Our proposal is to reformulate the identity of Iberoamerican missionaries working in development, cultural, and humanitarian projects. Instead of identifying themselves as development workers, which links them to the Western humanistic development model, we propose an identity as guests, ambassadors of *Isa al-Masih* (Jesus the Messiah) and promoters of Development-Salaam. Note that a guest does not necessarily have a message to give; they simply receive hospitality. But in this case, the idea is that the guest also brings a message from the King, the Lord of all, and is also a peaceful (not imposed) promoter of a different concept of society: the community of divine *shalom.*

---

[8] Attributed vs. acquired status is a common concept in cultural anthropology. Paul Hiebert and Charles Kraft call it ascribed vs. achieved while other authors prefer to speak of hierarchical societies, such as Carol R. Ember and Melvin Ember, *Cultural Anthropology*, 15th ed. (New York: Pearson Education, 2019). See also Robert H. Lavenda and Emily A. Schultz, *Core Concepts in Cultural Anthropology*, 7th ed. (New York: Oxford University Press, 2020).

[9] Frequently, teaching on technical subjects is conducted in the colonial language and with Western books. In contrast, humanities teachings such as literature, law, or mathematics, and of course theology, are taught in Arabic.

Therefore, we are talking about an identity that harmoniously combines three aspects or facets: the guest, the messenger, and the promoter of *salaam*.

5. Mission, Development, and Poverty

The *praxis*, the lived-out expression of the beliefs held by the missionary-development workers, has given rise to our commentary on the relationship between development, poverty, and mission. This has been particularly clear in two settings in North Africa: the project that serves and dignifies people living with disabilities and the water and rural development project. It is also one of the outstanding characteristics of some of the people we have interviewed. The fact is that they put into practice their mission and their way of understanding development by attending to and relating to poor and anonymous people as well as to rich and wealthy people. Such relationships with both rich and poor are not normal, even violating the unspoken rules of highly stratified societies such as Muslim societies.

This characteristic, which we have observed among the projects and people of our study, is in stark contrast with its absence in much of the development literature. That includes evangelical publications but especially that of liberation theology.

From our own reflection, we are surprised by the near absence of discussion of the rich in the writings of liberation theology except to condemn them. It seems as if salvation is not for them. It is as if the church that traditionally was on the side of the powerful and wealthy is now, in a pendulum swing, going to the opposite extreme (at least in word, but not in deed). Moreover, biblical passages that mention rich people and situations of wealth are excluded from theological reflection. This lack of balance seems serious to us, especially because poverty is a relative concept; it can only be evaluated in relation to its opposite, wealth. Therefore, to pretend to understand and sympathize with the poor by excluding the rich from the picture (or only condemning them) seems to us to be completely fallacious.

Also surprising is the practical absence of references to the diaconal, service action of the church of the first centuries, a church that launched a whole social movement directed towards the marginalized of its time. If anything characterized the Christian church of the first four centuries, it was its practical care for the needy, as well as the theological elaboration regarding diaconal solidarity and the sharing of goods. The duty of social and economic solidarity is the theme on which practically all Patristic authors agree. It is worth asking why this fact is virtually absent in the authors of liberation theology that we consulted. Could it be because the church of the first centuries, a church focused on the poor, was composed of both the poor and the rich, without class distinction?

Drawing on the perspective gained through a Christian's years of managing development projects, it is unthinkable for us to undertake a project, a concrete situation, without a careful analysis, as a team, of those involved or affected in one way or another by the project, the stakeholders. Would such a stakeholder analysis have helped some of the liberation theologians to avoid marginalizing the rich from their field of vision?

The subject of the poor and poverty is masterfully addressed by Bryant Myers, who has dealt closely with this subject throughout his career, in part as a vice president of World Vision International, one of the world's largest development agencies. After carefully analyzing the various schools or approaches to the issue of poverty, he concludes that, first, the *nature* of poverty is fundamentally relational and, second, that the *cause* of poverty is fundamentally spiritual.[10] One of his insights is to point out the difference between the poor, the non-poor (the one who is usually called rich) and the rich (the truly rich, according to the biblical understanding). He also exposes the poverty of the non-poor, who also suffer from a mistaken sense of identity, trapped in webs of lies and playing God in the lives of others.

By engaging, addressing, and challenging the rich, Myers avoids neglecting one of the two sides of the inseparable pair: poverty and wealth. Liberation theologians certainly clearly see the indissoluble relationship between wealth and poverty, and indeed they frequently explore the cause-and-effect relationships that link them. But by leaving the rich out of their pastoral attention and focusing too much on the option for the poor, they fail to offer a real solution to the problem. If we accept that poverty is a complex issue and that it is inextricably linked to wealth (since the two can only be measured relatively and in relation to each other), it is clear that the solution can never be found by addressing only one side of the problem. Myers' distinction between the non-poor and the rich provides a very adequate way of, on the one hand, addressing the damage that the accumulation of wealth causes to the poor and excluded and, on the other hand, offering pastoral care to a significant part of the problem, while allowing those who cause it to be an active part of the solution.

The concurrent relationship with rich and poor, as an inherent part of one's understanding of development and mission, is an important contribution to the concept and praxis of missiology that non-proselytizing missionaries attached to integral mission in *Islamia* bring to the field. In the future, it would be useful to take a few more steps: to be aware of the value of such practice, to reflect theologically on it, to reflect strategically on how best to implement it on the ground, and also how to disseminate this body of knowledge.

---

[10] Myers, *Walking with the Poor*, 2011, chap. 4; Bryant L Myers, *Engaging Globalization: The Poor, Christian Mission, and Our Hyperconnected World*, Mission in Global Community (Grand Rapids: Baker Academic, 2017).

Questions for Reflection and Discussion

1. In what ways is your church or organization involved in promoting biblical development and fighting poverty and injustice? In what ways could they do more?
2. If you are a development worker, what does the Development-Salaam proposal suggest you? What aspects are applicable in your environment? If you work in a Muslim setting, make a list of the advantages and disadvantages of this model.

For Further Reading

Baker, David L. *Tight Fists or Open Hands?: Wealth and Poverty in Old Testament Law*. Grand Rapids: Eerdmans, 2009.

Haar, Gerrie ter, ed. *Religion and Development: Ways of Transforming the World*. London: Hurst & Co, 2011.

Travis, Ted. *Building Cathedrals: Urban Discipleship That Works*, 2 ed. Urban Ministry in the 21st Century 7. Skyforest, Calif.: Urban Loft Publishers, 2016.

Yoder, Richard A., Calvin W. Redekop, and Vernont E. Jantzi. *Development to a Different Drummer: Anabaptist/Mennonite Experiences and Perspectives*. Intercourse, Penn.: Good Books, 2005.

16. Missionary Praxis

"The peace of Allah be upon you. May Allah bless you and keep you; may He make your house fruitful and put peace among your children; may the face of the Merciful One illuminate your life, and make you a truthful, peaceful, tolerant, and well-thinking man. May *Isa al-Masih* restore to you the hope you have lost."

Mario, as we shall call him, has just arrived in a small town and has begun to greet the group that awaited his arrival, the committee connected with the local association for the care of people with special needs. He started with the normal standard forms of greeting, "the peace of Allah be upon you", but as sometimes happens, led by the Holy Spirit his greeting became a tailored blessing, sometimes a prophecy, sometimes a word of wisdom. The joy and presence of the Lord Jesus flows into his life producing an impact that is difficult to explain to the people around him.

Mario's story began many years ago, in his native Colombia, when God called him to serve as a missionary among Muslims. He began to get involved in the various outreach initiatives of his church. After some years of preparation, his wife and he, newly married, arrived in North Africa. The beginnings were not easy. It seemed that all aspects of his profession, sports coaching, were carried out differently in this new country. But the couple dove headlong into studying the language and interacting with nationals. "It took us three years to accept or understand integrality," they told us.

Over the years, their ministry focused not on athletes but on people with disabilities, with special needs. His professional background has opened doors not only with the people he worked with but with their families, with professional associations, and with high profile personalities as well as with extremely humble people.

Mario is not concerned with gaining new believers or establishing churches; those are the least of his worries. He is oblivious to the missionary fads and to their terminology and strategies. In fact, he interacts very little with missionaries and instead spends most of his time among Muslims, very much integrated into the local culture, rituals, and religious vocabulary. He knows that God has called him to open doors, to be an aroma of God's presence. That is why he spends a lot of time with people, loving, serving, giving – and receiving. Because love flourishes in intimacy with people and in reciprocity. "They have as much to give me as I have to them," he says. That forms community, one of the keys to Mario's work.

Deep interpersonal bonds and a sense of belonging form community. Mutual help brings together people with and without special needs, the poor and the well-to-do, relatives and strangers. In the midst of them all, as he travels the country, Mario moves like a fish in water. Everyone knows that he is a follower of Jesus the Messiah, and everyone knows that his main purpose, the one that drives his daily actions, is to bless this country and its people in the name of *Isa al-Masih*, whom he names over and over again. But everyone also knows that he is not a proselytizer, and sincerely enjoys many Muslim values and ideals. His identity as a specialized trainer and advisor to associations blends perfectly with his role as a "man of God"; some call him *faqih*, someone versed in Islamic theology, someone wise in the things of God.

Therefore, when Mario begins to greet and speak in the name of God, the listeners extend their hands, palms up, to receive God's blessing. "You have God's word for us," they tell him.

1. Missionary Praxis: Elements

What elements does the analysis of missionary praxis add to this theologically responsible missiological paradigm, to the Development-Salaam we are proposing? Given that evangelical Iberoamerican mission to Islam is of recent origin, less than forty years old, the analysis of its practice is very important.

In this final chapter, we offer personal considerations, focused on applying on the ground an integral missiology of Development-Salaam. It is *personal* because it reflects our conclusions and thoughts. It summarizes the changes or recommendations we dare to make to our colleagues in the Muslim mission field. Much of what we mention in this chapter is valid, or very easily adapted, to other mission fields. It is *missiology*, since that is the focus of this book, more specifically Latin American missiology focused on the welfare of peoples, Muslim, Christian and secular. Finally, it is *integral* because of the considerations that we have formulated within three elements of the theoretical scaffolding: of integral mission, of transformational development, and starting from an integrative praxis.

Although all of the recommendations we have formulated are highly interrelated, we have grouped them into three practical sections: missionary agencies, workers, and projects. But first, let us highlight some lessons drawn from actual missionary context.

Context

Six Regions

We have suggested a grouping of the countries of the Muslim world, that is, the countries where Muslims form a majority of the national population, into six major regions: the Middle East, North Africa, the Arabian Peninsula, the Sahel, "exclusivist" Asia, and "pluralist" Asia. We believe that this classification, although with the limits inherent to any generalization, is useful in the missiological context because it helps to gauge the conditions under which certain conclusions can be extrapolated or not.

The stories we have considered are of people, projects, and churches that are located, for the most part, in North Africa and the Sahel, with some references also to the Middle East and "exclusivist" Asia. We have highlighted the great differences in the acceptance or non-acceptance of development projects across these locations along with the degree of religious freedom and social tolerance towards other faiths, and the different ways of doing mission in general and establishing churches in particular. What happens in Morocco or Tunisia cannot (or should not) uncritically be applied to Turkey or Uzbekistan. We have also seen how, in each of the areas we have considered, the churches studied have defined their identity differently. As noted in chapter eleven, the Global Consultation on Islam of the Lausanne Movement held at Accra in April 2014 defined five types or faces of Islam: mystical and popular Islam, missionary and polemical Islam, ideological and political Islam, militant and violent Islam, and progressive and liberal Islam. The combination of the zones and types will undoubtedly contribute to a better understanding and missionary practice towards Islam.

Latin-Muslim Hybridity

Our descriptions have moved between the cultural context of each community and the hybrid Latin-Muslim context arising from the interaction between the two cultures. We have highlighted the interactions between the two ways of thinking, some of their clashes (war-mongering language, sacred spaces) and their mutual enrichments (entrepreneurship, culture of honor and relationships) and even blind spots (*machismo*, purity-impurity).

In fact, as the missionaries have adapted to the host culture, even to the point of wanting to make it their own, they have achieved a sort of mixture, a cultural symbiosis manifested in the decoration of their homes, their way of dressing, their way of cooking, their way of speaking, and that often has transformed the very language and institutional culture of the missionary organization to which they belong. The Venezuelan has become a sort of *criollo* of North Africa, the Costa Rican has amalgamated with the Uzbek, and the Andalusian of Southern Spain has acquired a new Andalusian flavor. This process, voluntary and intentional in the parents, has been natural and spontaneous in the children of these missionaries. They are true hybrids, third culture kids who are neither Argentinean nor North African but a mixture of both. They feel at ease, and at the same time foreign, in both worlds; they use to perfection the best of each language (Arabic dialect, French, and Argentine Spanish). They have played with the children of the project, they have lived with the children of the national pastor, they have friends whose parents are high-ranking people of the city, and in short, they constitute a cultural and religious bridge forged in harmonious relationships of mutual trust.

This fact should not be overlooked. In the current times of polarization between Islam and the West, finding bridges of trust, both cultural and religious, is a very important fact. It has not been a post-colonial reaction, nor a challenge to the official culture as Homi Bhabha initially described hybridization,[1] but a quasi-planned, albeit unconscious, process.

Theoretically, parents have wanted to hybridize, and they have also wanted it for their children, but they did not always consciously prepare themselves for all the consequences that this process might entail, for example, their children marrying nationals. On the other hand, in these Muslim settings the churches with their pastors and leaders that for many years have lived alongside these missionaries, their children, and their many Latin American visitors have experienced a degree of hybridization. Obviously, it is not to the same degree – they are surrounded mostly by their own culture – but despite that, no less important. To some extent, they are "Creole churches." To their own spirituality has been added, mixed with, or incorporated varying degrees of the Iberoamerican spirituality they have known since they were born into the Christian faith. They pray, sing, and read the Bible with influences from a Latin American background. They are born as hybrid churches,[2] but with the passing of the years they will become more indigenous, leaving behind little by little the Latin influence.

For this reason, as missionaries we do everything possible so that the church we establish is indigenous, knowing, however, that our own presence involuntarily hinders this self-identity. But it is part of a process. If we do not plant the church, the process will not even begin. And in time, after we leave, perhaps even after a new generation takes leadership, the church will move – then, yes – toward a fully indigenous character. That was already the case for the mother church in the North African capital, the one that ordained and sent the national pastor to Gran Urbe. It had already taken decisive steps on the road to being autochthonous, "of the place."

Context and Hermeneutic

There is yet another contextual element that, in this case, affects Iberoamerican missionaries in certain Muslim areas; we have called it the hermeneutical element. Historically, the missionary agency of which were part, PM International (PMI), began its work in North Africa in 1984. The initial missionary group was made up of people from Latin America. Their immersion in the North African culture brought them closer to the Mediterranean cultures that were the crucible of the Bible. Very soon, daily events began to revolutionize

---

[1] Homi K. Bhabha, *Locations of Culture* (London: Routledge, 1994).

[2] Lamin Sanneh, *Translating the Message: The Missionary Impact on Culture*, 2nd ed. (Maryknoll: Orbis, 2008).

their reading of a Bible that they knew almost by heart, but from a great cultural distance. As Christian wrote earlier:

> The workers, including ourselves (who became part of this process in 1989) began to realize that the similarity between what they experienced in North Africa and life in biblical times went far beyond the external details. They found similarities in such expressions as "going in and out of the gate" (John 10:9). They saw judges sitting at the main gate of their cities (Ruth 4:1-2). They noted examples of the kind of hospitality that takes a whole day to cook a dinner from its living ingredients (Gen. 18:2-8), as well as using oil as medicine and for anointing (Luke 10:34; Ps. 23:5). Biblical images took on a new hermeneutical importance for them, an importance above ideas and theories.
>
> Moreover, they grasped the integrality that permeated everything in North Africa, just as it did for the biblical characters already familiar to them. The concepts of family, descendants, honor, belonging, reciprocity, blessing, and bargaining or barter blended harmoniously in North African daily life as in the Bible. They found new inspiration in studying Abraham, Joseph, David, Jeremiah, and others. They began to read their Bibles with new eyes, making different, at times novel interpretations in light of their new, adopted social context.[3]

This is not insignificant. The host cultural context affected our understanding of the Bible, which, in turn, had consequences on the way we understood life itself and the meaning of mission. We could say that it was an *accelerated contextual reading* because the constant jostling with daily life produced an accelerated eye-opener.

Of course, every context affects those who live in it. This could be said of virtually every reader everywhere. And yet, two circumstances make this particular factor stand out, make it different. First, it is common knowledge that for Latin American evangelicals the Bible is special. The Bible is loved, honored, and displayed in public. In few places in the Christian world does the annual Day of the Bible have as much resonance as in Latin America. Second, the missionaries discovered direct connections between their beloved Bible and the local culture; bi-directional connections, that is, connections that changed the way they read and also served to introduce the Bible to their Muslim friends. However, this hermeneutical process was not at first the fruit of theological reflection. They were not looking for "the meaning for the first readers" as is the case when using the historical-critical method of interpretation.[4]

---

[3] Christian Giordano, *Peregrinaje en la Misión*, Colección Musulmania 14 (Granada: PM International, 2009), 25, https://musulmania.com/resources/14_Peregrinaje_en_mision.pdf; trans. D. Greenlee.

[4] It could be that the fresh and new way of reading the Bible that characterizes Latin America may have had a preparatory effect on the missionaries themselves, even before arriving in Muslim lands. Professor Andrew Kirk, who is well acquainted with the

The changes the Latin American missionaries in North Africa began to experience in their way of seeing life and understanding mission were accepted relatively easily by their sending churches. They received them as biblical changes, as if, somehow, they came from the Palestine of New Testament times. This fact, together with the prestige that the intercultural missionary has in the Latin American evangelical world, contributed to the acceptance of these changes. This was the hermeneutical change that took place in the first years in PMI, and that was one of the steps in its "pilgrimage in mission."[5] We have described it in the past because, over the years, maturity in the field and greater cultural understanding have led to more critical approaches to local cultures. However, we have the impression that our colleagues in the field have not realized what a treasure they had, and still have to some extent, to their credit.

Political and Social Context

On the other hand, there is an important political and social element of the context that has an impact on the missionaries and projects that we are studying. For historical reasons, Arab countries have not had formal diplomatic relations with Latin American countries until late in their history. In 1947, thirteen of the twenty Latin American countries – which constituted at the time the largest bloc of the fifty-seven members of the UN – voted in favor of the partition of Palestine and soon after gave diplomatic recognition to the state of Israel. In response, many Arab states broke off, or did not establish, ties with them.

Cecilia Baeza clarifies that, from 1990 onwards, Latin American countries began to normalize their relations with Arab countries, moved by "the end of the Cold War and the emergence of a new unipolar order in 1990; the democratic stabilization of all countries in the region; and finally, the Palestinian-Israeli peace process and the creation of the Palestinian National Authority (PNA)."

Since the year 2000, this process has gone further with the election of leftist governments in Latin America and Brazil's aspirations to occupy a prominent place as an emerging power, especially during Lula da Silva's term of office (2003-2010).[6] It is precisely in this context of new diplomatic and commercial relations that the Latin American missionaries studied are present in North Africa, Senegal, and Uzbekistan, being the standard bearers of this new climate of understanding, while exploring new paths. The situation makes them very visible. Each visa in their passport opens up novel adventures – and not just for themselves; often the immigration officials have never dealt with a Latin

---

ecclesial reality of Latin America, argues this fact. Among other characteristics of the Latin American biblical reading, he says: "The contemporary meaning of the text is more important than the original." J. Andrew Kirk, *Mission under Scrutiny: Confronting Current Challenges* (London: Darton, Longman & Todd, 2006), 163.

[5] From the title of Christian's book, Giordano, *Peregrinaje en la Misión.*

[6] Cecilia Baeza, "América Latina y la Cuestión Palestina, (1947-2012)," *Araucaria. Revista Iberoamericana de Filosofía, Política y Humanidades* 14, no. 28 (July 2012): 11-131.

American before. They are invited to receptions in the embassies, they advise newly-formed businesses, or they might act as correspondents of the Latin American press. Latin American names such as Neymar, Messi, Maradona, and Pelé are made popular through soccer; in turn, they become recurring topics of conversation.

On a general level, we can affirm that Latin Americans are well received in Muslim countries. They represent a contrast to the growing clash of civilizations. They are not directly part of the conflict; they are people from the Global South living and serving in the Global South. This is what happened to one of the directors of PMI on one of his first visits to North Africa. When the customs officer saw his Argentinean passport, he smiled and said: "Argentina, poor like us, welcome!" Thus, nationality itself places Latin Americans on the fringes of the clash of civilizations and, instead, causes them to be seen among the bloc of sympathetic nations. From a missiological perspective, this may be an example, albeit for different reasons, of the rapprochement that David E. Singh describes as exchange, a rapprochement that distances itself from the common models of contact and conflict.[7]

The social-political context also shapes our approach to mission: mission from below. As Latin Americans, we do not belong to the group of countries considered powerful or influential. Our consuls or ambassadors are not going to fight for us or get us out of trouble. Likewise, even if the churches backing us were megachurches with abundant economic resources, the circumstances of currency exchange make meager at best the economic resources at our disposal. The context itself forces us to engage in mission from a position of weakness, from the periphery, from below. Unfortunately, mission from below is not always accompanied by mission *without conquest*. If this position of weakness is not well understood, it can aggravate the need to impose ourselves with other weapons, the spiritual ones, giving rise to so-called spiritual warfare and its companion, the warmongering language we have already mentioned.

Church-Related Elements

The diversity among the Protestant or evangelical churches in *Islamia* depends on where they are found among the six regions we have mentioned. The level of religious pluralism, religious tolerance or persecution, and the acceptance or rejection of the Western social model in their own societies determines whether the churches may, in turn, be more or less visible, evangelistically active, and involved in the social transformation of their societies.

Our study of several churches in North Africa, Senegal, and to a lesser extent in Uzbekistan and Turkey has highlighted the importance of two elements: first, the degree of integrality of the church, that is, its capacity to respond not only to

---

[7] David Emmanuel Singh, "Hundred Years of Christian-Muslim Relations," *Transformation* 27, no. 4 (September 2010): 225-38, https://doi.org/10.1177/0265378810378561.

the spiritual facets but to all facets of life, and to do so in a harmonious way. Second, a correct and intentional religious identity, oriented toward society, and inspired by the golden relationship.

Integrality of the Church

We have found that a one-dimensional typology of churches is insufficient and does not do justice to the diversity and complexity of the church communities studied. A "C-scale" spectrum approach falls short of our intended purpose: to understand the churches arising in Muslim contexts. Instead, we have proposed and used a matrix of twenty-three qualities and thirteen situations, as a springboard for a *qualitative* study, without getting bogged down in the combinations that the matrix might yield. Our purpose has always been to go beyond the quantitative, to *understand* the churches, not just typify them.

Those churches that have adopted more missional and integral identities seem to have more vitality, visibility, and social impact than those that have opted for inward-looking identities, whether that means they are secretive or perhaps only focused on proclamation. That is to say, those churches that are more oriented to blessing their community than themselves, and that attend to all (or several) facets of life (spiritual, material, social, economic, relational) in a balanced way, could be considered more solid and successful. This conclusion, rarely touched on or analyzed in other works we have read, is very revealing. In fact, we have not found any other similar statement in the literature focused on churches with a Muslim background.

Identify of the Church

Identity is a complex matter. It is not only about what the church believes itself to be, but also about how it is perceived by others, by outsiders. We suggest that some aspects of positioning, a marketing concept per say, could be applied to the construction of church identity.

Positioning is oriented outward, toward customers. The construction of a healthy identity is a conscious, consensual, and relational task. It is built among all and must be shared, lest a few ruin the identity of the church, bringing it into disrepute. We advocate a *national, internal, or endogenous identity that is honorable, credible, beneficial to the community, transparent, relational and promotes salaam.*

If the church is to have a chance for the future, it must be national, in the sense of not being foreign. The nationals must be at the forefront even if there are foreigners supporting it. A further step is that it must be autochthonous, endogenous, from within the culture. That is to say that both the local members and their surrounding community perceive it as "something that is ours," not as a foreign religion.

The identity of the church must be honorable and gain respect (1 Thess. 4:11-12) so that its testimony has validity. It should also be credible and transparent to outsiders, not giving rise to a suspicion that its motives are different from what they claim to be. The identity of the church will be perceived as useful or beneficial to the community if it has a real interest in the welfare of the community, if it contributes to the common good and not only to its own interest and growth. It will be relational, that is, it will maintain healthy relationships with the community, with its members, with the authorities and institutions.

Finally, the promotion of *salaam* will be an important part of a healthy ecclesial identity in a Muslim context. *Salaam*, in its elements that are equivalent to biblical *shalom*, is generous, communitarian, altruistic, integral and is religious in essence, since ultimately it can only come from God.

2. Mission Agencies

The Goal of Mission

Now we must distance ourselves a little from the day-to-day details and short-term thinking to ask again what the goal of mission is. Related to that, what is the purpose of the missionary agency? One element of Iberoamerican activism urges us to establish churches in Muslim countries. It would seem that this is the quintessence of the Iberoamerican missionary model, heroic and conquering, planting the flag of Latin American Christianity in Islamic territory. Islam is the enemy to be defeated as we snatch followers and plant churches. Unfortunately, there is too much of this attitude at present. Iberoamerican missionary agencies are tempted to not confront this mentality but to take advantage of it, trying to raise funds at the expense of such thinking, seeking to recruit new personnel, participating in conferences and prayer vigils loaded with "anti-Muslim Christian imperialism," and so on, instead of strengthening a balanced and mature vision.

In a way that few others can, Johannes Verkuyl helps us to clarify the goal of mission. His first-hand experience of imperialism, World War II and wars of independence, living among Muslims, and dealing with Christian paternalism as well as his far-sightedness as a missiologist are an invaluable help. In a chapter titled "The Goal and Purpose of Mission"[8] he reviews the seven answers that different missionary approaches have given to this question.

- The goal of saving individual souls,
- Church-centered goals,
- The "three-self" formula,
- The goal of church growth,
- The goal of forming a Christian society,
- The goal of the social gospel, and of improving the macrostructures.

[8] Johannes Verkuyl, *Contemporary Missiology: An Introduction* (Grand Rapids: Eerdmans, 1978), chap. 7.

Finally, he offers a biblical, integral, and current alternative centered on the coming of the kingdom of God in each specific situation.

The establishment of the church, although an important component of the purpose of mission, is neither the only nor the final purpose. The goal of mission must be seen in the broader context of the kingdom of God. Mission agencies need, again and again, to reconsider the ultimate goal and their own role as part of that ultimate goal. Only from that perspective does the daily work of establishing churches, managing development projects, or discipling people make sense.

Resisting Pragmatism and a Results-Orientation

There is constant pressure at all levels of a mission agency (leadership, members, supporters, and others) to adopt a pragmatic vision of missionary work; pressure to adopt a results-orientation is very strong. It comes not only from those providing financial resources, the foundations and churches, it is also the constant bombardment launched by articles in missions-focused magazines and the themes of workshops and plenaries in numerous conferences.

The voices in favor of an integral mission model are in the minority compared to those others – many and strong – that advocate successful methodologies, results, application of more technologies and knowledge, reduction of missionary drop-out, and the like. If mission, in general, should not be primarily guided by the search for short-term results, how much less should this be the case in Muslim contexts?

So how do we deal with these constant pressures? The answer seems obvious, even if we rarely see it put into practice. We must periodically identify these pressures and design concrete strategies not only to resist them, but to the extent possible to combat them. Therefore, we ask ourselves, in what way are the Latin missionary agencies to Islam resisting such short-sighted pressures?

Deepening Integral Mission

If, as we have pointed out, integral mission not only does justice to the biblical model of mission, but is a *sine qua non* condition in Muslim cultures, integral in themselves, what should missionary agencies do to deepen it, strengthen it, and apply it more and better every day?

The first thing must be to **put integral mission into practice**. As the text of Romans 15:18-19 makes clear, this includes words and deeds, as well as signs of God's power, coupled with incarnation, which our Lord Jesus Christ taught us by his own example. These are the four ingredients: word, deed, incarnation, and the power of the Spirit, an expanded concept of integral mission that Christian succinctly developed in his 2009 *Pilgrimage in Mission*.

The next step, unavoidable if integral mission is to be consolidated, is to **disseminate, explain, and promote** integral mission among the churches that support us and the Iberoamerican Christian public in general. This must be done by all means: books, videos, testimonies, formal and informal teaching, articles in magazines, web pages, and so on. We must not avoid this. As experts in cooperation and development emphasize, *NGOs exist to do and communicate*, "to raise awareness here and work there."[9] If disseminating, explaining, and promoting is an inherent part of the missionary agency's task, each agency should have a communication department, staffed by trained professionals and, of course, an important part of the agency's budget – we suggest no less than a third – should be allocated to this task.

If we limit ourselves to *putting integral mission* into practice in the field, without dedicating sufficient effort to disseminating, explaining, and promoting it in Iberoamerica, we will face significant problems both for the mission agency itself and in the field. If this happens, the agency will continue to receive new missionary candidates who have not internalized integral mission. At the most, they will have picked up a dose of holism, something we have described as the sum of social work (generally relief) and evangelism but carried out without integration. It becomes just a complement to evangelism or, worse, a hook to catch people. New workers like this come with activist hearts, coupled with the task of "planting churches" assigned by their sending church, often done from a reductionist perspective. It is obvious that this will cause serious detriment to the advances that may have been achieved in the field. This situation, this approach, is aggravated by the growing tendency of shorter stays of missionary personnel in the field. The very dynamics of globalization and the acceleration of life lead to a shortening of the time spent in the field, and turnover within teams increases. As these workers assume leadership positions, workers who themselves have not sufficiently internalized integral mission, the integrality of the missionary team, of the project, and of the church suffer.

Global Dialogue

Nevertheless, mission agencies are uniquely qualified to contribute to a global dialogue on integral mission. We mentioned earlier that the Latin American Theological Fraternity has tended to deal exclusively with the Latin American context. The agencies could contribute their own intercultural perspective, from the hybrid Latin-Muslim point of view. This would enrich the dialogue and understanding of the integral mission. The twenty-first century is characterized by *glocality*, the practice of thinking globally and acting locally.

Along these lines, Latin American mission agencies could enrich the wider understanding of integral mission in the twenty-first century by adding to Latin America's existing understanding the vision of Hispanics in North America and the vision of Latin American missionaries in *Islamia*. All of them are Iberoamerican visions, but from the wider world. We are not saying that Latin Americans need to see the world through Anglo-Saxon or African eyes. What we are talking about is the way we see the world – the whole world, not just to

---

[9] S. Baiges et al., *Las ONG de Desarrollo en España: Dilemas de la Cooperación* (Barcelona: Flor del Viento Ediciones, 1996), 191ff.

the coastlines of the continent – with Latin eyes, and, from that viewpoint what we can share with our African, Asian, European, and other colleagues. In this way, we can enrich each other with a truly glocal vision.[10]

They could also contribute valuable elements to interreligious dialogue, a field that is still in its infancy in the ecclesial and missionary spectrum of Iberoamerica. Noteworthy work is being done in this regard by the Christian-Muslim Relations Team of the Mennonite mission and Andrés Prins, one of the founders of PMI, fostering friendly encounters between evangelical and Muslim leaders throughout Latin America and also in the Muslim world.

3. The Workers

Discipleship

The history of the people, projects, and churches presented in this book has highlighted the importance of discipleship. Since there is much confusion about the term discipleship, we clarify here the meaning and practical use of the term. Discipleship is the personal process in which a more mature believer teaches and helps a younger believer grow in the likeness of the Master, Jesus Christ. It is not just a few preparatory classes for baptism. It goes beyond that, focusing on Christian character formation. It is teaching a disciple in a practical way to obey everything Jesus commanded (Matt. 28:20). That is, the main emphasis is not only on communicating biblical knowledge but also on life transfer. The goal is Christian maturity. Paul said: "He [Christ] is the one we proclaim, admonishing and teaching everyone with all wisdom, so that we may present everyone fully mature in Christ. To this end I strenuously contend with all the energy Christ so powerfully works in me" (Col. 1:28-29).

It is worth highlighting some factors in the discipleship process. First, there must be a teacher. Jesus Christ is the supreme Teacher, but the process of discipleship is based on human teachers, capable of saying "so I encourage you to follow my example" (1 Cor. 4:16 CEB) "I urge you to imitate me" (1 Cor. 4:16). Likewise, there must be a disciple who wants to learn from his master. Too often this seemingly obvious fact is overlooked. The relationship between the two and the goals must be clear and known to both. Finally, discipleship is a reproducible process: "Take the things you heard me say in front of many other witnesses and pass them on to faithful people who are also capable of teaching others" (2 Tim. 2:2 CEB). Discipleship is a relationship of mutual trust and friendship, tailored to each situation and involving a lot of shared time. How long should it last? It does not seem to us that there is an equal rule for all, but between a few months and a few years seems reasonable if we look at the examples of Jesus Christ and Paul with their teams.

---

[10] We owe this thought to missionary and anthropologist Peter Jones.

Disciple-making should be one of the priority goals of Latin American workers serving among Muslims, preparing themselves in advance for this aspect of service. Similarly, the missionary team and the agency should support, stimulate, and encourage the discipleship processes. For those who are focused on starting new churches, discipleship of key people is fundamental for the development of home groups and true leadership. But not only that, for those dedicated to managing projects, whether development, business, cultural, humanitarian, or social, a priority should be to not do anything alone, but to have disciples by their side. That is, to be training others not only in the tasks related to the project, but also in reproducing the kind of spiritual person, those with a servant's heart, fit to carry out such a task.

We have also mentioned the need to train agents of social welfare, who propagate and consolidate the advances of the Jubilee, of Development-Salaam. In other words, the task is not limited to "spiritual" discipleship, but encompasses all aspects of life, leadership, and projects; we call it *integral discipleship*. In the social reality of Muslim communities, integral discipleship is a widely accepted concept. Parents expect the master carpenter, for example, to teach their son not only the trade, but also to show him how to be an upright and religious person. We are not proposing something foreign or culturally challenging, but unfortunately experience has shown a lack in its implementation from the missionary side, which tends to be quite accustomed to preaching but little inclined to discipleship.

Investing in Identity

If, as we have shown in this book, the identity of the worker is so important for the success of mission among Muslims, each worker should consciously invest in creating and strengthening their personal and family identity. We are aware that this is no easy process. It has many nuances as it is lived out. Forming such an identity will be a topic for future study: how to create a solid, true, credible, and viable identity. This might best be carried out by those who are adept in the disciplines of psychology and sociology.

Our study has taken a first step: defining the overall goal. Personally, the goal is an integrated, mono-vocational, transparent identity, supported by a real job or occupation, and free from the pressures of exaggerated activism. Socially, this identity takes the form of guests with a message, ambassadors of *Isa al-Masih* (Jesus the Messiah) and promoters of Development-Salaam.

4. The Projects

Who Does the Project Serve?

As we have already mentioned, in many countries that restrict access for missionaries, projects are used as an entry strategy. These strategies are often an elaborate plan, with the full organizational support of the mission agency, to obtain legal residence in the country, deceiving the immigration officials who have to issue the visa and the host society in general. These approaches arise from the need sensed by missionaries and agencies to "do missions." They allow them to execute the plans they have designed, plans set up even before arriving on the field.

This type of approach must be clearly denounced. It violates biblical ethics and pretends to carry the gospel by relying on institutional deception. Any entry strategy must be ethical, transparent, based on the real needs of the beneficiaries and, moreover, developed on the basis of what they, the beneficiaries, have asked for. We should not be naïve about the long-term consequences and ultimate motives that the project may entail. Therefore, it seems to us vital to promote both a true integral development, based on biblical principles, as well as to establish strict and long-term criteria regarding the purpose, sustainability, ownership, and motivations of each project.

Social Transformation

Finally, we would like to put on record some considerations regarding the transformation of society. Integral mission includes an undeniable transforming social dimension. Charles Van Engen adds a fourth element to the purpose of the mission that was enunciated long ago by Gisbertus Voetius: "the transformation of the Church and, through the Church's ministries, the transformation of the contexts and nations in which the churches are to be found."[11]

In the first place, the theme of social transformation requires a change in the theology of salvation of a part of the evangelical Christian sector, and therefore of its missionaries. Many believe that salvation is a matter addressed to human beings, to individuals, in such a way that the conversion of the individual will bring, by itself, the transformation of their environment. This is the idea behind the slogan "change the world, one person at a time." This is a reductionist theology that assumes that sin only affected individuals.

This is a broad topic; this is not the place to deal with it in depth. Suffice it to say, at a general level, that both daily reality and a serious study of the Bible show that not only the individual needs salvation, but also interpersonal relationships, the structures of society, as well as nature itself. Sin has contaminated the entire cosmos, including the economic, judicial, political, commercial, and other systems, as well as the structures and relationships of marriage, school, work, and more. Each one of these structures needs the integral salvific work of the triune God, although the concrete way of doing so is different in each case.

In any case, social transformation does not come by itself, in an almost magical way. If the projects are to contribute to social transformation focused on the model of the kingdom of God, the missionaries who initiate and manage such

---

[11] Charles E. Van Engen, *Transforming Mission Theology* (Pasadena: William Carey Library, 2017), chap. 6.

projects must overcome the aspects of the reductionist theology we have mentioned and must seriously approach the study of social transformation.

Having made the above clarification, the theme of integral social transformation that the gospel brings is being studied and put into practice in some sectors of evangelical Christianity in Latin America. For those serving in Muslim communities, however, the circumstances are quite different. On the one hand, the missionaries are "strangers in a foreign land"; they have to learn to behave as quality guests, ambassadors of the King, as we have proposed. This condition of guest makes it necessary to think twice before proposing changes in a "stranger's house." Both sociocultural ignorance and ethnocentric prejudices can easily lead to false conclusions.

Likewise, since the church finds itself as a minority and often persecuted, it may not be able to pursue an aggressive approach toward transformation. Still, there are many facets of the "ideal Muslim society" that are fully consistent with the gospel. What we have called explicitly religious concepts of the language and ideals of the kingdom of God can be wisely combined to introduce social and relational changes. However, we will have to be vigilant, since the biblical and Muslim motivations for the same action may be very different.

Finally, the missionaries will have to sow the seed of social transformation (not revolution) in the nascent church with much tact, without pressuring them. The goal should be to help the church and the believers avoid becoming a subculture. On the contrary, they must become an acceptable counterculture, in the sense that the rest of Muslim society tolerates or accepts this degree of nonconformity, seeking micro-social transformations in areas including the family, work, and intra-family relations.

5. Final Conclusion

At the beginning of this book, we asked ourselves: is there a possibility of Christian evangelism in Muslim lands that is both frank and respectful, without religious confrontation? Moreover, is it ethically permissible to combine development projects with the establishment of Christian churches?

Yes, it is possible! We have shown the stories of several individuals, projects, and churches as examples. We have analyzed their stories to understand the keys to the ways they work and serve, and the reasons for their strengths and weaknesses. In these closing lines, then, we thank them for their good will, for opening to us their homes, projects, celebrations and, above all, their hearts and desires. Thank you for allowing us to observe and study.

True, these individuals, projects, and churches constitute a minority example among the multitude of examples of religious confrontation that is part of current Iberoamerican missionary outreach. But this does not diminish their importance; rather, it enhances their value. We believe that they shine with their own light and that they show another way, a responsible way of carrying out the task of evangelism and mission. They are an alternative, in this case non-governmental alternative, to the clash of civilizations and they demonstrate the possibility that people of Christian faith and Muslim faith can and do collaborate, with joy and harmony, for the common welfare of peoples.

Their way of doing things has revealed changes, changes in the conception of Christian mission and in missionary identity as well as changes in the procedures and approaches of mission agencies. Furthermore, the analysis has led us, as authors, to propose a theology, identity models, and practical guidelines that, in some aspects, go beyond the experiences of the people, churches, and projects whose stories we have narrated.

Of course, the responsibility for this proposal is ours alone, not theirs. Therefore, we understand our work as a first step. The analysis and the proposal should be followed by public review, as well as the nuances and counterproposals of the missionary community, both Iberoamerican and global. We put forward our conclusions for debate within the missionary community; we are eager to learn more, and to discover better ways for Christian mission among Muslims.

Further, we have tried to bridge the gap between mission among Muslims and the specific missionary situation of our readers through questions for reflection and discussion at the end of each chapter. The intention has been that readers can apply the lessons and principles mentioned throughout the book to their own circumstances and in their own communities.

Finally, if this work contributes to a more respectful and frank understanding between followers of Islam and Christians, it will have more than served its purpose.

Questions for Reflection and Discussion

1. For you, what is the goal of mission? What do you think your church's or organization's goal of mission is?
2. If you are a development or social worker, what religious or spiritual elements characterize or are part of the projects you work in? How could its Christian identity be made more evident, or its Christian values?
3. If you are serving among Muslims, what would you suggest regarding our ideas about a changed identity? Make a list of the pros and cons.
4. What do the proposed changes for mission agencies suggest to you regarding integral mission?

The authors welcome comments and your reflections. Please send them to desarrollo-salaam@losgiordano.org. Thank you.

For Further Reading

Horst, Willis, Frank Paul, and Ute Paul. *Mission without Conquest: An Alternative Missionary Practice*. Carlisle: Langham, 2015.

Newbigin, Lesslie. *The Open Secret: An Introduction to the Theology of Mission*. Rev. ed. Grand Rapids: Eerdmans, 1995.

Shenk, David W. *God's Call to Mission*. Scottdale, Penn.: Herald Press, 1994.

Walls, Andrew F., and Cathy Ross, eds. *Mission in The Twenty-First Century: Exploring the Five Marks of Global Mission*. Maryknoll: Orbis, 2008.

Bibliography

ACT Alliance. "ACT Alliance: Founding Document." ACT International, 2009. https://actalliance.org/wp-content/uploads/2015/09/ACT-Founding-document-ENG.pdf.

Adeney, Miriam. *Kingdom without Borders: The Untold Story of Global Christianity*. Downers Grove: InterVarsity, 2009.

———. *Wealth, Women, and God: How to Flourish Spiritually and Economically in Tough Places*. Pasadena: William Carey Library, 2015.

Agencias. "Sánchez: España, Con un 27% de Niños Pobres, Está entre los Países de UE con Datos 'Más Alarmantes.'" Qué! February 3, 2021. https://www.que.es/2021/02/03/sanchez-espana-ninos-pobres-datos-alarmantes/.

Albertz, Rainer. *A History of Israelite Religion in the Old Testament Period*. 2 vols. Louisville, KY: John Knox Press, 1994.

Allen, Scott D., and Darrow L. Miller. *The Forest in the Seed*. Phoenix: Disciple Nations Alliance, 2006. https://faith2share.net/perch/resources/forest-in-the-seed-1.pdf.

Alonso Schökel, Luis. "Shalom." In *Diccionario Bíblico Hebreo-Español*. Madrid: Editorial Trotta, 1994.

Amado, Marcos. "Declarando Paz al Islam." PM Internacional, 2001.

Anastasios, Archbishop (Yannoulatos). *Mission in Christ's Way: An Orthodox Understanding of Mission*. Brookline, Mass. and Geneva: Holy Cross Orthodox Press and World Council of Churches Publications, 2010.

Anderson, Royce. "A Definition of Peace." *Journal of Peace and Psychology*, 2004.

Arendonk, C. van, and D. Gimaret. "Salām." In *Encyclopaedia of Islam*. Leiden: Brill Online, 2013. https://referenceworks.brillonline.com/browse/encyclopaedia-of-islam-2/alpha/s?s.rows=100&s.start=200.

Assmann, Hugo, and Franz J Hinkelammert. *A Idolatria do Mercado*. Coleção Teologia e Libertação. Série V, Desafios da Vida Na Sociedade 5. Petrópolis, Brazil: Vozes, 1989.

Baeza, Cecilia. "América Latina y la Cuestión Palestina, (1947-2012)." *Araucaria. Revista Iberoamericana de Filosofía, Política y Humanidades* 14, no. 28 (July 2012): 11-131.

Baiges, S., D. Dusster, E. Mira, and R. Viladomat. *Las ONG de Desarrollo en España: Dilemas de la Cooperación*. Barcelona: Flor del Viento Ediciones, 1996.

Bailey, Kenneth E. "Arabic-speaking Christianity: A Glorious Past and a Challenging Present and Future." In *Middle Eastern Presbyterian Caucus Banquet*, 1-11. Richmond, Vir.: 2004. http://www.pcusa.org/media/uploads/worldmission/pdfs/arabic_speaking_christianity_rev_dr_kenneth_e_bailey.pdf.

Baker, David L. *Tight Fists or Open Hands?: Wealth and Poverty in Old Testament Law*. Grand Rapids, MI: Eerdmans, 2009.

Bammel, Ernst, and Friedrich Hauck. "Ptochós." In *Theological Dictionary of the New Testament*, VI:885-915. Grand Rapids: Eerdmans, 1964.

Bartley, James, José Luis Martínez, and Rubén O. Zorzoli, eds. *Nuevo Comentario Bíblico: Siglo Veintiuno*. 1st Spanish ed., ESword. El Paso, TX: Casa Bautista de Publicaciones, 1999.

Baumer, Christoph. *The Church of the East: An Illustrated History of Assyrian Christianity*. London: I.B. Tauris, 2006.

Bavinck, Johan Herman. *An Introduction to the Science of Missions*. Phillipsburg, NJ: P & R Publishing, 1960.

Bedford, Nancy Elizabeth. "The Flight to Egypt: Toward a Protestant Mariology in Migration." In *Latinxs, the Bible, and Migration*, edited by Efraín Agosto and Jacqueline M. Hidalgo, 109-31. The Bible and Cultural Studies. Cham, Switzerland: Cham Springer, 2018. https://doi.org/10.1007/978-3-319-96695-3_6.

Befus, David R. *Kingdom Business: The Ministry of Promoting Economic Activity*. Miami: Latin America Mission, 2002.

Belser, Patrick. "The Economics of Slavery, Forced Labor and Human Trafficking." In *The Encyclopedia of Law and Economics*, 1-36. Rochester: Elgar Publishing, May 11, 2008. https://papers.ssrn.com/abstract=1838369.

Bendor-Samuel, Paul. "Epilogue: Called to Undivided Witness." In *Undivided Witness: Jesus Followers, Community Development, and Least-Reached Communities*, edited by David Greenlee, Mark Galpin, and Paul Bendor-Samuel, 163-68. Regnum Practitioner Series. Oxford: Regnum, 2020.

Berrtuzzi Historical Archive. "Consulta Misiológica FTL-COMIBAM, 1995: Comunicado de Prensa." In *Comunicado de Prensa*. Miami: FTL and COMIBAM, 1995. http://recursosmisioneros.com/docs/eventos/Miami_1995.pdf.

Bertuzzi, Federico A., ed. *Latinos en el Mundo Islámico*. Miami: UNILIT, 1991.

———, ed. *Ríos en la Soledad: Latinos Respondiendo al Llamado Macedónico de los Pueblos Islámicos*. CLAME 90. Santa Fe, Argentina: Proyecto Magreb, 1991.

———. *Ríos en Tierra Seca: Europeos, Latinos y Exmusulmanes Evangelizando a los Hijos de Ismael en el Viejo Continente*. Granada: Musulmania, 2012. http://musulmania.com/resources/Rios_en_tierra_seca_INTRO.pdf.

Bhabha, Homi K. *Locations of Culture*. London: Routledge, 1994.

Blaut, J.M. "Where Was Capitalism Born?" *Antipode* 8, no. 2 (1976): 1-11. https://doi.org/10.1111/j.1467-8330.1976.tb00633.x.

Blomberg, Craig L. *Neither Poverty nor Riches: A Biblical Theology of Material Possessions*. New Studies in Biblical Theology 7. Leicester and Downers Grove: Apollos and InterVarsity, 1999.

Boff, Leonardo. *Cry of the Earth, Cry of the Poor*. Ecology and Justice. Maryknoll: Orbis, 1997.

Bonhoeffer, Dietrich. *Letters and Papers from Prison*. Edited by Eberhard Bethge, Renate Bethge, C. Gremmels, Ilse Tödt, and John W. De Gruchy. Minneapolis: Fortress, 2010.

Bosch, David J. *Transforming Mission: Paradigm Shifts in Theology of Mission*. Maryknoll: Orbis, 1991.

———. *Witness to the World: The Christian Mission in Theological Perspective*. Eugene, OR: Wipf & Stock, 2006.

Bradshaw, Bruce. *Bridging the Gap: Evangelism, Development and Shalom*. Innovations in Mission 5. Monrovia, Calif.: MARC, 1994.

Brislen, Mike. "A Model for a Muslim-Culture Church." *Missiology* XXIV, no. 3 (July 1996): 355-67.

Brueggemann, Walter. *Peace*. Atlanta: Chalice Press, 2001.

———. *Theology of the Old Testament: Testimony, Dispute, Advocacy*. Minneapolis: Fortress Press, 2005.

Bryant, Katharine, and Todd Landman. "Combatting Human Trafficking since Palermo: What do We Know about what Works?" *Journal of Human Trafficking* 6, no. 2 (March 14, 2020): 119-40. https://doi.org/10.1080/23322705.2020.1690097.

Bullón, H. Fernando. *El Pensamiento Social Protestante y el Debate Latinoamericano sobre el Desarrollo*. Grand Rapids, MI: Libros Desafío, 2013.

———. *Ética Cristiana y Responsabilidad Social*. Vol. 1. 3 vols. Misión Cristiana y Responsabilidad Social 1. Buenos Aires: Kairos, 2009.

———. *Historia de la Iglesia y Responsabilidad Social*. Vol. 2. 3 vols. Misión Cristiana y Responsabilidad Social. Buenos Aires: Kairos Ediciones, 2009.

———. *Misión, Economía y Desarrollo Humano: Desafíos Avanzando el Siglo 21*. Grand Rapids: Libros Desafío, 2016.

———. *Misión y Desarrollo en America Latina: Desafíos en el Umbral del Siglo 21*. Cuadernos FTL 8. Buenos Aires: Ediciones Kairos and FTL, 2000.

———. *Protestant Social Thought in Latin America: The Debate on Development*. Regnum Studies in Global Christianity. Eugene, OR: Wipf & Stock, 2015.

———. *Transformación de América Latina y Responsabilidad Social*. Vol. 3. 3 vols. Misión Cristiana y Responsabilidad Social. Buenos Aires: Kairos Ediciones, 2009.

Cano Pérez, María José. "Paz en el Antiguo Testamento." In *Cosmovisiones de Paz en el Mediterráneo Antiguo y Medieval*, edited by Francisco A. Muñoz and Beatriz Molina Rueda, 29-61. Granada: Universidad de Granada, 1998.

Carr, G. Lloyd. "Shalom." In *Theological Wordbook of the Old Testament*, edited by Gleason L. Archer, Bruce K. Waltke, and R. Laird Harris. Chicago: Moody, 1999.

Carrillo Luna, Pablo. "El Desafío del Islam en el Siglo XXI." *Kairós: Iglesia y Misión*, 2004. https://repository.globethics.net/bitstream/handle/20.500.12424/202961.

———. *Huellas en el Desierto*. Granada: PM Internacional, 2010.

———. *Seminario Raimundo Lulio*. Granada: LAM and PMI, 2005.

Chapman, Colin. "Christians in the Middle East – Past, Present and Future." *Transformation* 29, no. 2 (April 2012): 91-110. https://doi.org/10.1177/0265378812439955.

Chauvel, Geneviève. *Aïcha: La Bien-aimée du Prophète*. 7th ed. Paris: Librairie Générale Française, 2009.

Chávez, Moisés. *La Ishah: Un Estudio Etnohistoriográfico. La Mujer en la Biblia y en el Pensamiento Hebreo.* Miami: Caribe, 1976.

Cherian, Joyson K. "An Interreligious Initiative for Peace and Harmony: A Christian Perspective:" *Transformation* 36, no. 2 (May 16, 2019): 100-112. https://doi.org/10.1177/0265378819844874.

Christian, Jayakumar. *God of the Empty-Handed: Poverty, Power and the Kingdom of God.* 2nd ed. Brunswick East, Vic., Australia: Acorn Press, 2011.

Clarke, Colin. "The Latin American Structuralists." In *The Companion to Development Studies*, edited by Vandana Desai and Robert B. Potter, 2nd ed. London and New York: Routledge, 2002.

Coenen, Lothar, and H.H. Esser. "Pobre." In *Diccionario Teológico del Nuevo Testamento*, II:380-85. Salamanca: Sígueme, 1985.

Cogswell, James A. "Relief and Development: Challenges to Mission Today." *International Bulletin of Missionary Research* 11, no. 2 (April 1987): 72-76.

"Consulta Misiológica FTL-COMIBAM, 1995: Comunicado de Prensa." Miami: FTL and COMIBAM, 1995. http://recursosmisioneros.com/docs/eventos/Miami_1995.pdf.

"Consultation on Mission Language and Metaphors." Fuller Theological Seminary, June 1, 2000. http://www.ad2000.org/re00620.htm.

Cooperrider, David L, Diana Kaplin Whitney, and Jacqueline M Stavros. *Appreciative Inquiry Handbook: For Leaders of Change*. 2nd ed. San Francisco: Berrett-Koehler, 2008.

Costas, Orlando E. *Christ Outside the Gate: Mission beyond Christendom*. Maryknoll: Orbis, 1982.

———. *Liberating News: A Theology of Contextual Evangelization*. Eugene, OR: Wipf & Stock, 2002.

———. *The Integrity of Mission: The Inner Life and Outreach of the Church.* San Francisco: Harper & Row, 1979.

Coulon, Christian. "The Grand Magal in Touba: A Religious Festival of the Mouride Brotherhood of Senegal." *African Affairs* 98, no. 391 (April 1, 1999): 195-210. https://doi.org/10.1093/oxfordjournals.afraf.a008007.

Cragg, Kenneth. *The Call of the Minaret*. 3rd rev. Oxford: Oneworld, 2008.

Crespo, Rafael. "Los 'Móodu-Móodu' y Su Impacto en la Sociedad de Origen." In *Empresariado Étnico en España*, edited by Joaquín Beltrán, Natalia Ribas, and Laura Oso, 12:249-61. Documentos Observatorio Permanente Inmigración. Madrid: Ministerio de Trabajo y Asuntos Sociales, Fundació CIDOB, 2006. http://www.cidob.org/es/content/download/4587/46036/file/12_crespo.pdf.

Croatto, J. Severino. *Biblical Hermeneutics: Toward a Theory of Reading as the Production of Meaning*. Maryknoll: Orbis, 1987.

Cruz, Antonio. "Bienaventuranza." In *Gran Diccionario Enciclopédico de la Biblia*, 347-49. Viladecavalls, Barcelona: CLIE, 2013.

Daou, Fadi, and Nāylā Tabbārah. *Divine Hospitality: A Christian-Muslim Conversation*. Translated by Alan J. Amos. Geneva: World Council of Churches, 2017.

deCarvalho, Levi, Ninette Jiménez, Carlos González, and Samuel Guerrero. "Fortalezas y Debilidades del Movimiento Misionero Iberoamericano." Equipo Investigación Misiopedia, 2006. http://recursosmisioneros.com/resources/Fortalezas_debilidades.pdf.

Dennett, Bill, and John R. Reid. *Sharing the Good News with Muslims*. Homebush West, NSW, Australia: Anzea, 1992.

Desai, Vandana, and Robert B. Potter, eds. *The Companion to Development Studies*. 2nd ed. London and New York: Routledge, 2002.

DeSilva, David Arthur. *Honor, Patronage, Kinship & Purity: Unlocking New Testament Culture*. Downers Grove: InterVarsity, 2000.

Dillon, John. "The Root Causes of the Current Financial Crisis." In *Justice not Greed*, edited by Pamela Brubaker and Rogate R. Mshana, 86-103. Geneva: WCC Publications, 2010.

Douglas, James Dixon, ed. *Let the Earth Hear His Voice: International Congress on World Evangelization, Lausanne, Switzerland: Official Reference Volume: Papers and Responses*. Minneapolis: World Wide Publications, 1975.

Dovlo, Elom and Alfred Ofosu Asante, "Reinterpreting the Straight Path: Ghanian Muslim Converts in Mission to Muslims," Exchange 32, no. 3 (January 2003): 214-38.

Dowsett, Rose, ed. *Global Mission: Reflections and Case Studies in Contextualization for the Whole Church*. Globalization of Mission. Pasadena: William Carey Library, 2011.

Duchrow, Ulrich, and Franz J. Hinkelammert. *Transcending Greedy Money: Interreligious Solidarity for Just Relations*. New York: Palgrave Macmillan, 2012.

Ebin, Victoria. "International Networks of Trading Diaspora: The Mourides of Senegal Abroad." In *La ville à Guichets Fermés*, edited by Philippe Antoine and Abdoulaye Bara Diop, 323-36. Dakar: IFAN / ORSTOM, 1995. http://horizon.documentation.ird.fr/exl-doc/pleins_textes/pleins_textes_7/carton01/010004580.pdf.

Eichrodt, Walther. *Theology of the Old Testament*. Translated by John Baker. 2 Vols. London: SCM, 1983.

Ekklesia. "Archbishop Urges Christians and Muslims to Create Fairer Lending," October 21, 2008. https://old.ekklesia.co.uk/node/7816.

Ember, Carol R., and Melvin Ember. *Cultural Anthropology*. 15th ed. New York: Pearson Education, 2019.

Entz, Donna. "Burkina Faso." In *Anabaptists Meeting Muslims: A Calling for Presence in the Way of Christ*, edited by J. R Krabill, D. W Shenk, and L. Stutzman, 197-207. Scottdale, Penn.: Herald Press, 2005.

Escobar, Arturo. *Encountering Development: The Making and Unmaking of the Third World*. Reprint. Princeton: Princeton University Press, 2012.

———. *Territories of Difference: Place, Movements, Life, Redes*. Durham, NC: Duke University Press, 2008. https://doi.org/10.1215/9780822389439.

Escobar, Samuel. "Beyond Liberation Theology: Evangelical Missiology in Latin America." *International Bulletin of Missionary Research* 6, no. 3 (1982): 108-14.

———. *In Search of Christ in Latin America: From Colonial Image to Liberating Savior*. Downers Grove: InterVarsity, 2019.

———. *La Fe Evangélica y las Teologías de la Liberacíon*. El Paso: Casa Bautista de Publicaciones, 1987.

———. *Liberation Themes in Reformational Perspective*. Sioux Center, IA: Dordt College Press, 1989.

———. *The New Global Mission: The Gospel from Everywhere to Everyone*. Downers Grove: InterVarsity, 2003.

Europa Press. "La Trata de Personas en el Mundo, en Datos y Gráficos." Datos, October 2020. https://www.epdata.es/datos/trata-personas-mundo-datos-graficos/427.

———. "El Tráfico de Personas en el Mundo en Diez Datos." Europa Press, May 6, 2016. https://www.europapress.es/internacional/noticia-trafico-personas-mundo-diez-datos-20170506174236.html.

Eurostat. "Glossary: At Risk of Poverty or Social Exclusion (AROPE)." Eurostat, June 29, 2021. https://ec.europa.eu/eurostat/statistics-explained/index.php?title=Glossary:At_risk_of_poverty_or_social_exclusion_(AROPE).

Evans, Alex, Richard Gower, and Tearfund. "The Restorative Economy: Completing our Unfinished Millennium Jubilee." Tearfund, 2015. https://learn.tearfund.org/~/media/files/tilz/research/tearfund_therestorativeeconomy_summary.pdf.

Evans, Wendel P. *Church-planting in the Arab-Muslim World*. Mimeograph. AWM, 1986.

Familia Rocha no Senegal. "Centro Medico Social Keru Barkeel: Paredes do Térreo Levantadas!!" *Centro Medico Social Keru Barkeel* (blog), August 19, 2013. http://centrosocialdakar.blogspot.com/2013/08/paredes-do-terreo-levantadas.html.

Feingold, David A. "Trafficking in Numbers: The Social Construction of Human Trafficking Data." In *Sex, Drugs, and Body Counts: The Politics of Numbers in Global Crime and Conflict*, 46-74. Ithaca: Cornell University

Press, 2011. https://www.degruyter.com/document/doi/10.7591/9780801458309-005/html.

Fileta, Jason, Tearfund, and Micah Challenge. *Live just.ly: Global Edition*. Portland, Ore.: Micah Challenge and Tearfund, 2017. https://learn.tearfund.org/en/resources/tools-and-guides/live-justly-global-edition.

Foerster, Werner. "Eirene." In *Theological Dictionary of the New Testament*, edited by Gerhard Kittel and Geoffrey William Bromiley, 2:400-417. Grand Rapids: Eerdmans, 1964.

Foulkes, F. "Paz." In *Nuevo Diccionario Bíblico*, edited by James D. Douglas. Barcelona: Certeza Unida, 1991.

Francis. *The Joy of the Gospel: Evangelii Gaudium*. Frederick, MD: The Word Among Us Press, 2014. https://www.vatican.va/content/francesco/en/apost_exhortations/documents/papa-francesco_esortazione-ap_20131124_evangelii-gaudium.html.

Franco Sánchez, Francisco. "La Noción de Paz en el Pensamiento Religioso Islámico y su Plasmación en al-Andalus." In *Idees de Pau a l'Edat Mitjana: Reunió Científica. XIII Curs d'Estiu Comtat d'Urgell Celebrat a Balaguer els Dies 2, 3 i 4 de Juliol de 2008; Sota la Direcció de Flocel Sabaté i Maite Pedrol.*, edited by Flocel Sabaté, 161-84. Collecció Aurembiaix d'Urgell 13. Lleida: Pagès, 2010. http://hdl.handle.net/10045/16616.

FTL-Brasil. "Seguir a Jesus em seu Caminho de Vida. Reflexiones para CLADE V." FTL-Brasil, June 25, 2012. https://ftl-al.com/download/seguir-a-jesus-em-seu-caminho-de-vida-documento-da-ftl-brasil/#.

Galilea, Segundo. "Teología de la Liberación: Ensayo de Síntesis." Edited by Teodoro Balle. *Selecciones de Teología* 19, no. 76 (December 1980). http://www.seleccionesdeteologia.net/selecciones/llib/vol19/76/076_galilea.pdf.

García-Johnson, Oscar. *Mestizo/a Community of the Spirit: A Postmodern Latino/a Ecclesiology*. Princeton Theological Monograph Series 105. Eugene: Pickwick Publications, 2009.

———. *The Beatitudes: To Evangelize as Jesus Did*. Translated by Robert R. Barr. Maryknoll: Orbis, 1987.

García-Pelayo y Gross, Ramón, ed. *Diccionario Moderno Español-Inglés Larousse*. Paris: Larousse, 1986.

Garrison, V. David. *Church Planting Movements: How God Is Redeeming a Lost World*. Midlothian, Vir.: WIGTake, 2004.

Geertz, Clifford. *Islam Observed: Religious Development in Morocco and Indonesia*. Chicago: University of Chicago, 2008.

Gern, Wolfgang. "Development." In *Dictionary of Mission: Theology, History, Perspectives*, edited by Karl Müller. American Society of Missiology Series, no. 24. Maryknoll: Orbis, 1997.

Giordano, Christian. "Identidad, Contexto y Mensaje." In *Rios en Tierra Seca*, edited by Federico A. Bertuzzi, 275-86. Granada: Musulmania, 2012.

———. "Identity, Context and Message: Iberoamerican Mission in Muslim lands." M.Th., Brunel University, London School of Theology, 2008. https://doi.org/10.13140/RG.2.1.2644.4241.

———. *Peregrinaje en la Misión*. Colección Musulmania 14. Granada: PM Internacional, 2009. http://musulmania.com/resources/14_Peregrinaje_en_mision.pdf.

Gómez Camarero, C., B. Molina Rueda, C. Perez Beltran, and A. R. Vidal Luengo. "Una Lectura del Corán desde la Paz." *Miscelánea de Estudios Árabes y Hebraicos* 46 (1997): 113-48.

Gottwald, Norman K. *The Tribes of Yahweh: A Sociology of Religion of Liberated Israel, 1250-1050 B.C.E.* Maryknoll and London: Orbis and SCM, 1979.

Greenlee, David, ed. *From the Straight Path to the Narrow Way: Journeys of Faith*. Downers Grove: InterVarsity, 2006.

———. "Growing Churches in Resistant Areas." *Evangelical Missions Quarterly* 38, no. 4 (October 2002): 456-62, also in *Envisioning Effective Ministry: Evangelism in a Muslim Context*, edited by Laurie Fortunak Nichols and Gary R. Corwin, 259-64. Wheaton: Evangelism and Missions Information Service, 2010.

———, ed. *Longing for Community: Church,* Ummah*, or Somewhere in Between?* Pasadena: William Carey Library, 2013.

———. *One Cross, One Way, Many Journeys: Thinking Again about Conversion*. Tyrone, Ga.: Authentic, 2007.

Greenlee, David, and Rick Love. "Conversion through the Looking Glass: Muslims and the Multiple Facets of Conversion." In *From the Straight Path to the Narrow Way: Journeys of Faith*, edited by David Greenlee, 35-50. Waynesboro, Ga.: Authentic Media, 2006.

Gutiérrez, Gustavo. *A Theology of Liberation: History, Politics, and Salvation*. Translated by Caridad Inda and John Eagleson. Rev. Maryknoll: Orbis, 1988.

———. "Situación y tareas de la teología de la liberación." *Theologica Xaveriana* 143 (2002): 503-24. https://revistas.javeriana.edu.co/index.php/teoxaveriana/article/view/20913.

———. *The Power of the Poor in History*. Translated by Robert R Barr. Eugene, OR: Wipf & Stock, 2004.

Guzmán, Andrés. "Ourselves as Servants." In *Perspectives on the World Christian Movement*, 4th ed., 700-702. Pasadena: William Carey Library, 2009.

Haar, Gerrie ter, ed. *Religion and Development: Ways of Transforming the World*. London: Hurst & Co, 2011.

Harnack, Adolf von. *The Mission and Expansion of Christianity in the First Three Centuries*. Translated by James Moffatt. The cloister library TB92. New York: Harper Torchbooks, 1962.

Hauck, Friedrich, and Gerhard Kittel. "Pénes." In *Theological Dictionary of the New Testament*, translated by Geoffrey William Bromiley, VI:37-40. Grand Rapids: Eerdmans, 1964.

Hickel, Jason, and Martin Kirk. "Are You Ready to Consider that Capitalism is the Real Problem?" *Fast Company* (blog), July 11, 2017. https://www.fastcompany.com/40439316/are-you-ready-to-consider-that-capitalism-is-the-real-problem.

Hiebert, Paul G. *Anthropological Reflections on Missiological Issues*. Grand Rapids: Baker, 1994.

Hill, Harriet S, and Margaret Hill. *Translating the Bible into Action: How the Bible Can Be Relevant in All Languages and Cultures*. Carlisle: Piquant, 2008.

Hoffman, Valerie J. "Hospitality and Courtesy." In *Encyclopaedia of the Qur'an*. Washington, DC: Georgetown University, 2013. https://referenceworks.brillonline.com/entries/encyclopaedia-of-the-quran/hospitality-and-courtesy-EQCOM_00086?s.num=12.

Holwerda, David E. *Jesus and Israel: One Covenant or Two?* Grand Rapids and Leicester: Eerdmans and Apollos, 1995.

Hookway, Esther, and Christopher Francis. *From Inter-Church Aid to Jubilee: A Brief History of Ecumenical Diakonia in the World Council of Churches*. Edited by Alexander Belopopsky. Geneva: World Council of Churches Diakonia and Solidarity Team, 2002. http://www.wcc-coe.org/wcc/europe/diakoniahistorybook.pdf.

Horst, Willis, Frank Paul, and Ute Paul. *Mission without Conquest: An Alternative Missionary Practice*. Carlisle: Langham, 2015.

Huang, Nellie. "Senegal Travel: A Detailed Guide & Itinerary," July 17, 2019. https://www.wildjunket.com/senegal-travel-guide-itinerary/.

Ingleby, Jonathan. "Does Development Work? The Question the Mission People Forgot to Ask!" *Encounters Mission Ezine*, October 2006.

International Institute of Islamic Thought, ed. *The Meaning of the Holy Qur'ān: Complete Translation with Selected Notes*. Translated by Abdullah Yusuf Ali. Washington, DC: Amana Corporation, 1989.

Internet Movie Database. "Kashf: The Lifting of the Veil." IMDb, 2008. http://www.imdb.com/title/tt1253580/.

Jenkins, Philip. *The Lost History of Christianity: The Thousand-Year Golden Age of the Church in the Middle East, Africa, and Asia – and How It Died*. New York: Harper One, 2008.

Jewett, Paul King. *Man as Male and Female: A Study in Sexual Relationships from a Theological Point of View*. Grand Rapids: Eerdmans, 1990.

John Paul II. *Sollicitudo Rei Socialis*. Vatican City: Editrice Vaticana, 1987. http://www.vatican.va/content/john-paul-ii/en/encyclicals/documents/hf_jp-ii_enc_30121987_sollicitudo-rei-socialis.html.

Kässmann, Margot. "Creative Thinking for Peace or Blessed Are the Peacemakers." *The Ecumenical Review* 63, no. 1 (2011): 5-15. https://doi.org/10.1111/j.1758-6623.2010.00088.x.

Kateregga, Badru, and David W. Shenk. *A Muslim and a Christian in Dialogue*. 2nd ed. Harrisonburg, Vir.: Herald Press, 2011.

Kenny, Peter. "Muslim World League Leader Tells World Council of Churches, 'We Must Combat Extremists.'" *Ecumenical News*. November

10, 2017, Online edition, sec. Church. https://www.ecumenicalnews.com/article/muslim-world-league-leader-tells-world-council-of-churches-we-must-combat-extremists/60451.htm.

Kim, John. "Muslim Villagers Coming to Faith in Christ: A Case Study and Model of Group Dynamics." In *From the Straight Path to the Narrow Way: Journeys of Faith*, edited by David Greenlee, 239-54. Waynesboro, Ga.: Authentic, 2006.

———. "The Anotoc Story Continued: Group Dynamics within an Insider Movement." In *Longing for Community: Church,* Ummah*, or Somewhere in Between?*, edited by David Greenlee, 169-80. Pasadena: William Carey Library, 2013.

Kirk, J. Andrew. *Mission under Scrutiny: Confronting Current Challenges*. London: Darton, Longman & Todd, 2006.

Lausanne Global Consultation on Islam. "Five Faces of Islam." Lausanne Global Consultation on Islam, April 2014. https://www.lausanne.org/news-releases/global-consultation-on-islam.

Lausanne Movement. "Lausanne Covenant," 1974. https://www.lausanne.org/content/covenant/lausanne-covenant#cov.

———. "The Cape Town Commitment." LCWE, January 25, 2011. https://www.lausanne.org/content/ctcommitment.

Lavenda, Robert H., and Emily A. Schultz. *Core Concepts in Cultural Anthropology*. 7th ed. New York: Oxford University Press, 2020.

Leipoldt, Johannes, and Walter Grundmann. *El Mundo del Nuevo Testamento*. Translated by Luis Gil. 2nd ed. Vol. I. 3 vols. Madrid: Ediciones Cristiandad, 1977.

Logan, Chantal. "Is the Gospel Good News for Muslim women?" In *Anabaptists Meeting Muslims: A Calling for Presence in the Way of Christ*, edited by James R. Krabill, David W. Shenk, and Linford Stutzman, 141-53. Scottdale, Penn.: Herald Press, 2005.

Madrigal Mir, Carlos. *Reassembling the Mission with Jesus: Reflections on the Global Task and Its Effects on the World*. Translated by Mónica Calderon, 2019.

Malina, Bruce J. *The New Testament World: Insights from Cultural Anthropology*. 3rd ed. Louisville, KY: Westminster John Knox Press, 2001.

Malina, Bruce J., and John J. Pilch. *Social-Science Commentary on the Book of Revelation*. Minneapolis: Fortress Press, 2000.

———. *Social-Science Commentary on the Letters of Paul*. Minneapolis: Fortress, 2006.

———. *Social-Science Commentary on the Book of Acts*. Minneapolis: Fortress, 2008.

Malina, Bruce J., and Richard L. Rohrbaugh. *Social-Science Commentary on the Gospel of John*. Minneapolis: Fortress, 1998.

———. *Social-Science Commentary on the Synoptic Gospels*. 2nd ed. Minneapolis: Fortress, 2003.

Max-Neef, Manfred. *La Dimensión Perdida: La Deshumanización del Gigantismo*. Montevideo and Barcelona: Nordan and Icaria, 2007. https://www.max-neef.cl/descargas/Max_Neef-La_dimension_perdida.pdf.

McCurry, Don. *Healing the Broken Family of Abraham: New Life for Muslims*. 2nd ed. Colorado Springs: Ministries to Muslims, 2011.

———. *Tales that Teach*. Colorado Springs: Ministries to Muslims, 2009.

Micah Network. "The Micah Network Declaration on Integral Mission," September 21, 2001. https://live-micah-global.pantheonsite.io/wp-content/uploads/2020/10/integral_mission_declaration_en.pdf.

Michel, Otto. "Oikodoméō" and "Oikonomía." In *Theological Dictionary of the New Testament*, V:119-53. Grand Rapids: Eerdmans, 1964.

Mises, Ludwig von. *Socialism: An Economic and Sociological Analysis*. Translated by J. Kahane. Indianapolis, IN: Liberty Fund, 1992.

Müller, Karl, ed. *Dictionary of Mission: Theology, History, Perspectives*. American Society of Missiology Series, no. 24. Maryknoll: Orbis, 1997.

Muller, Roland. *Honor and Shame: Unlocking the Door*. 1st ed. Philadelphia, Penn.: Xlibris Corporation, 2001.

———. "In search of Community: Islam, Christianity, and MBBs in the Middle East." *Evangelical Missions Quarterly* 49, no. 1 (January 2012): 44-51.

———. *The Messenger, the Message, the Community: Three Critical Issues for the Cross-Cultural Church-Planter*. Osler, Sask., Canada: CanBooks, 2006.

Muller, Roland, and Abdallah Hawatmeth. *Tools for Muslim Evangelism*. Hamilton, Ont. Canada: WEC Canada, 2000. http://www.rmuller.com/tools.html.

Murton, Zoe, and Tearfund. "Land Rights." *Paso a Paso*, 2018. https://learn.tearfund.org/-/media/learn/resources/footsteps/2018-tearfund-footsteps-105-land-rights-en.pdf.

Myers, Bryant L. *Engaging Globalization: The Poor, Christian Mission, and Our Hyperconnected World*. Mission in Global Community. Grand Rapids: Baker Academic, 2017.

———. *Exploring World Mission: Context and Challenges*. Monrovia, Calif.: World Vision, 2006.

———. "Holistic Mission: New Frontiers." In *Holistic Mission: God's Plan for God's People*, edited by Brian Woolnough and Wonsuk Ma, 119-27. Regnum Edinburgh 2010 Series. Oxford: Regnum, 2010.

———. *Walking with the Poor: Principles and Practices of Transformational Development*. Rev. ed. Maryknoll: Orbis, 2011.

Neill, Stephen. *Creative Tension: The Duff Lectures, 1958*. London: Edinburgh House Press, 1959.

Nerfin, M., ed. *Another Development: Approaches and Strategies*. Uppsala: Dag Hammarskjöld Foundation, 1977.

Newbigin, Lesslie. *The Open Secret: An Introduction to the Theology of Mission*. Rev. Grand Rapids: Eerdmans, 1995.

Niles, D. Preman. "Justice, Peace and the Integrity of Creation." In *Dictionary of the Ecumenical Movement*, edited by Nicholas Lossky. World Council of Churches, 2003. http://www.wcc-coe.org/wcc/who/dictionary-article11.html.

Nordstokke, Kjell. "Diakonia and Diaconate in the World Council of Churches." *International Journal for the Study of the Christian Church* 13, no. 4 (November 1, 2013): 286-99. https://doi.org/10.1080/1474225X.2013.867653.

Padilla, C. René, ed. *Bases Bíblicas de la Misión: Perspectivas Latinoamericanas*. Buenos Aires and Grand Rapids: Nueva Creación and Eerdmans, 1998.

———. "Holistic Mission." In *Dictionary of Mission Theology: Evangelical Foundations*, edited by John Corrie, 157-62. Downers Grove: IVP Academic, 2007.

———. *Mission between the Times: Essays on the Kingdom*. 2nd ed. Carlisle: Langham Monographs, 2010.

———. *The Local Church, Agent of Transformation: An Ecclesiology for Integral Mission*. Buenos Aires: Ediciones Kairos, 2004.

Pate, Larry. "Escala de Evaluación de Idioma." In Larry Pate, *Misionología: Nuestro Cometido Transcultural*, 415-22. Miami: Vida, 1987.

Paul VI. *Populorum Progressio: Encyclical of Pope Paul VI on the Development of Peoples*. Boston: Pauline Books and Media, 1963. http://www.vatican.va/content/paul-vi/en/encyclicals/documents/hf_p-vi_enc_26031967_populorum.html.

Peet, Richard, and Elaine Hartwick. *Theories of Development: Contentions, Arguments, Alternatives*. 2nd ed. New York and London: Guilford Press, 2009.

Protestante Digital. "Se Ahonda aún más la Brecha Social en España." *Protestante Digital, AC Press*. March 11, 2016, sec. España. http://protestantedigital.com/espana/38833/Se_ahonda_la_brecha_social_en_Espana.

Rad, Gerhard von. "Peace-Shalom (OT)." In *Theological Dictionary of the New Testament*, edited by Gerhard Kittel and Geoffrey William Bromiley, 402-6. Grand Rapids: Eerdmans, 1995.

Raheb, Mitri. "Sailing through Troubled Waters: Palestinian Christians in the Holy Land." *Dialog* 41, no. 2 (2002): 97-102. https://doi.org/10.1111/1540-6385.00105.

Ramachandra, Vinoth. "What is Integral Mission?" Micah Network Integral Mission Initiative, 2012. https://www.yumpu.com/en/document/view/33518643/what-is-integral-mission-by-vinoth-ramachandra-micah-network/3

Reyes, Miguel. "Violence in Times of Peace: A Reading of Jubilee from the Northern Triangle of Central America." *Transformation* 36, no. 2 (May 16, 2019): 76-88. https://doi.org/10.1177/0265378819839601.

Ricciotti, Giuseppe. *The Acts of the Apostles: Text and Commentary*. Translated by Laurence E Byrne. Milwaukee, WI: The Bruce Publishing Company, 1958.

Roa Buitrago, Jairo. *Desarrollo y Liberación: Política, Economía y Religión*. Madrid: Dykinson, 2009.

Rocha Júnior, José. "Dois Cafés da Manhã." Privately circulated manuscript. Dakar, Senegal, April 21, 2005.

Rojo, David. "Jean Ziegler: 'La Solución al Hambre no es Dar Más, Sino Robar Menos.'" Attac Acordem, September 27, 2011. http://www.acordem.org/2010/09/27/jean-ziegler-la-solucion-al-hambre-no-es-dar-mas-sino-robar-menos/.

Ropero Berzosa, Alfonso. "Economía," "Jubileo," and "Pobre-Pobreza." In *Gran Diccionario Enciclopédico de la Biblia*. Viladecavalls, Barcelona: CLIE, 2013.

Ross, Eric. "Globalising Touba: Expatriate Disciples in the World City Network." *Urban Studies* 48, no. 14 (November 1, 2011): 2929-52. https://doi.org/10.1177/0042098010391300.

Ross, Kenneth R, Jooseop Keum, Kyriaki Avtzi, and Roderick R Hewitt, eds. *Ecumenical Missiology: Changing Landscapes and New Conceptions of Mission*. Regnum Edinburgh Centenary Series 35. Oxford: Regnum, 2016.

Samuel, Vinay. "The Development Movement: An Overview and Appraisal." *Transformation* 13, no. 4 (December 1996): 12-16.

Samuel, Vinay K, and Chris Sugden, eds. *Mission as Transformation: A Theology of the Whole Gospel*. Oxford: Regnum, 1999.

———. *The Church in Response to Human Need*. Grand Rapids and Oxford: Eerdmans and Regnum, 1987.

Sanneh, Lamin. *Translating the Message: The Missionary Impact on Culture*. 2nd ed. Maryknoll: Orbis, 2008.

Schirrmacher, Christine. *The Islamic View of Major Christian Teachings: The Role of Jesus Christ, Sin, Faith, and Forgiveness; Essays*. Edited by Ruth Baldwin. Vol. 2. The WEA Global Issues Series. Bonn: Verlag für Kultur und Wissenschaft, 2008. https://iirf.eu/site/assets/files/91402/wea_gis_2_-_christine_schirrmacher_-_the_islamic_view_of_major_christian_teachings.pdf.

Schumacher, E. F. *Small Is Beautiful: Economics as If People Mattered*. Reprint. New York: Harper Perennial, 2010.

Seedat, Fatima. "When Islam and Feminism Converge." *The Muslim World* 103, no. 3 (July 2013): 404-20. https://doi.org/10.1111/muwo.12022.

Segura Carmona, Harold. "A Clean Slate!" *Transformation* 36, no. 2 (May 16, 2019): 135-40. https://doi.org/10.1177/0265378819839605.

———. "La Misión Integral: 41 Años Después." *El Blog de Bernabé* (blog), October 11, 2011. http://www.elblogdebernabe.com/2011/10/la-mision-integral-41-anos-despues-por.html.

———. "La Misión Integral Treinta y Cinco Años Después." *Espacio de Diálogo*, March 2005. http://www.cenpromex.org.mx/revista_ftl/ftl/textos/harold_segura.htm.

———. *Ser Iglesia en la "Era del Vacío."* El Paso: Mundo Hispano, 2011.

———. "Y después de Ciudad del Cabo, ¿Qué? Documento de Trabajo." *Lupa Protestante*, October 28, 2010. https://www.elblogdebernabe.com/2010/10/documento-de-trabajo-y-despues-de.html.

Sen, Amartya. *Development as Freedom*. Oxford: Oxford University Press, 2001.

———. *The Idea of Justice*. Cambridge: Belknap Press of Harvard University Press, 2011.

Shelley, Louise. *Human Trafficking: A Global Perspective*. Cambridge: Cambridge University Press, 2010.

Shenk, David, and Ahmed Haile. "Peacemaking and Church Formation." In *From Seed to Fruit: Global Trends, Fruitful Practices, and Emerging Issues among Muslims*, edited by J. Dudley Woodberry, 325-35. Pasadena: William Carey Library, 2008.

Shenk, David W. *Christian, Muslim, Friend: Twelve Paths to Real Relationship*. The Christians Meeting Muslims. Harrisonburg, Vir..: Herald Press, 2014.

———. *Global Gods: Exploring the Role of Religions in Modern Societies*. 2nd ed. Scottdale, Penn.: Herald Press, 1999.

———. *God's Call to Mission*. Scottdale, Penn.: Herald Press, 1994.

———. "Three journeys for Peace: Jesus, Constantine and Muhammad." In *Anabaptists Meeting Muslims*, Scottdale, Penn.: Herald Press, 2005. 25-39. http://www.mwc-cmm.org/sites/default/files/website_files/mis_com_fd_shenk_d._three_journeys2.pdf.

Shomali, Mohammad Ali. "Shi'a Muslims and the World Council of Churches." *Islam Today*. December 25, 2018, online edition, sec. Reports. http://ijtihadnet.com/shia-muslims-and-the-world-council-of-churches/.

Sider, Ronald, ed. *Evangelicals and Development: Toward a Theology of Social Change*. Philadelphia, Penn.: Westminster Press, 1982.

Simon, David. "Neo-Liberalism, Structural Adjustment and Poverty Reduction Strategies." In *The Companion to Development Studies*, edited by Vandana Desai and Robert B. Potter, 2nd ed. London and New York: Routledge, 2002.

Singh, David Emmanuel. "Hundred Years of Christian-Muslim Relations." *Transformation* 27, no. 4 (September 2010): 225-38. https://doi.org/10.1177/0265378810378561.

Smith, Adam. *An Inquiry into the Nature and Causes of the Wealth of Nations*. Edited by Edwin Cannan. Great Books of the Western World 39. Chicago: Encyclopaedia Britannica, 1984.

Stam, Juan B. "El Año de Jubileo." *Blog de Juan Stam* (blog), December 19, 2007. https://juanstam.com/posts/el-ano-de-jubileo-i.

Stark, Rodney. *The Rise of Christianity: How the Obscure, Marginal Jesus Movement Became the Dominant Religious Force in the Western World in a Few Centuries*. 1st pbk. San Francisco: HarperSanFrancisco, 1997.

Steuernagel, Valdir. *Obediencia Misionera y Práctica Histórica*. Buenos Aires and Grand Rapids: Nueva Creación and Eerdmans, 1996.

———. "Wholistic Mission," Mission Commission of the World Evangelical Alliance, Global Missions Summit, June 18-24, privately circulated manuscript. 2006.

Sung, Jung Mo. *Desire, Market and Religion*. London: SCM Press, 2007.

———. "El Pobre después de la Teología de la Liberación." *Concilium: Revista Internacional de Teología*, no. 361 (2015): 79-90.

———. "Greed, Desire and Theology." *The Ecumenical Review* 63, no. 3 (October 2011): 251-62. https://doi.org/10.1111/j.1758-6623.2011.00119.x.

———. "Mercado Religioso e Mercado Como Religião." *Horizonte* 12, no. 34 (June 25, 2014): 290-315. https://doi.org/10.5752/P.2175-5841.2014v12n34p290.

———. *Se Deus Existe, por qué há Pobreza? A Fe Cristã e os Excluídos*. 3rd ed. Sao Paulo: Paulinas, 2000.

———. "The Human Being as Subject: Defending the Victims." In *Latin American Liberation Theology: The Next Generation*, edited by Ivan Petrella, Maryknoll: Orbis, 2005. 1-19. https://www.academia.edu/5259533/The_Human_Being_as_Subject_Defending_the_Victims_-_Liberation_Theology_Next_Generation.

Suter, Heinz, and Marco Gmür. *Business Power for God's Purpose: Partnership with the Unreached*. Greng, Switzerland: VKG, 1997.

Taylor, William D., Antonia Van der Meer, and Reg Reimer. *Sorrow and Blood: Christian Mission in Contexts of Suffering, Persecution, and Martyrdom*. Pasadena: William Carey Library, 2012.

The Royal Aal al-Bayt Institute for Islamic Thought. "A Common Word between Us and You." Royal Academy of The Royal Aal al-Bayt Institute for Islamic Thought, October 13, 2007. https://www.acommonword.com/wp-content/uploads/2018/05/ACW-English-Translation.pdf.

Tiessen, Calvin. "Jubilee, Discipleship and Social Rest." *Transformation* 36, no. 2 (May 16, 2019): 113-26. https://doi.org/10.1177/0265378819837763.

Tomaselli, Keyan G., Lauren Dyll, and Michael Francis. "'Self' and 'Other': Auto-Reflexive and Indigenous Ethnography." In *Handbook of Critical and Indigenous Methodologies*, 347-72. Los Angeles and London: Sage, 2008.

Travis, John. "Must All Muslims Leave 'Islam' to Follow Jesus?" *Evangelical Missions Quarterly*, (October 1998). https://missionexus.org/must-all-muslims-leave-islam-to-follow-jesus/.

Travis, Ted. *Building Cathedrals: Urban Discipleship that Works*. 2nd ed. Urban Ministry in the 21st Century 7. Skyforest, CA: Urban Loft Publishers, 2016.

Truman, Harry S. "Inaugural Address." Edited by Gerhard Peters and John T. Wolley. The American Presidency Project, January 20, 1949. https://www.presidency.ucsb.edu/documents/inaugural-address-4.

Van Engen, Charles E. *Mission on the Way: Issues in Mission Theology*. Grand Rapids: Baker, 2000.

———. *Transforming Mission Theology*. Pasadena: William Carey Library, 2017.

———. *God's Missionary People: Rethinking the Purpose of the Local Church*. Grand Rapids: Baker, 2003.

Van Seters, John. *The Pentateuch: A Social-Science Commentary*. 2nd edition. London and New York: Bloomsbury T&T Clark, 2015.

Vanoni, Gottfried. "Schalom als zentrale biblische Botschaft." *Theologisch-praktische Quartalschrift* 141, no. 1 (1993): 3.

Verkuyl, Johannes. *Contemporary Missiology: An Introduction*. Grand Rapids: Eerdmans, 1978.

Verkuyl, Johannes, Philip Potter, Lesslie Newbigin, and José Míguez Bonino. "Emilio Castro: Servant of World Mission and Evangelism." *International Review of Mission* 73, no. 289 (January 1984): 106-17. https://doi.org/10.1111/j.1758-6631.1984.tb03257.x.

Vine, William E., Merrill F Unger, and William White. "Peace/Eirene" and "Poor/Needy." In *Vine's Complete Expository Dictionary of Old and New Testament Words: With Topical Index*. Nashville, TN: Nelson, 1996.

Walls, Andrew F. "The Mission of the Church Today in the Light of Global History." *Word & World* XX, no. 1 (2000): 5. http://wordandworld.luthersem.edu/content/pdfs/20-1_20th_Century/20-1_Walls.pdf.

Walls, Andrew F., and Cathy Ross, eds. *Mission in the Twenty-first Century: Exploring the Five Marks of Global Mission*. Maryknoll: Orbis, 2008.

Warren, Max. *Social History and Christian Mission*. London: SCM Press, 1967.

Waugh, Earle H. "Peace." In *Encyclopaedia of the Qur'an*, edited by Jane Dammen McAuliffe. Washington, DC: Georgetown University, 2013.

Widjaja, Paulus S. "Peace." In *Dictionary of Mission Theology: Evangelical Foundations*, edited by John Corrie. Downers Grove: InterVarsity, 2007.

Wilber, Charles K., and Amitava Krishna Dutt, eds. *New Directions in Development Ethics: Essays in Honor of Denis Goulet*. Notre Dame: University of Notre Dame Press, 2010.

Wit, Hans de. *En la Dispersión el Texto es Patria: Introducción a la Hermenéutica Clásica, Moderna y Posmoderna*. San José, Costa Rica: Universidad Bíblica Latinoamericana, 2002.

Woodberry, J. Dudley, ed. *From Seed to Fruit: Global Trends, Fruitful Practices, and Emerging Issues among Muslims*. Pasadena: William Carey Library, 2008.

Woods, Timothy J. "Islam, Peace and the Quest for Justice." *Theology* 109, no. 852 (November 1, 2006): 412-20. https://doi.org/10.1177/0040571X0610900603.

World Council of Churches. "São Paulo Statement: International Financial Transformation for the Economy of Life." World Council of Churches, October 5, 2012. https://www.oikoumene.org/resources/documents/sao-paulo-statement-international-financial-transformation-for-the-economy-of-life.

Wright, Christopher J. H. *Exodus*. The Story of God Bible Commentary Series. Grand Rapids: Zondervan Academic, 2021.

———. *God's People in God's Land: Family, Land, and Property in the Old Testament*. Grand Rapids: Eerdmans, 1990.

———. "Lamentations: A Book for Today." *International Bulletin of Missionary Research* 39, no. 2 (April 2015): 59-64.

———. *Old Testament Ethics for the People of God*. Downers Grove: InterVarsity, 2004.

———. *The Mission of God: Unlocking the Bible's Grand Narrative*. Downers Grove: IVP Academic, 2006.

Zamorano, Enrique. "La Pobreza se Agudiza en España mientras los más Ricos ya se han Recuperado de la Crisis, Según Oxfam Intermón." *El Confidencial*. January 25, 2021, sec. Alma, Corazón y Vida. https://www.elconfidencial.com/alma-corazon-vida/2021-01-25/informe-oxfam-intermon-espana-ricos-social_2921204/.

Ziegler, Jean. *Betting on Famine: Why the World Still Goes Hungry*. Translated by Christopher Caines. Chicoutimi, Quebec: Bibliothèque Paul-Émile Boulet, Université du Québec, 2018.

Index